Against Theatre

Performance Interventions

Series Editors: **Elaine Aston,** University of Lancaster, and **Bryan Reynolds,** University of California, Irvine

Performance Interventions is a series of monographs and essay collections on theatre, performance, and visual culture that share an underlying commitment to the radical and political potential of the arts in our contemporary moment, or give consideration to performance and to visual culture from the past deemed crucial to a social and political present. *Performance Interventions* moves transversally across artistic and ideological boundaries to publish work that promotes dialogue between practitioners and academics, and interactions between performance communities, educational institutions, and academic disciplines.

Titles include:

Alan Ackerman and Martin Puchner (*editors*)
AGAINST THEATRE
Creative Destructions on the Modernist Stage

Elaine Aston and Geraldine Harris (*editors*)
FEMINIST FUTURES?
Theatre, Performance, Theory

Leslie Hill and Helen Paris (*editors*)
PERFORMANCE AND PLACE

Forthcoming titles:

Lynette Goddard
STAGING BLACK FEMINISMS
Identity, Politics, Performance

Amelia M. Kritzer
POLITICAL THEATRE IN POST-THATCHER BRITAIN

Performance Interventions
Series Standing Order ISBN 1–4039–4443–1 Hardback 1–4039–4444–X Paperback
(*outside North America only*)

You can receive future titles in this series as they are published by placing a standing order. Please contact your bookseller or, in case of difficulty, write to us at the address below with your name and address, the title of the series and the ISBN quoted above.

Customer Services Department, Macmillan Distribution Ltd, Houndmills, Basingstoke, Hampshire RG21 6XS, England

---

Against Theatre

Creative Destructions on the Modernist Stage

Edited by

Alan Ackerman and Martin Puchner

First published 2006 by
PALGRAVE MACMILLAN
Houndmills, Basingstoke, Hampshire RG21 6XS and
175 Fifth Avenue, New York, N.Y. 10010
Companies and representatives throughout the world

PALGRAVE MACMILLAN is the global academic imprint of the Palgrave
Macmillan division of St. Martin's Press, LLC and of Palgrave Macmillan Ltd.
Macmillan® is a registered trademark in the United States, United Kingdom
and other countries. Palgrave is a registered trademark in the European
Union and other countries.

ISBN-13: 978–1–4039–4491–7 hardback
ISBN-10: 1–4039–4491–1 hardback

This book is printed on paper suitable for recycling and made from fully
managed and sustained forest sources.

A catalogue record for this book is available from the British Library.

Library of Congress Cataloging-in-Publication Data
Against theatre : creative destructions on the modernist stage / edited by
    Alan Ackerman & Martin Puchner.
        p.   cm. — (Performance interventions)
    Includes bibliographical references and index.
    ISBN 1–4039–4491–1 (cloth)
    1. Experimental theater—History—20th century.   2. Performing arts—
    History—20th century.   3. Experimental drama—History and criticism.
    I. Ackerman, Alan L. (Alan Louis)   II. Puchner, Martin, 1969–
    III. Series.
    PN2193.E86A33 2006
    792.02′23—dc22   2005055291

Printed and bound in Great Britain by
CPI Antony Rowe, Chippenham and Eastbourne

For Barbara Johnson and Elaine Scarry

Contents

Part III   Values

Illustrations

Acknowledgements

We gratefully acknowledge the journal *Modern Drama* for granting us permission to reprint four chapters of this volume as well as parts of the introduction and afterword, which first appeared in a special issue entitled 'Modernism and Anti-Theatricality' (Fall 2001). Thanks also to the editors of the journal at that time, Ric Knowles, Joanne Tompkins and W. B. Worthen, who allowed us to serve as guest-editors. Also at *Modern Drama*, Kim Solga and Sylvia Hunter were indispensable in seeing the articles to press.

We are also pleased for our book to inaugurate Palgrave's 'Performance Interventions' series and wish to extend special thanks to Bryan Reynolds for helping to make that possible. We gratefully acknowledge those at Palgrave who have contributed to this project along the way: Paula Kennedy, Helen Craine and Penny Simmons. We are delighted to take this opportunity to thank Andrea Most and Amanda Claybaugh for reading drafts of the introduction and for their support in innumerable ways as we worked on this project.

Finally, we wish to express our deep gratitude to two of our finest teachers, Elaine Scarry and Barbara Johnson, to whom we dedicate this book. They taught us that to think *against* can also be a way of thinking *for* and that to resist representation is to challenge assumptions about the world and, at the same time, to intervene in it.

The jacket reproduces Picasso's 'Harlequin' © 2006 Estate of Pablo Picasso/Artists Rights Society (ARS), New York.

Note on the Contributors

Alan Ackerman is an Associate Professor of English at the University of Toronto. He is author of *The Portable Theater: American Literature and the Nineteenth-Century Stage* and editor of the journal *Modern Drama*.

Arnold Aronson is Professor of Theatre at Columbia University. He has written on both avant-garde theatre and scenography. His books include *The History and Theory of Environmental Scenography*, *American Set Design, American Avant-Garde Theatre: A History* and *Looking into the Abyss: Essays on Scenography*. He will be the Commissioner General of the 2007 Prague Quadrennial.

Herbert Blau is Byron W. and Alice L. Lockwood Professor of the Humanities at the University of Washington. He has also had a distinguished career in the theatre, as co-founder and co-director of The Actor's Workshop of San Francisco, then co-director of the Repertory Theater of Lincoln Center in New York, and as artistic director of the experimental group KRAKEN, the groundwork for which was prepared at California Institute of the Arts, of which he was founding Provost, and Dean of the School of Theater and Dance. Among his books are *Take Up the Bodies: Theater at the Vanishing Point, The Audience, To All Appearances: Ideology and Performance* and, recently, *Sails of the Herring Fleet: Essays on Beckett*. He has also published a book recently on fashion, *Nothing in Itself: Complexions of Fashion*, and a new collection of essays, *The Dubious Spectacle: Extremities of Theater, 1976–2000*. He is currently working on *As If: An Autobiography*.

Elin Diamond is Professor of English at Rutgers University. She is the author of *Unmaking Mimesis: Essays on Feminism and Theater* and *Pinter's Comic Play*, and editor of *Performance and Cultural Politics*. Her essays on performance and feminist theory have appeared in *Theatre Journal, ELH, Discourse, TDR, Modern Drama, Kenyon Review, Cahiers Renaud-Barrault, Art and Cinema, MASKA* and in anthologies in the United States, Europe and India. She is at work on a new book on modernism and performance.

Elinor Fuchs is Professor of Dramaturgy and Dramatic Criticism at the Yale School of Drama. She is author of *The Death of Character: Perspectives* *on Theater after Modernism*, winner of the George Jean Nathan Award for Dramatic Criticism, and the *Choice* Outstanding Academic Book citation. She is co-editor of *Land/Scape/Theater* and co-author of the documentary play *Year One of the Empire*, which won the *Drama-Logue* "Best Play" award for its Los Angeles production. Her articles and essays on theatre have appeared in numerous journals and anthologies. She has taught at Columbia, Harvard and Emory universities, and has been the recipient of Rockefeller and Bunting Fellowships. Her most recent book is *Making an Exit*, a memoir about her mother.

Charlie Keil is Associate Professor in the History Department and the Cinema Studies Programme at the University of Toronto. He is the author of *Early American Cinema in Transition: Story, Style and Film-making, 1907–1913* and co-editor, with Shelley Stamp, of *American Cinema's Transitional Era: Audiences, Institutions, Practices*. In addition to numerous essays on early cinema, he has published on documentary and contemporary cinema.

Herbert Lindenberger is Avalon Foundation Professor Humanities Emeritus at Stanford University. Besides books on Wordsworth, Büchner and Trakl, his writings includes studies of historical drama and critical theory. He has published two books on opera, *Opera: The Extravagant Art* and *Opera in History: From Monteverdi to Cage*. He is currently writing a series of essays on the interactions of various art forms.

Patrick McGuinness is Fellow and Tutor in French at St Anne's College, Oxford. His books include *Maurice Maeterlinck and the Making of Modern Theatre*, *Symbolism, Decadence and the Fin de Siècle* and *Anthologie de la poésie symboliste et décadente*. He has also edited T. E. Hulme's *Selected Writings* and written a book of poems, *The Canals of Mars*.

Marjorie Perloff is Sadie D. Patek Professor Emerita of Humanities at Stanford University and currently Scholar-in-Residence at the University of Southern California. She is the author of a dozen books, among them, co-edited with Charles Junkerman, *John Cage: Composed in America* and, most recently, *The Vienna Paradox* and *Differentials: Poetry, Poetics, Pedagogy*.

Martin Puchner is Associate Professor of English and Comparative Literature at Columbia University and author of *Stage Fright: Modernism, Anti-Theatricality and Drama* as well as *Poetry of the Revolution: Marx,*

Manifestos, and the Avant-Gardes. He has written introductions to works by Henrik Ibsen, Karl Marx and Lionel Abel and is co-editor of the *Norton Anthology of Drama.* He is also the associate editor of *Theatre Survey.*

David Savran, distinguished Professor of Theatre and Vera Moury Roberts Chair in American Theatre, CUNY Graduate Center, is author of *A Queer Sort of Materialism, Taking it Like a Man, Communists, Cowboys, and Queers: The Politics of Masculinity in the Works of Arthur Miller and Tennessee Williams, Breaking the Rules: The Wooster Group* and co-editor of *The Masculinity Studies Reader.*

Julie Stone Peters is Professor of English and Comparative Literature at Columbia University. A specialist in early modern and modern comparative drama, her most recent book is *Theatre of the Book: Print, Text, and Performance in Europe, 1480–1880* (winner of the ACLA Harry Levin Prize, among others). She is currently working on a study of the historical relationship between theatre and the law.

Rebecca L. Walkowitz is Assistant Professor of English at the University of Wisconsin-Madison, and an editor of six books in the field of literary and cultural studies, including *The Turn to Ethics* and the forthcoming *Bad Modernisms,* and author of the forthcoming *Cosmopolitan Style: Modernism Beyond the Nation.*

Kirk Williams teaches at the Yale School of Drama. He has published work on German literature and culture, modern drama and the role of technology in the humanistic disciplines. He is currently finishing a book that explores the relationship between the German stage and military theory and practice from the eighteenth century to the Third Reich.

1
Introduction: Modernism and Anti-Theatricality

Alan Ackerman and Martin Puchner

Being one's self means slaying one's Self.

(Ibsen, *Peer Gynt*[1])

This volume of essays takes its starting point from a special issue of the journal *Modern Drama* on the topic, 'Modernism and Anti-theatricality'. In turning the special issue into a larger collection, we have expanded its conceptual scope, though modernism remains a central point of reference. What we have retained from the special issue is its emphasis on the critique of specific aspects of theatrical presentation and reception. Modern theatre emerges as a field marked by competing, and often contradictory, impulses and developments. Competition *from within* is the process that the economist Joseph Schumpeter has called 'creative destruction', and the technological changes and inventiveness of the past century and a half have been crucial factors in fashioning new methods of *production* in both theatrical and economic senses.[2] In referring to Schumpeter, the dark theorist of capitalism, we want to indicate how modernist theatre responds to, represents and critiques the forces unleashed by rapid industrialization and the capitalist mode of production. And yet a critique, even destruction, of certain types of theatre is, this book will show, a productive force within modernism and a force that led to the most successful reforms of modern theatre and drama. The chapters that follow insist on a historical grounding of any understanding of anti-theatricalism, exploring various forms of a specifically modernist critique of theatre. Theatre is understood sometimes as a medium, sometimes as trope or idea, but always as a crucial configuration of relationships between 'actors' and 'audiences' that cannot be taken for granted and is subject to question from a variety of perspectives, including aesthetic, political, legal and technical ones.

1

Twenty years ago, Jonas Barish identified a disposition within Western culture that he termed the anti-theatrical prejudice. He cites instances, from the Greeks to the present, of a bias against the expressive, the imitative, the deceptive, the spectacular and the subject that arouses, or even acknowledges, an audience. Exposing the philosophical, moral and aesthetic assumptions made by the enemies of the theatre throughout the centuries, his *Antitheatrical Prejudice* sought to fortify theatre's defences against its detractors. This volume argues that Barish's trans-historical notion of anti-theatricalism and, by extension, of the theatre is in need of a number of revisions. *The Antitheatrical Prejudice* is itself an important historical document, a product not only of Barish's own humanistic sensibility but also of his historical moment. A Jewish New Yorker, Barish fought in World War II before embarking on a career as a Renaissance scholar in the Department of English at the University of California, Berkeley, from 1954 until his retirement in 1991. His book associates anti-theatricality with fascism, from Plato to Nietzsche, and with anti-Semitism. The argument, earlier advanced by Horkheimer and Adorno in *Dialectic of Enlightenment* (1944) and developed by Barish, that Jews, nomads, players are perceived as 'other' and that their very existence is a provocation, a projection of a false mimesis, will be further investigated and complicated in this book. In its analysis of Schoenberg's *Moses und Aron*, Herbert Lindenberger's contribution, 'Anti-Theatricality in Twentieth-Century Opera', shows that Moses not only challenges theatricality but also becomes an embodiment of a spirit of anti-theatricality. From the work of Freud and Joyce to that of Schoenberg, in fact, Moses, for whom God is *unvorstellbar* or unrepresentable, appears as a paradigmatic modernist figure. And in the antithesis between Moses and Aron, Lindenberger sees a tacit critique of the theatrically seductive and popular Arons (read Hitlers) of the world. On the other hand, Rebecca L. Walkowitz, in 'Narrative Theatricality: Joseph Conrad's Drama of the Page', shows ways in which 'foreigners' in cosmopolitan Europe appropriated (or were perceived to appropriate) modes of theatricality that were fundamental to the construction of modernism and cosmopolitanism.

This book argues that anti-theatricalism always emerges in response to a specific theatre and, by extension, that the modernist form of anti-theatricalism attacks not theatre itself but the value of theatricality as it arose in theoretical and practical terms throughout the nineteenth century. Several crucial developments brought particular pressures to bear on the theatre. On the one hand, there was the emergence of what one might call theatrical or pro-theatrical theatre, epitomized by

Wagner and his conception of the total theatre. Trying to impose theatre on the other arts, Wagner effectively turned theatricality into a quality that could be found not only in the theatre but in each individual art as well. Lindenberger in Chapter 4 demonstrates to what extent the modernist, anti-theatrical opera looks to Wagner as its key antagonist. On the other hand, we have what one could call, with reference to George Mosse, the theatrical mobilization of the masses.[3] Mosse and others have detailed the manner in which the mass politics of the first half of the twentieth century, in particular fascist politics, proceeded through a systematic exploitation of theatrical presentation. There has certainly never been a system of political power that has not, in one way or another, presented itself through various theatrical means; one example is, as Karl Marx noted, the theatrics of the French Revolution and its nineteenth-century imitations, especially in the Second Empire of Napoleon III.[4] But even if theatrical politics was nothing new in principle, the mass parades of Italian and German fascism, the ritualistic repetition of scenes from the October Revolution and so on encouraged a renewed suspicion of the theatre. It would be wrong to claim a simple historical causality between fascist or Soviet theatrical politics and modernist anti-theatricalism, but the history of theatrical politics reinforced a pre-existing anti-theatricalism and also perhaps supplied it with a new imperative.

In Barish's book, 'theatricality' is continually associated with the possibilities of self-determination. 'Freedom' is *The Antitheatrical Prejudice*'s most pervasive term. However, a deep ambivalence, not unlike the antithesis within Schoenberg's opera *Moses and Aron*, informs the work. Barish notes that Plato's prescriptions may appear confining, '[b]ut we can hardly help finding their opposite, the spectacle of frenetic metamorphosis, disquieting'.[5] And, in this respect also, *The Antitheatrical Prejudice* is an unmistakably post-war American work. Written in the midst of the counter-cultural movements of the 1960s, the war in Vietnam and the crisis of Watergate, *The Antitheatrical Prejudice* is alert to 'the conditions of our time, to the breakdown of longstanding patterns of culture, . . . the mass media, and above all to the menace of nuclear war, with its dissolving of the boundaries of destruction and its consequent threats to the self and the traditional symbolism of the self' (p.471). American public life of the 1970s presented ample reason for a heightened concern about theatricality and authenticity. '[T]he individual flirts desperately with the world at large', writes Barish, 'all the while cynically disbelieving in any reality behind his own impersonations' (p.474). Yet, as Walkowitz argues, Barish's model of theatricality is embedded in a pre-modernist conception of culture. Barish defined theatre as the 'representation of the observed and the actual, intelligible configurations of character, narrative coherence, meaningful patterns of action' (p.464). This idea of theatre assumes an objective world independent of human imagining, an opposition between fact and fiction, history and literature, a world characterized by categories such as national distinctiveness that can be represented. But Conrad, Walkowitz claims, imagines a theatre that is 'constructive rather than mimetic', and, as a result, a notion of theatre that becomes integral to the production of culture.

The Antitheatrical Prejudice concludes with an acknowledgment that, at least in a superficial sense, the 'battle of the theatre' has been 'won': 'Actors now win knighthoods in England, inhabit seats of government in America, and are revered as sages in France' (p.475). In 1966, the American movie actor Ronald Reagan ran for and won the position of Governor of the state of California with an agenda that included combating the radicalism of the Berkeley campus where Barish taught. Of course, the notion that the actor's victory was superficial has proved prescient, for it has been a central irony of public life that Republicans of the past 40 years have repeatedly campaigned on what has come to be known as 'the character issue'. So Reagan's political triumph, and more recently that of Arnold Schwarzenegger, signifies less a new privileging of the actor than a rhetorical shift whereby the very idiom of theatricality has shifted from the marginal to the normative. 'We're using up prime time', Reagan began his acceptance speech for the Republican nomination for President in 1980. 'Well, the first thrill tonight was to find myself for the first time in a long time in a movie on prime time.'[6] And this discursive shift, from actor as 'other' and marginal to 'prime time', marks, in effect, the culmination of a phenomenon that the present collection of essays sets out to investigate. Theatricality has become central to our imagining of the historical *real*, and modernism provides a set of co-ordinates within which to map aspects of that imagining.

We employ the term 'modernism' in order to define our field in at least three crucial and interrelated ways: (1) an insistence on authenticity that can ultimately only uncover its own artifice; (2) a newly heightened aesthetic self-reflexivity or attention within art to its artness, its media and, especially in theatre, to the constituting role of the audience; and (3) an emphasis on pluralism or multiplicity that is both internal and external to art and a consequent perspectivism.[7] The destruction of the Apollonian world of appearances, the rending of the veil of Maya, the shattering of illusion is a recurrent theme of modernist literature and art. Yet Conrad, like other modernist authors, under-mines the notion that darkness has an *authentic* heart, an origin outside of cultural practices, that could be 'natural'. Our investigation of modernist anti-theatricality thus includes a reassessment of Naturalist drama, which was particularly invested in exposing artifice with the hope of reaching the real. In Chapter 6, 'Anti-Theatricality and the Limits of Naturalism', Kirk Williams shows that if the first question of anti-theatricalism is the self or subject as such, 'Naturalism claims this self as the elusive object of its dramatic quest.' Focusing on material detail, Naturalists aimed to expose hypocrisy and idealism for what they were and, within the drama, to reject metaphor. But the irony of naturalism's putatively empirical mode is that naturalism is itself an aesthetic strategy. Naturalist theatre, therefore, provides a crucial scene for our analysis of modernist practices, since it proves 'that the theatre is never more theatrical, more metaphorical, than when it attempts to transcend its own conditions of representation'.

Anti-theatricality, in this sense, is opposed to the banal keeping up of appearances required by modern, middle-class culture, represented in the unreflective pieties of characters ranging from Torvald Helmer to Pollyanna or Willy Loman. Belief of such characters and theatregoers in supra-individual ideals, from the religious to the national, collapses as writers from Freud to Beckett compel patients and characters to tell and retell personal narratives that return continually to the untellable, the unnameable. In short, the oscillation between the concrete detail of realism and a poetics of abstraction is a constructive tension of the modern stage. An idealization of theatre as a repository of 'beauty and truth', in the American drama critic George Jean Nathan's words, is simultaneously both created and destroyed by pressures of the market-place and changes wrought by immigration including the radical mobility of individuals and the instability of communities. A key socio-historical aspect of the 'unnameable' is the problem of defining (setting limits about, maintaining frames for) specific forms of cultural produc-tion and reception. As audiences change so too must notions of cultural hierarchicalism. Thus, as David Savran writes in his contribution, Chapter 11 'The Curse of Legitimacy', the category of 'legitimate' theatre is especially vexed in America in the 1920s, as it appears in the works of highbrow critics such as Nathan to sanctify a European tradi-tion in opposition to an implicitly 'illegitimate' yet popular other, only to become unnameable itself in the writings of iconoclastic critics, such as Gilbert Seldes, for whom 'serious plays' cannot compete in an economic and cultural marketplace of 'lively arts', including comic strips, movies and vaudeville. Falling between art and commerce, Savran writes, 'the legitimate theatre became a kind of battleground in which a "higher literary" theatre was growing increasingly hostile to and isolated from "the theatre of the people"'. Each new frame, each restrictive strategy, acquires significance, as Schumpeter writes, 'in the perennial gale of creative destruction, a significance which they would not have in a stationary state or in a state of slow and balanced growth' (Schumpeter, *Capitalism, Socialism, and Democracy*, p.87). In the case of the legitimate theatre, as in the case of retail trade, the competition that matters arises not from additional dramas of the same type (or, in trade, from similar shops), but from jazz, from cinema, from radio and from the funny pages. 'Now a theoretical construction which neglects this essential element of the case', notes Schumpeter, 'is like Hamlet without the Danish prince' (p.86).

A central problem of the modern theatre, therefore, the question of what it can and cannot represent, is the crucial topic of modern (that is to say cosmopolitan, socially mobile and post-colonial) identity. Should identity be understood in terms of essence or performance? Elin Diamond, in Chapter 7, 'Deploying/Destroying the Primitivist Body in Hurston and Brecht', shows how, making visible the commodification of the primitivist body on stage, Zora Neale Hurston and Bertolt Brecht 'develop a technique of representation, in contradistinction to the tired conventions of bourgeois naturalism, which could render the dynamism of working-class life – for Hurston, the experience of blacks "farthest down" '. Yet the anti-mimetic attitude of Hurston, Brecht, or of Gilbert Seldes is not simply an inversion of the Naturalist experiments of the late-nineteenth century European stage that they ostensibly critique; rather, they are tacitly dependent on, even constituted by, the sense of difference always already at play within *anti*-theatricality. So, in contrast to the overtly performed identity, Williams in Chapter 6 demonstrates a proto-Freudian 'return of the repressed' in the anti-theatricality of Hauptmann. The Romantics had pioneered personal experience, subjectivity and inwardness as subjects of art. The modernists do not abandon that project but find a self fractured in both spatial and temporal senses, driven by a death instinct, amoral and out of sync with the natural or exterior world. In short, by the late nineteenth century it had become the contradictory task of theatre (from *theatron*, or 'space of seeing') and drama (from *dran*, 'to do') to depict human interiority.

Alongside the fracturing of the subject we find the destruction of its external manifestation: the individual body. The modern theatre witnessed an unprecedented resurgence of physicality, including a new emphasis, in actor training, on physical fitness, gymnastics, bio-mechanics and other body techniques. This development is often associated with Antonin Artaud and his campaign for an anti-literary and pro-physical theatre. But it would be misleading to identify modern theatre simply with the resurgence of the body. Embodiment, too, is subject to the process of creative destruction that characterizes modern theatre throughout. In the theatre, bodies often lose their organic integrity and become fragments, vehicles or signs. As Diamond argues in Chapter 7 in her discussion of Hurston and Brecht, bodies on stage are never just given and natural, but on the contrary are made and remade, framed and reframed. Estrangement is one term for this process, and Brecht himself once described his theory and practice of the theatre as being derived from a deeply rooted 'suspicion of the theatre', an anti-theatricalism that allowed him to find in the theatre's destruction material for his own epic theatre.

The challenge to conventional structures characterizes a theatre, as Barish remarks, against itself. But, in fact, theatre has come only belatedly to theorize what Roland Barthes termed the 'reality effect', a notion already much explored in philosophical writing, poetry and the novel. The notion that terror, like 'the horror', resists representation has been a major concern since 9/11, but this problem is continuous with modernism. In her contribution to this book, Chapter 3, 'Clown Shows: Anti-Theatricalist Theatricalism in Four Twentieth-Century Plays', Elinor Fuchs details that, in *Hamletmachine*, the ultimate rejection of the 'Hamlet drama is itself a drama within the Western tradition', the drama of the avenger Elektra, who summons Lady Macbeth, Medea, the Manson gang and Conrad's 'heart of darkness' speech to her aid. Whether in the dramaturgy of Genet and Müller or in State Department documents, as Fuchs remarks, terror places itself on the disputed boundary between representation and invisibility. If modernism extends Romantic concerns with interiority, modernist artists also decentre the subject and shift emphasis from an individual person on to the texture of the work itself. And an aesthetic or formal self-reflexivity is the second key feature of modernist theatre as understood here. As Charles Taylor puts it, 'the epiphanic centre of gravity begins to be displaced from the self to the flow of experience, to new forms of unity, to language conceived in a variety of ways – eventually even as a "structure".'[8]

The most recurring objection to the theatre is not to display as such, for some form of display is involved in all the arts and their systems of presentation, from the museum to the book, from the concert hall to architectural space. What seems particularly objectionable in the theatre is that it presents, displays and exhibits not objects, but human beings. While concerns about the display of human beings to the eager eyes of an audience are usually moralistic, in particular when women are concerned, in modernism they are replaced by a set of aesthetic categories, centred on a critique of personalized mimesis. One could, of course, speculate about whether the aesthetic critique of the human being on stage is but the latest form of the older moralistic prejudice, an aesthetic veiling of a system of social control. But such a speculation would nevertheless also have to take into account a more general modernist celebration of an impersonal art, from Stéphane Mallarmé to T. S. Eliot. Be this as it may, it is remarkable that the modernist incarnation of these objections against human beings on display, which seems to aim at the very heart of the theatre, has not left the modernist stage in paralysis. In fact, modernist directors, from E. G. Craig to Oskar Schlemmer, have directly applied this ideal of an impersonal art to the theatre, instructing actors to impersonate machines or replacing actors altogether with puppets and objects. These developments testify to the productive and transformative effects of anti-theatricalism on the modernist theatre. Another way of putting this is to say that in no period before modernism has the theatre been more ready to take to heart the arguments and obsessions of its detractors.

This creative destruction of the subject and the human actor was vital, in particular, to the project of symbolism. 'Of all the anti-theatrical literary movements', Patrick McGuinness writes in Chapter 9, 'Mallarmé, Maeterlinck and the Symbolist *Via Negativa* of Theatre', 'French Symbolism was the most avowedly extreme, yet it furnishes the best example of how a systematically thought out anti-theatrical position can produce constructive and innovative engagements with theatre.' Symbolist plays manifest a phobia of materiality; in the works of Mallarmé and Quillard poetry recoils from the body as virginal women recoil from sexuality. And yet the Symbolists return obsessively to theatre and theatricality. As Arnold Aronson shows in Chapter 2, 'Avant-Garde Scenography and the Frames of the Theatre', it was the 'intrusion of elements of the everyday into the realm of the theatrical that led Symbolists to call for the detheatricalization of the theatre'. The Symbolist theatre, Aronson argues, aimed to dissolve the proscenium frame, collapsing stage and auditorium, implicitly challenging the spectators' apparently orderly perception of a separate world. The composer John Cage epitomizes one of the purest forms of this strain of creative destruction in the performance of 'silence' in his famous composition *4′33″*. As Marjorie Perloff's contribution, Chapter 8 'John Cage's Living Theatre, shows not just *4'33"* but Cage's entire theatrical *oeuvre* is marked by a critical probing of the limits of the theatre. Perloff's analysis of *James Joyce, Marcel Duchamp, Erik Satie: An Alphabet*, which was first produced as a radio play, establishes how Cage systematically questions central categories of the theatre, including that of the actor/character. Part of the logic of this play is textual, based on the act of reading, on a sequence of letters. And yet Cage transposes this textualism on to some kind of stage with some kind of actors engaging in some kind of action. At the end of modernism, we thus have a destruction of the theatre that nevertheless leads to entirely new theatrical and para-theatrical forms.

While Cage, Artaud and many others have sought to dissolve, transgress or supercede the frame that defines the space of the stage, Brecht sought to expose, foreground and overdetermine not only the proscenium frame but also the various framing devices of the stage and of the drama, thereby heightening the sense of scenic divisions and theatrical constructedness. In text and performance, as Diamond suggests, Zora Neale Hurston, much like Brecht, imposed both literal and figurative quotation marks, exposing the theatricality of putatively realistic and folk vocabularies. Frames situate both the observer and the object observed, making the latter visible by defining what there is to see, a 'scopic regime', in the words of Christian Metz. If pictorial frames developed in conjunction with the art of perspective in the Renaissance, modernist attacks upon the frame represent an assault on the idea of the simulacrum and *trompe-l'oeil* and, by extension, the authority of the artist and the implicit power of the spectator. Cinema's relationship to theatre, in this respect, has been one of creative destruction since the younger medium's inception at the end of the nineteenth century. Charles Keil writes in his contribution, Chapter 5, that 'making a case for cinema's development as an aesthetically distinct medium often meant...delineating the ways in which cinema's formal specificity denied a dependency on "theatricality"'. Modernist self-consciousness about cinematic form, Keil argues, typified by the French impressionists' theories of 'photogénie' or the Soviet montage school's elevation of editing as a formal dominant, aimed to eliminate vestiges of the 'antiquated' art of theatre. In this respect, cinema provides the most explicit instance of competition within the arts. This competition is vitally related to the revolutionary process of competitive technological capitalism and, as Philip Fisher puts it, the 'acceleration of frame-making and frame-breaking because of technology'.[9] The result, contrary to the long-standing pessimism of critics and intellectuals, has been a remarkably dynamic, self-reflexive and experimental field of cultural production in which practitioners of modern theatre, driven by a mission to overcome the old, continue to expand the horizons of the possible in form and content. In the visual arts, this neo-Kantian emphasis on modern art's self-critical tendency is famously described by Clement Greenberg in 'Modernist Painting', an essay that has had important ramifications for the development of modernist anti-theatricality. 'The self-criticism of Modernism grows out of but is not the same thing as the criticism of the Enlightenment', Greenberg writes. 'The Enlightenment criticized from the outside, the way criticism in its more accepted sense does; Modernism criticizes from the inside, through the procedures themselves of that which is being criticized.'[10] To say that modernist art criticizes itself from the inside means that 'the unique and proper area of competence of each art coincided with all that was unique in the nature of its medium' (Greenberg, 'Modernist Painting', p.86). Modernist painting *uniquely* orients itself to the 'ineluctable flatness of the surface' (p.87). To define modernist art in this way is immediately to place theatre at a severe disadvantage, not only because theatre does not employ a single medium but also because fundamental to theatre is a feature that cannot easily be located in art *per se*, namely the audience. Theorists, dating back at least to Francisque Sarcey in 1876, have posited an odd analogy between the flatness of painting and the audience of theatre.[11] Of course, the audience can hardly be said to be a medium like a canvas, and the spectator would seem to be required for paintings just as much as for plays. However, this problem of defining the forms (and the ineluctability of the audience in theatre) is precisely where the anti-theatrical prejudice enters a broader set of modernist projects.

Theatre becomes an inherently pejorative term for the situation that includes a beholder; 'theatre' now implies a work of art that postures for an observer external to it. This form of anti-theatricality is influentially articulated by the art historian Michael Fried, whose early essay 'Art and Objecthood' has often been cited in regard to twentieth-century theatre. '[T]he imperative that modernist painting defeat or suspend its objecthood is at bottom the imperative that it *defeat or suspend theater*. And *that* means that there is a war going on between theater and modernist painting, between the theatrical and the pictorial.'[12] Fried goes on to claim that

> [t]he success, even the survival of the arts has come increasingly to depend on their ability to defeat theater. This is perhaps nowhere more evident than within the theater itself, where the need to defeat what I have been calling theater has chiefly made itself felt as the need to establish a

drastically different relation to its audience. (The relevant texts are, of course, Brecht and Artaud.) For theater has an audience – it exists for one – in a way that other arts do not; in fact, this more than anything else is what modernist sensibility finds intolerable in theater generally.

(Fried, 'Art and Objecthood', p.163, original emphasis)

Fried's theory, which aims at a 'continuous and perpetual' presentness in the temporal and spatial experience of art (p.167), concludes with the quasi-religious remark, 'Presentness is grace' (p.168). The being of art effectively overcomes the dualism of observer and object. And this reorientation of the subject–object relationship harks back not only to the phenomenology of Maurice Merleau-Ponty but also to the aesthetic theory of Stephen Dedalus in *A Portrait of the Artist as a Young Man*. Beauty, in Stephen's immature conception, is made up of wholeness, harmony and radiance:

The dramatic form is reached when the vitality which has flowed and eddied round each person fills every person with such vital force that he or she assumes a proper and intangible esthetic life. [...] The esthetic image in the dramatic form is life purified and reprojected from the human imagination.[13]

Stephen Dedalus's and Fried's compelling attempts to redress the separation or detachment of the audience from the event remain one of the goals of an anti-theatrical aesthetic prevalent within modernism.

The boundaries within the theatre (such as the line between actors and spectators) and the boundaries that define the circumference of theatre or that separate theatre from the outside world are continually challenged and eroded, just as historical events of the twentieth century lose clarity or evade definition. 'It is the anomalous nature of modernist events', Hayden White writes, 'that undermine [*sic*] not only the status of facts in relation to events but also the status of the event in general'.[14] The Holocaust, for example, has been described as the paradigmatic modernist event, the epitome of the unrepresentable. The historical consciousness that White describes explodes conventional forms of representation and, thus, ways of knowing. In Beckett's *Endgame*, Hamm remarks: 'The whole place stinks of corpses.' Clov responds: 'The whole universe.'[15] It is not only the stage that the characters find inadequate to give coherence or meaning to their experience but words themselves. Stanley Cavell writes: '[I]n Beckett there *is* no role towards which the actor can maintain intelligence, and he has nothing more to *tell* his audience [...]; damnation lies not in a particular form of theater, but in theatricality as such.'[16] And yet Beckett continued to write plays and his actors to speak their lines. His theatre brings us most unforgivingly to what he identifies in 'Three Dialogues' as the 'ferocious dilemma of expression' within modernism, 'the expression that there is nothing to express'.[17]

The different art forms create their own versions of anti-theatricalism. Barish's discussion of nineteenth-century anti-theatricality draws its evidence almost exclusively from the novel, without considering the novel's characteristic ways of knowing, the significance of its cultural hegemony in that century, or the ways in which the novel and theatre have shaped each other in the twentieth. This is not the place to develop a theory of literary genre or cultural forms. But it may be noted briefly that the novel, founded upon philosophical realism, privileging the representation of individual consciousness, and experienced in secluded reading, may appear in its very form to be in tension with theatre *per se*. The contentious relation between the novel and the theatre is most directly engaged in Cage's use of the novel, as Perloff demonstrates in her multi-layered reading in Chapter 8. And Walkowitz shows in Chapter 10 the extent to which the conflict between drama and novel marked the work of Conrad. However, the greatest clash between literature and theatre surfaces in symbolism, whose anti-theatricalism, McGuinness argues in Chapter 9, derived directly from the movement's emphasis on poetry. Even Artaud, a champion of the theatre against the literary text, had been an admirer of literary symbolism and once promoted an anti-theatrical aesthetic derived from Maurice Maeterlinck. Once more, literature and theatre, anti-theatre and theatre, are not simply opposed to one another but multiply intertwined.

Noticing the multiplicity of anti-theatricalisms means that we can no longer isolate different attacks on the theatre and hold them up as examples of an ingrained prejudice. Instead, we must ask which particular understandings of the theatre stand behind the various forms of anti-theatricalism, what draws them to the theatre that they would bother to attack it so vehemently, what values motivate these attacks, and from what position or discipline are they launched. As the essays in this collection show, each anti-theatricalism tends to construct its own horror fantasy of the theatre, its own version of the inherent limits of theatrical representation, so that we can know each form of anti-theatricalism by the phantasm of the theatre it has created. Anti-theatricalism certainly describes an opposition to theatre as such and not just to some historically contingent theatre. At the same time, however, any such general attack on the theatre takes its point of departure from a critique of a historically specific theatre, from which a general understanding of theatre is then distilled. We must therefore examine, in each case, what kind of theatre stands in for this construction of the 'theatre as such', who personifies it, and what specific theatrical practice defines its limits and excesses. For Naturalist theatre, for example, it is the melodrama that represents the theatre; while for the Symbolist theatre and opera, it is naturalism. Collectively, the following chapters reveal this historical dynamic behind the seemingly ahistorical nature of anti-theatricalism.

Once we have historicized the tendency to abstract a general theatre from a particular one, we can move on to investigate the mode in which the theatre, thus stabilized and generalized, is to be opposed. Are we faced with a strategic opposition, one that uses the rhetoric of anti-theatricalism in order to differentiate itself from contemporary rivals? This type of opposition typically emerges inside the theatre, when playwrights and directors speak about their chosen medium in the most dismissive terms, without implying that they too will, as a consequence, give up on the theatre altogether. At other times, anti-theatricalism seems to create a paranoid image of the theatre, of a theatre that is at work everywhere, infiltrating and corrupting everything, and which therefore demands the greatest vigilance. This type of anti-theatricalism can most often be found outside the theatre – it is the one to which Barish pays most of his attention – in the discipline of philosophy, as in the case of St Augustine or Jean-Jacques Rousseau, or among critics of rival art forms, as in the case of Fried or Adorno.

From a reflection on the mode of opposition we are thus led to ask from what position and discipline different forms of anti-theatricalism are voiced. The longest and most constitutive tradition of anti-theatricalism is indeed that of philosophy, infused by various forms of religious iconoclasm, and it is tempting to dismiss philosophical anti-theatricalism as an ideology that attacks the theatre from afar. However, more often than not, even this philosophical anti-theatricalism is not simply a critique from a distance but a critique that, on the contrary, testifies to the centrality of the theatre for philosophy. While Plato opposes both theatre and drama, playwrights such as Agathon and actors such as Ion are central figures in his texts, which, furthermore, are written in the dramatic form of the dialogue. Philosophy, here, seems to be a special form of theatre that must therefore differentiate itself from the regular modes of tragedy and comedy.[18] A similarly ambiguous relation can be seen in another anti-theatrical philosopher, Nietzsche, who not only sought a revival of Greek tragedy in Richard Wagner's *Gesamtkunstwerk* but also introduced notions such as masks and acting into the very terminology of his philosophical texts.[19] Indeed, we can plot a trajectory of theatrical philosophy, from Nietzsche to Walter Benjamin, Kenneth Burke and Gilles Deleuze, that testifies to the contentious but constitutive struggle between theatre and philosophy.[20] The convergence of theory and theatre is exemplified in Chapter 13 by Herbert Blau, whose career as theatre artist and as theorist shows just how closely those two endeavours can be intertwined. The search for the impossible theatre, the anti-theatre, the point zero of the theatre leads not only to ever-new theatres, but also to new forms of thinking and writing about theatre. Perhaps it is one of the after-effects of the creative destructions of the modernist theatre that manifestos, theatres and theories can no longer be neatly kept apart.

The theatre of modernism was intensely admired and reviled not only by the other arts and philosophy, but also by politics and law. In Chapter 12, 'Performing Obscene Modernism', Julie Peters claims that the rise of obscenity as a specific juridical category had contradictory goals: on the one hand, censorship aimed to protect morals from modern pornography and mass entertainment and, on the other, spokesmen for modern art, such as Oscar Wilde, who were themselves labelled (and in Wilde's case legally convicted) as 'indecent', invoked the same category to protect art for art's sake. 'Where art was disinterested, an end in itself, above the world of commerce and exchange, finer as it became more disembodied, and ultimately a stimulus for the rational and contemplative faculties', Peters writes, 'pornography was unabashedly a product of commerce, catering purely to self-interest, instrumental, frankly embodied, and a stimulus for bodily pleasure. Thus, obscenity as a moral and legal concept arose, in part at least, as a kind of watchdog for the aesthetic.' There is, she shows, a deep historical and structural affiliation between theatricality and obscenity (expressed in the etymology sometimes proffered: *ob* (against) and *skene* (stage) – obscenity is that which is against or off the stage). If theatre was troubling in part because it always verged on the obscene, obscenity was troubling in part because it always verged on the theatrical. Thus, in the name of obscenity, some of the most important works of early theatrical modernism – Ibsen's *Ghosts*, Strindberg's *Miss Julie*, Wedekind's *Spring Awakening* and the Lulu plays, Wilde's *Salomé*, Schnitzler's *La Ronde*, Shaw's *Mrs Warren's Profession* – were banned. Yet censorship led to the creation of the independent theatre movement, and playwrights such as Wedekind and Shaw wrote in continual dialogue with the censors. Modern art had declared itself, in Shaw's paradoxical phrase, 'conscientiously immoral', and, in France, Great Britain, Germany and the United States, theatre was central to debates about obscene art in this period.

These varied forms of anti-theatricalism suggest that we can no longer take for granted that anti-theatricalism merely means an opposition to the theatre. If anti-theatricalism appears inside the theatre, what is being opposed cannot simply be everything that happens on the stage and for an audience. Rather, *theatrical* becomes an adjective that describes a condition or value rather than solely the essence of one art form. As is suggested forcefully by Fuchs, anti-theatricalism can be thought of as a subset of what Lionel Abel called 'metatheatre', the critical version of the theatre's tendency towards self-commentary and self-reflection.[21] When seen within this tradition, which is an integral part of the history of theatre from Euripides and Calderón to Bertolt Brecht and Beckett, anti-theatricalism presents itself as a paradoxical way of affirming the capacious powers of the theatre: far from fearing its own extinction, the theatre can host its own critique and profit in the process.

The anti-theatricalist self-critique of the theatre is a trend that does not stop with modernism. Happenings and performance art are forms that have developed out of a radicalized self-critique of the theatre; they are developments fuelled by modernist anti-theatricalism, as Perloff's analysis of Cage shows. This history emerges not only from the practices of happenings and performance art that seem intent on violating every aspect of the stage but also from the explicitly anti-theatrical pronouncements of its defenders and practitioners, who often do not seem to have a single good thing to say about the theatre.[22] For all its difference from modernist theatre, performance art must be understood not only as a celebration of theatricality, as is often assumed, but rather as a combination of celebration and critique. Even as *Against Theatre* is devoted to locating the diverse forms of modernist anti-theatricalism, it may point toward an analysis of performance art and thereby also contribute to the newly expanded mission of Theatre Studies in general.

Notes

1. Henrik Ibsen, *Peer Gynt: A Dramatic Poem*, trans. Peter Watts (London: Penguin Books, 1966), p.210.
2. Joseph A. Schumpeter, *Capitalism, Socialism, and Democracy*, 3rd edn (New York: Harper & Brothers, 1950).

3. George L. Mosse, *The Nationalization of the Masses: Political Symbolism and Mass Movements in Germany from the Napoleonic Wars through the Third Reich* (Ithaca, NY: Cornell University Press, 1991).

4. Karl Marx, *The 18th Brumaire of Louis Bonaparte* (New York: International Publishers, 1963).

5. Jonas Barish, *The Antitheatrical Prejudice*. (Berkeley: University of California Press, 1981), p.469.

6. Reagan, Ronald. 'Acceptance of the Republican Nomination for President, 1980'. 1 May 2002 <http://www.pbs.org/wgbh/amex/reagan/filmmore/index.html>.

7. Perspectivism, which Alexander Nehamas describes in his important book, *Nietzsche: Life as Literature* (Cambridge: Harvard University Press, 1985), holds that 'every view is only one among many possible interpretations', and also bears on the first two ways in which we aim to define modernism. For perspectivism 'is both something that must be understood and something that suggests that understanding may be impossible', holding that 'there are no facts that are independent of interpretation' (pp.1–3). Nehamas's reading of Nietzsche serves as an important corrective to essentialist or non-contingent theories of self or of truth (as opposed to illusion). For instance, Benjamin Bennett argues for a theory of 'drama as knowledge, as authentic, anguished self-confrontation' which runs through Nietzsche, Strindberg, Brecht, and the German expressionists. He writes: 'The principle of modern drama, in all of these cases, is neither the imitation of reality nor the alleviation of human anguish, but rather the intensification of our condition, precisely in its most difficult and disturbing aspects' (p.247).

8. Charles Taylor, *Sources of the Self: The Making of the Modern Identity* (Cambridge: Harvard University Press, 1989), p.465.

9. Philip Fisher, *Still the New World: American Literature in a Culture of Creative Destruction* (Cambridge: Harvard University Press, 1999), p.4.

10. Clement Greenberg, 'Modernist Painting', in *The Collected Essays and Criticism, Volume 4: Modernism with a Vengeance, 1957–1969* ed. John O'Brian (Chicago: University of Chicago Press, 1993), p.85. 'Modernist Painting' was first published in *Forum Lectures* (1960).

11. Francisque Sarcey, 'Essai d'une esthétique de théatre', in *Quarante ans de théâtre*, vol. 1 (Paris: Bibliothèque des Annales Politiques et Littéraires, 1900), pp.125–33.

12. Michael Fried, 'Art and Objecthood' [1967], *Art and Objecthood: Essays and Reviews* (Chicago: The University of Chicago Press, 1998), p.160.

13. James Joyce, *A Portrait of the Artist as a Young Man*, ed. Seamus Deane (New York: Penguin Books, 1992), p.233.

14. Hayden White, *Figural Realism: Studies in the Mimesis Effect* (Baltimore, MD: The Johns Hopkins University Press, 1999), p.70.

15. Samuel Beckett, *Endgame* (New York: Grove Press, 1958), p.46.

16. Stanley Cavell, 'Ending the Waiting Game: A Reading of Beckett's *Endgame*', in *Must We Mean What We Say? A Book of Essays* (Cambridge: Cambridge University Press, 1976), p.160

17. Samuel Beckett, *Disjecta: Miscellaneous Writings and a Dramatic Fragment*, ed. Ruby Cohn (New York: Grove Press, 1984), pp.138, 139.

18. The first to recognize the extent to which Plato not only rejected, but also directly competed with, the theatre was Friedrich Nietzsche, who described

Plato's dialogues as a composite of Greek tragedy and comedy, the creation of a new, synthetic genre, namely the novel. Friedrich Nietzsche, *Die Geburt der Tragödie aus dem Geiste der Musik* (1872; Stuttgart: Kröner, 1976), p.122. This argument was to be repeated by Bakhtin, who does not attribute it to Nietzsche. M. M. Bakhtin, *The Dialogic Imagination*, ed. Michael Holquist, trans. Caryl Emerson and Michael Holquist (Austin: University of Texas Press, 1981), p.22.

19. This theatrical reading of Nietzsche has become a standard reading, thanks to Deleuze's subsequent book on Nietzsche and a number of other commentators, from Gianni Vattimo to Peter Sloterdijk, who casts Nietzsche as a 'thinker on stage'. Peter Sloterdijk, *Der Denker auf der Bühne: Nietzsches Materialismus* (Frankfurt am Main: Suhrkamp Verlag, 1986). Gianni Vattimo, *I Sogetto e la Maschera: Nietzsche e il problema della liberatzione* (Milano: Bompiani, 1974).

20. Several philosophers concerned with the intersection of theatre and psychoanalysis, such as Jean-François Lyotard, Philipe Lacoue-Labarthe and André Green, are collected in *Mimesis, Masochism, and Mime: The Politics of Theatricality in Contemporary French Thought*, ed. Timothy Murray (Ann Arbor: The University of Michigan Press, 1997).

21. Lionel Abel, *Metatheatre: A New View of Dramatic Form* (New York: Hill & Wang, 1963).

22. Philip Auslander, for example, noted an affinity of performance art and the anti-theatricalism of Michael Fried in *From Acting to Performance: Essays in Modernism and Postmodernism* (London: Routledge, 1997).

Part I
Frames

2
Avant-Garde Scenography and the Frames of the Theatre

Arnold Aronson

> Over some fifteen years a growing number of minds have been more or less actively seeking a way towards a new type of theatre, They have been abusing the picture-frame stage, stamping on the footlights, pulling out the front of the apron, pushing the actors into the loges, down the orchestra pit, into the prompter's box, out upon the runways or up the aisles. They have gone clear out of the playhouse and into circuses, open air theatres, and public parks, All to set up a new and mutual relationship between the actor and the audience.
>
> (K. Macgowan and R. E. Jones, *Continental Stagecraft*, 1922[1])

How do we know we are watching theatre and not simply observing the world around us? In *The Contrast*, Royall Tyler's play of 1787 (usually considered the first American comedy), the good-hearted but simple character Jonathan is tricked into going to the theatre – an activity that he perceives as immoral, but of which he has had no experience. Questioned afterward, he comments on the peculiar architecture to be found in New York City that permits one to peer into neighbouring buildings, and acknowledges that he would not mind having a bit of cider with one of the individuals he observed. It is an amusing conceit precisely because of its metatheatricality. As a theatrically competent audience we may laugh at a naïf who is unaware of the presence of a frame and thus perceives the on-stage action as an extension of his own world, no matter how peculiar. The situation in this play serves to demonstrate that without a frame there can be no theatre. And equally important, the spectator must be able to identify the presence of the frame because the frame not only creates the theatrical event, it creates the spectator – the one who observes what is in the frame. Classical Sanskrit performance theory identifies two modes of behaviour: *lokadharmi* or everyday behaviour, and *natyadharmi*, the specialized and heightened activity of performance.[2] Although we might presume that the latter – what Eugenio Barba calls the 'extra-daily' – would be recognizable simply by its differences from the quotidian, this is not always the case; it is the presence of a frame that separates performance from daily life and foregrounds it. Guy Debord, in an admittedly different context, states this eloquently: 'The phenomenon of separation is part and parcel of the unity of the world, of a global social praxis that has split up into reality on the one hand and image on the other.'[3] 'Separation', he further proclaims, 'is the alpha and omega of the spectacle.'[4]

A frame, of course, is that which surrounds, borders, limits and defines an image or object. Its existence creates difference and as such it distinguishes the theatrical from the non-theatrical, that which is on stage from that which is off. In regard to the theatre, the term 'frame', today, at least in the West, most probably evokes some variant of the proscenium arch, but it need not be so literal. In the traditional English mumming play, for instance, the performers entered a home or inn, sometimes literally sweeping the occupants of the room into a circle with a broom, while chanting, 'Room, room, brave gallants all,/Pray give us room to rhyme.'[5] The performers created a stage by re-framing the space of the room and transformed the occupants of the room into spectators, but there is no permanent or concrete stage space. Between the amorphous space of the folk performance and the elaborate proscenia of baroque opera houses are all manner of stages, many of which may not have overt frames but whose very existence functions as a frame. The edges of an arena or thrust stage are frames, just as much as the pictorial frames of the late nineteenth century. So too are the invisible but often inviolable edges of the spaces carved out by folk performers or street buskers. But while all stages function as frames, frames are not limited to the physical stage. As Patrice Pavis points out:

> The frame or framework of the theatre performance is not only the type of stage or space in which the play is performed. More broadly, it also refers to the set of the spectators' experiences and *expectations*, the contextualization of the fiction represented. *Frame* is to be taken both literally (as a "boxing-in" of the *performance*) and abstractly (as a contextualization and foregrounding of the action.)[6]

While I am concerned with the physical manifestation of the frame, I am here using the term to refer as well to the aesthetic structure and system of signification that allows us, as with *lokadharmi* and *natyadharmi*, to distinguish that which is performance from that which is 'life'.

Just as nineteenth-century artists began to interrogate the function of the (physical) frame in painting, so too did nineteenth-century practitioners begin to challenge the notion of the frame in the theatre. The elimination of the proscenium, the emergence of thrust, arena and fragmented stages, as suggested by Macgowan and Jones above, can be seen as part of a modernist project to transgress the traditional boundaries of the stage. In fact, it is this attack upon the stage itself – the very signifier of the theatrical event – that constitutes a significant aspect of modernist theatre. And thus, if we can say that stage/frame = theatre (and its corollary: stage/frame creates the spectator), then the creation of a fragmented or porous frame, or the elimination of the frame altogether, is an anti-theatrical gesture.

The Renaissance frame

The peculiar goal of the enframed stage, from the Renaissance through the nineteenth century, was to recreate a physical simulacrum of the experiential world. The artistic frame emerged as a crucial device in the early Renaissance because of the technical development of the art of perspective. Renaissance art foregrounded the frame as a fundamental mechanism for the capturing of reality. As Rudolph Arnheim has noted, the Renaissance frame functioned as 'figure' while the painting within it was seen as 'ground'. 'As pictorial space emancipated itself from the wall and created deep vistas', he explained, 'a clear visual distinction became necessary between the physical space of the room and the world of the picture.'[7] The invention of mathematically precise perspective painting is generally attributed to Filippo Brunelleschi and Leon Battista Alberti, and it was the latter who delineated his technique in *Della Pittura* (On Painting) in 1436. Describing his approach, Alberti explained: 'First of all, on the surface on which I am going to paint, I draw a rectangle of whatever size I want, which I regard as an open window through which the subject painted is seen.'[8] The figure of the open window, of course, has become a classic metaphor for pictorial realism in all the arts. Not only does it posit a separation of viewer on one side and subject on the other, but it establishes the notion of the frame through which the subject is seen. A frame serves to create the necessary aesthetic distance required for apprehending a work of art, and at the same time it limits what is seen by the viewer. The subject is whatever fits within the frame – the rest of the cosmos may be implied but is at least visually excluded. As Arnheim explained: 'This world came to be conceived of as boundless – not only in depth, but also laterally – so that the edges of the picture designated the end of the composition, but not the end of represented space.'[9]

The window, however, was only the first step for Alberti. In order to accurately (perspectively) recreate what he saw, he described the creation of a grid within this window which, significantly, he called a veil:

> a veil loosely woven of fine thread, dyed whatever colour you please, divided up by thicker threads into as many parallel sections as you like, and stretched on a frame, I set this up between the eyes and the object to be represented, so that the visual pyramid passes through the loose weave of the veil.[10]

For the artist, then, the window is not transparent; the image is mediated. The life seen through the window is transformed into geometric patterns and, amazingly, possibly tinted by the colors of the veil. Presumably, Alberti could have simply suggested a grid over a window, yet he proposed a kind of *veil of maya* that prevents the viewer from seeing pure reality. Yet the idea of pictorial realism as life viewed through a window (or a fourth wall in nineteenth-century theatrical terms) retains, even today, its aura of scientific objectivity.

In baroque theatre the simulacrum was achieved through the application of perspective painting to the stage, a technique that is at once mathematical and metaphorical and functions by deceiving the eye. Painted flats and drops, often placed in forced-perspective arrangements, created a sense of depth (and by implication, time) in an essentially two-dimensional space. Significantly, the most ambitious of these techniques were employed for the creation of allegorical spaces rather than those that might actually be encountered in nature or human creation. The fantastical scenes of the *intermezzi* would not have been seen through any known window. But by the nineteenth century, first in melodrama and then in naturalistic productions, perspectively painted flats and drops were largely replaced or supplemented by actual, tangible objects borrowed from the experiential world of the spectator, or else by a stage filled with hidden technology that allowed the recreation of natural phenomena ranging from cascading waterfalls to earthquakes. Theatre thus became not the domain of the actor, and certainly not of the text, but became instead the realm of the visual and spectacular. Aristotle's 'imitation of an action' gave way to what Christian Metz referred to, in regard to film, as a 'scopic regime'.[11]

The emergence of perspective, came to symbolize, as Martin Jay points out, 'a harmony between the mathematical regularities of optics and God's will'.[12] That is, the image that was depicted not only functioned as a world observed through a window, but it also connected the viewer to divine *lux*, the light emanating from God.[13] As science replaced religion, substituting what was understood as a rational order for a theocratic one, the perspective image embodied the scientificism of the *ocular*. Perspective, it must be emphasized, is not a copy of the world as much as it is a strategy for organizing the perception and understanding of space – a strategy that is entirely dependent on the perceived presence of a frame.

The creation of perspective, however is problematized in the theatre for two reasons. Instead of a single, flat, painted canvas, there are multiple canvases in a perspectival relation to each other on the three-dimensional space of the stage. Second, the presence of the live actor exponentially complicates reception, not only through the physical dimensionality of the performer, but through the emotional and psychological effect that the actions of one living being have on another. (Even here, Alberti obviously understood the theatricality of the perspective image while seemingly anticipating the twentieth-century acting theories of Stanislavski and Strasberg. Saying that the purpose of painting is 'historia' – a term which he does not really define – he notes that: 'A "historia" will move spectators when the men painted in the picture outwardly demonstrate their own feelings as clearly as possible.'[14] In other words, the clear delineation of emotion by the subjects of the painting will evoke appropriate emotion from the spectators.)

As Jay points out, in the move from the Renaissance to the modern, 'canvases were filled with more and more information that seemed unrelated to any narrative or textual function' and the figural function of the painting was foregrounded over the narrative resulting in the 'increasing autonomy of the image from any extrinsic purpose, religious or otherwise'.[15] Like the artist's canvas, the stage by the mid-nineteenth century was becoming increasingly filled with 'information' which likewise overwhelmed the narrative function of the stage. It was, in fact, the clutter, detail, technology, and the intrusion of elements of the everyday into the realm of the theatrical (furniture, food, 'real' people rather than actors) that led Symbolist poet Stéphane Mallarmé to call for a kind of 'detheatricalization' of the theatre. If ever there was a crusade 'against theatre', this was it and it would echo through the avant-garde movements of the early twentieth century.

The deconstruction of the spectator

If the frame produces not only the stage but the spectator, then to detheatricalize the theatre is to call into question the role of the spectator within that construction. While the interrogation of the spectatorial role was first made overt by the Symbolists, the seeds may have been planted earlier. Jonathan Crary has identified 'a reorganization of the observer' that begins early in the nineteenth century as a result of 'an uprooting of vision from the stable and fixed relations incarnated in the camera obscura'.[16] Although Crary is looking at the social construction of vision in the nineteenth century and makes only passing reference to the theatre, the stage actually seems to be one of the prime contested sites for the very issues he raises. Although the elaborate proscenium frame is a product of the baroque, it is not until the mid-nineteenth century that the stage opening is completely bordered on all four sides by what is known as a picture-frame proscenium or sometimes a peep-show stage. But prior to this development, the stage picture itself – that which is contained within the frame – began to lose its stability. The fixed positions of the wings, drops and borders – essential for the perspective vista – and, consequentially, the fixed position of the privileged spectators, gives way to the increasingly random placement of two- and three-dimensional objects on the stage (sometimes known as 'free plantation'). The necessity of the duke's box, the centrally situated site for the primary observer, was obviated.

It was Richard Wagner, of course, who in his theatre at Bayreuth, instituted the most radical reorganization of the spectator while, ironically, simultaneously reinforcing the stage frame with his famous double proscenium that encased the mystic gulf. By eliminating the auditorium boxes, which were essentially mini-proscenia that transformed spectators into performers, and more importantly, by turning off the houselights and plunging the spectators into darkness, Wagner eliminated the individuated and privileged audience and turned it into an undifferentiated community. But whereas Wagner envisioned the audience projecting itself through the mystic gulf into the world of the stage, the symbolists, so profoundly influenced by Wagner, sought to eliminate the separation through more direct means. The symbolist theatre would seek to dissolve the proscenium frame in order to unify the stage and auditorium. Crary suggests that 'over the course of the nineteenth century, an observer increasingly had to function within disjunct and defamiliarized urban spaces'.[17] Wagner's attempt to deconstruct the audience (and his decision to create his festival theatre in the small town of Bayreuth) was one response to the increasing alienation of urban life. Mallarmé's challenge to dematerialize the stage, and the similar calls of those who followed, might also be understood as part of an attempt to reintegrate the spectator into the shifting dynamics of the modernist urban world.

The issue of the spectator and the frame (or the individual within society) has remained a potent one. More than half a century later Jean-Paul Sartre provides a metaphorical means of approaching these issues. In Section 3 of *Being and Nothingness* ('The Existence of Others'), Sartre articulates the scopic regime of being alone in a park[18] and describes the objects in his view: 'those things in my universe; grouped and synthesized *from my point of view* into instrumental complexes'[19] (italics in original). Sartre's gaze is absolute; he is at the centre of the universe or, more properly, the centre of the visual field which amounts to the same thing in this case. He is, in a sense, the embodiment of Descartes's *cogito*, the self as universal centre. The spectator in the baroque theatre, looking through the metaphoric window at perspective vistas, was not unlike Sartre in the park with a god-like, self-centred view. But the introduction of three-dimensional objects complicated the visual field. We exist in cubic space, as it were, in the midst of a fully dimensional world. But a spectator viewing a simulacrum of human space on a stage (through a window/frame) must have the objects arranged for visual access. Thus, on the traditional box set – a development of the late eighteenth and early nineteenth centuries – all furniture faces the curtain line. (Just as in Leonardo's painting of the Last Supper Jesus and all the disciples sit, improbably, on one side of the table.) Three-dimensionality is flattened within the frame and spatial and kinetic logic are dismissed or reappropriated.

André Antoine, director of the Naturalist Théâtre Libre in Paris, began to rebel against this arrangement of furniture and to arrange the stage as if there were no missing fourth wall or even a single line of sight. Multiple spectators create multiple perspectives (which would seem to challenge the Cartesian view). In a sense this disruption of the gaze seems to be embodied in Sartre's scenario as well. Into his public park comes a second individual. And because this is a person and not an inanimate object, Sartre is no longer the master of the gaze, an omnipotent observer, but becomes an object of another's gaze. And furthermore, this 'other' disrupts the lines of vision. No longer do all lines of sight connect the first observer equally with the horizon and all objects in the park; the intruder becomes the focal point from whom all lines of sight emanate. 'The distance', Sartre declares, '*is unfolded starting from the man whom I see* ... instead of a grouping *toward me* of the objects, there is now an orientation *which flees from me.*'[20] Modernist scenography, can be read as the introduction of an 'other' into the frame which thereby destabilizes the frame in relation to the viewer. The self-centered gaze is disrupted, the singular, unchanging objectification of vision is destroyed. Modern, that is, post-Renaissance, theatre was based upon the controlled, unifying vision of the frame (window) which implied a singular or unified spectator and a mono-directed gaze. Just as Sartre's second park denizen disrupts the notion of a frame by interrogating the position of the viewer, so too does the modernist project, through its attempts to alter or eliminate the frame, throw the whole notion of theatre into question.

Roland Barthes, in an essay on the theatre of Baudelaire, defined theatricality as 'theatre-minus-text'.[21] For Barthes, in other words, theatricality is the totality of non-textual elements: the spectacular and the physical. The Symbolists of the 1880s wanted to strip theatre of its theatricality which, they implied, was extraneous to the purposes of theatre and interfered with its spiritual aspect. Yet, if what makes the theatre theatrical (as opposed to literary) is, in fact, the visual-physical – the spectacular – then to detheatricalize is nothing less than to deny the existence of theatre itself. In its historical context, the Symbolist project is understandable, of course. A theatre that had become the domain of stage managers and technicians, a theatre of erupting volcanoes, burning buildings, storm-tossed ships at sea, trap doors and special effects had already done the reverse – that is, it had de-literacized the theatre. Language, poetry and philosophy were minimized if not totally eradicated on the melodramatic stage and, arguably, on certain naturalistic stages as well. But the Symbolists were not simply opposed to the technological aspects of theatre; the very presence of the human actor was anathema to them. Maurice Maeterlinck, in 'Menus propos – le théâtre', claimed that 'the great poems of humanity', such as *Lear, Hamlet, Othello, Macbeth* and the like, could not, in fact, be represented on the stage. 'The stage is where masterpieces die', he proclaimed, 'because the presentation of a masterpiece by *accidental* and *human* means is a contradiction. All masterpieces are symbols, and the symbol never withstands the active presence of man.'[22] Similarly, Mallarmé, commenting on Wagner, declared that 'a static set and a real actor' interfere with the true spiritual intention of theatrical art.[23] If there is no actor, there is no need for a stage and theatre retreats back into the spiritual realm of the text.

Disintegration of the frame: Symbolism, Futurism and beyond

Despite the symbolists' attacks on theatricality, they seemingly were unable to let go of the idea of theatre altogether, continuing to create performance texts while simultaneously permeating or eroding the frame. One of the most notable – if ultimately unsuccessful – examples was the attempt to release perfumes into the air at the Théâtre d'Art production of *Song of Songs* base on Solomon's Biblical poem. To evoke the scents mentioned in the text, and perhaps to reference the 'perfumes' of Baudelaire's sonnet 'Correspondences', several Symbolist poets standing at the front of the stage and in the balcony sprayed the audience with perfumes from hand-held atomizers.[24] While one might argue that visual and aural elements, by definition, emanate from the stage and thus suffuse the audience as well, when the private senses (smell, touch, taste) are subsumed into the performance, the fourth wall has truly been ruptured. The text was, to borrow a later futurist phrase, a 'net of sensations' which, ideally, enveloped the audience in an effort to minimize the differentiation between auditorium and stage, thereby implicating the spectators within the performance.

At the same time, performances were being moved from the play-house into nature which, in its time, also served to dissolve the sense of frame. Maurice Pottecher, for instance, created The People's Theatre, an open-air theatre at Bussang, in 1895. Alfred Vallette, editor of *Mercure de France*, suggested that such theatres would allow playing 'those pieces unplayable in a theatre'.[25] Presumably, playing in the pure environment of nature would allow the 'non-theatrical' to flourish in a way impossible on the theatrical stage. Even Alfred Jarry praised 'natural décors' while suggesting that spectators could reach such theatres by bicycle.[26] If the recreation of the natural world on the stage through illusionistic techniques was antithetical to art, then the reintroduction of the performer (and the text) into nature itself served to dispel the corrupting influences of the stage while still deriving the spiritual benefits that theatre had to offer. This is certainly what Edward Gordon Craig, inspired by Eleanore Duse, had in mind when he suggested 'playing in the Open Air' as the Greeks had done. Doing so, he proclaimed, would eliminate the 'humbug' and 'trickery' of the theatre. 'The open air is at once the most lawful and the most illegal place in creation. All is allowed there except for the unnatural.'[27] If Baudelaire is the spiritual father of the Symbolists, then his sonnet, 'Correspondences', not only anticipates the central Symbolist notion of synesthesia, but in its opening lines makes the connection to nature explicit. 'Nature is a temple in which living pillars/ Sometimes emit confused words;/ Man crosses it through forests of symbols....'[28] The Symbolist theatre artists, in certain instances, rejected the physical theatre in order to move into the temple of nature, to move into the forests. Of course, as with so many revolutionary movements, the rejection of the established order, when seen in retrospect, was far from complete. Just as with Pottecher's outdoor stage, the move into nature most often meant little more than the recreation of the stage structure in a park setting. But even so, part of the frame – the architecture of the theatre building – was eliminated so that nature itself became the frame, thereby incorporating the spectator rather than erecting a barrier.

But even when the Symbolists did not dispense with the frame, they were in some way tampering with the idea of framing. Playwright Pierre Quillard stated the famous Symbolist dictum: 'Language creates the scenery like everything else.'[29] If the traditional frame of the stage provided an Alberti-like window on reality, a window profusely populated with the objects and images of the observable world, then the Symbolists fully rejected this notion. Their frame contained comparatively minimalist and suggestive scenic elements, often little more than a painted backdrop or some scrims. In his 1886 essay, 'Wagnerian Painting', critic Teodor de Wyzewa declared that 'art must consciously re-create, by means of *signs*, the total life of the universe, that is to say the soul.'[30] He then went on to posit that the most fundamental element of the 'life of our soul' is 'sensation'. Thus, the apprehension of a work of art (and by implication a work of theatre) is not limited to rational and objective depictions within the frame but rather, to quote Wyzewa, 'there arises in the soul something akin to an immense flow, whose waves lose themselves in confusion.' The frame, in other words, dissolves, and the spectator/observer becomes one with the work. Boundaries cease to exist as suggested by the line from Quillard's *The Girl with Cut-Off Hands*: 'O world, O life, O senses, fade away!'[31]

In *The Art of Description*, an analysis of seventeenth-century Dutch painting, Svetlana Alpers suggests that Italian Renaissance painting was an art of narrative, whereas 'the Dutch present their pictures as describing the world seen rather than as imitations of significant human actions.'[32] One result is to decentre the spectator, or even to seemingly ignore the presence of the spectator. As Martin Jay notes, 'this world, moreover, is not contained entirely within the frame of the Albertian window, but seems instead to extend beyond it.'[33] As he goes on to explain, frames continue to exist – these are still paintings after all – 'but they are arbitrary and without the totalizing function they serve in Southern art'. A similar analysis might be applied to Symbolist scenography, especially the famous décor for Alfred Jarry's *Ubu Roi*. Although enframed by the stage, the scenery is no longer mimetic; it no longer relates in any scientific or objective way to the external world. Painted by an artistic dream team including Vuillard, Sérusier and Toulouse-Lautrec, the scene depicted, in Jarry's words, 'doors opening onto snow-covered plains under blue skies, mantelpieces with clocks on them swinging open to turn into doorways, and palm trees flourishing at the foot of beds so that little elephants perching bookshelves can graze on them'.[34] Alpers's description of the distinctions between Northern and Southern Renaissance art could be applied equally to the setting for *Ubu*:

> Attention to many small things versus a few large ones; light reflected off objects versus objects modeled by light and shadow; the surface of objects, their colors and textures, dealt with rather than their placement in a legible space; an unframed image versus one that is clearly framed; one with no clearly situated viewer compared to one with such a viewer.[35]

In a purely technical sense the *Ubu* scenography does not violate the frame of the stage. One might contend that the frame, in fact, is necessary in order to make any sense of the seemingly disconnected and disparate objects and styles accumulated in this décor. But this famous design was radically different from any scenography that preceded it. (It might be argued that the true scandal, and the true revolution of *Ubu* was in its scenography even more than in the text or the acting.) The total disregard of unity seemed to mock the very idea of a frame. If the major purpose of a frame is to contain and unify that which is found within it, then this décor defied the totalizing function of the frame and in that sense challenged the notion of order and perception of the world held by the spectators.

But it was the Futurists who, as in so many things, radically challenged the conventions of theatre practice and, in this regard became the embodiment of a modernist anti-theatricality. The majority of their theatrical work fell into three broad categories. The form that most closely resembled traditional theatre was the *sintesi* or syntheses which, in their definition were 'very brief, [intended] to compress into a few minutes, into a few words and gestures, innumerable situations, sensibilities, ideas, sensations, facts, and symbols'.[36] These were skits and playlets ranging from a few lines to a few pages in length. They challenged conventional dramatic structures and deconstructed genres, and although these were generally performed within a traditional stage setting – thereby engendering a series of expectations on the part of the audience that would then be subverted – their intention was to shatter all preconceptions of the very nature of the frame. The Futurist Synthetic Theatre Manifesto declared that they would:

> Symphonize the audience's sensibility by exploring it, stirring up its laziest layers with every means possible; eliminate the preconception of the footlights by throwing nets of sensation between stage and audience; the stage action will invade the orchestra seats, the audience.[37] [All capital letters in the original.]

The manifesto blatantly rejected 'the prejudice of theatricality' in favour of 'life itself'.[38] The Futurists also presented *serate* or evenings which were performances in the form of provocative lectures that often resulted in riots or at least energetic exchanges between performers and spectators; and they created events or happenings in public places – staging fist fights in train stations, for instance – that would engage unsuspecting passersby. The aim of the Futurists was to blur if not obliterate the distinction between stage and auditorium, and in the process to obscure the distinction between life and art.[39] One of the significant transformations of Western theatre through the eighteenth and nineteenth centuries was the move from the court to the city. As theatre became bourgeois it became urban. The Futurists were taking that to the next logical step – to dissolve the walls of the theatre so that the urban environment itself *was* the theatre.

From here one could simply recite a litany of avant-garde events in which the frame of the stage was permeated if not entirely dissolved: the cabaret performances of the Dadas, the urban Dada events such as Dadatours, and the proto-performance art of Tristan Tzara who would, among other things, sit in a tree in front of his home reciting an invented bird language. Some early Expressionist performances, such as Kokoschka's *Murderer, the Hope of Women*, were presented in natural surroundings, much as Vallette and Jarry had advocated. Meyerhold's Symbolist projects in St Petersburg, the later work of Nikolai Okhlopkov at Moscow's Realistic Theatre, and the stagings of Andrzej Pronaszko and Szymon Syrkus in Poland, all to one degree or another challenged the stage frame. Max Reinhardt, as early as 1901, stated that 'for me the frame that separates the stage from the world has never been essential...and everything that breaks that frame open, strengthens and widens the effect, increases contact with the audience, whether in the direction of intimacy or monumentality, will always be welcome to me.[40] In his outdoor stagings at Salzburg, and in the original designs for the so-called 'Theater of Five Thousand' (though not so completely in its final manifestation as the Grosses Schauspielhaus), Rheinhardt put these ideas into practice. Architecturally, Emile Jacques-Dalcroze's theatre at Hellerau (where he developed eurhythmics and worked with Appia), Copeau's Vieux Colombier, the several theatre projects of Norman Bel Geddes, and many of the productions of Erwin Piscator, to cite only the best known, all bridged the divide between stage and auditorium.[41]

The two great theoreticians of the first half of the twentieth century Artaud and Brecht, both, of course, challenged the theatrical frame. Artaud famously called for theatre in alternative spaces: 'We abolish the stage and the auditorium and replace them by a single site, without partition or barrier of any kind, which will become the theater of the action.'[42] Brecht, on the other hand, did not want to eliminate the frame; by doing away with the curtain and exposing the technical elements of the stage he was instead foregrounding the frame, forcing the audience to be aware of the theatrical devices employed by the drama. In doing so, the audience could reframe, or resituate the content so as to respond actively. In the years following World War II, theatre artists in the United States and Europe created an experimental or avant-garde theatre that was largely inspired by one or both of these writers, particularly in the new approaches to staging and scenography.

The assumption underlying all these alternative stagings was that theatre, as commonly practised, was increasingly ineffective in engaging an audience and conveying meaning – as if Alberti's net across the window no longer provided a means of analysing the image but served only to obscure it. Thus, the primary signifier of the theatre, the stage, had to be eliminated in favour of a physical form that was more like life. In reality, of course, these projects bore no more relationship to the 'real world' than the proscenium or other conventional stages. By substituting a new set of signs for the stage, they simply referenced the perceived structure of daily existence and therefore, for a brief time, suggested (created an illusion of) a greater reality.

In 1971 the Parisian newspaper *Le Monde* published a chart entitled 'Two theories of popular theatre'. The chart, clearly echoing Brecht's famous comparison of epic and dramatic theatre, consisted of two columns, the left categorizing theatre of the 1950s and the right that of the 1970s. Under the heading 'Where' was the following:

New premises	The street, the place of work
Without proscenium arch	Without any fixed structure
Towards the public	Amidst the public[43]

As perceived from that moment in time, the theatre had moved from the incremental steps away from the proscenium to a full-fledged abandonment of the theatre for the streets. If we take the phrase 'towards the public' in the sense of lines of vision as in both Alberti as well as in Sartre's organization of space, then the post-war theatre was simply challenging the centrality and ocular-centrism of the spectator. By the seventies, however, any spatially organizing principle seems to have been abandoned in favour of a decentralized anarchy in which all perspectives are possible, and in which the focal point might be continually shifting with the energy of the flow of traffic in the streets. From the vantage point of the mid-1970s, all notion of the traditional stage had seemingly been destroyed by the work of Grotowski, Kantor, Schechner, Schumann (Bread and Puppet Theatre) and others. Much of this work was termed 'environmental theatre' which might be seen as a phenomenological equivalent to John Cage's notion of 'chance' in that it mimicked nature in its 'method of operation'. When I wake up in the morning I am *in* my bed, not observing it; at mealtimes I am *in* my kitchen, handling food and utensils, and I then sit at a table and eat. Again, I do not observe, I experience. If, since the Renaissance if not since ancient Greece, the theatre had transformed the spectator into a passive observer of a simulation of life, this rejection of theatre through the elimination of the frame (or in some cases, more precisely, the incorporation of the spectator *within the frame*) was intended to re-engage the spectator in an active role in the performance in order not simply to entertain but to transform.

John Cage reframes the performance

There is perhaps no better exemplar of modernist theory and practice than the composer John Cage. (It is perhaps worth noting that two of the giants who book-end modernism – Wagner and Cage – come from the world of music, which may say something about the differing relations of music and visual arts to the notion of framing. But that is a topic for another essay.) And it was precisely through the strategy of foregrounding or subverting the frame that Cage created some of his most famous and influential works. No doubt the best known of these is *4'33"* whose title defines a particular length of 'silence'. This composition is divided into three movements, each of which functions as a device to frame the ambient sound of the concert hall, thereby redirecting the listeners to hear sounds that would normally be excluded from the notion of a concert and asking them to reconceive the very notion of music. The frame in this case transforms 'noise' into music. But Cage's compositions and use of framing are also emblematic of the modern notion of transgressing or eliminating the frame. Cage, in many of his works, is asking the audience to refocus outside the bounds of the visible stage (whether theatrical or musical) and the activities normally performed upon the stage, and become aware of the sounds/ activities both inside and outside the concert hall/theatre. In a certain sense, Cage foregrounds the frame but then leaves it empty in order to encourage the audience to see (hear) that there is no difference between what is inside and what is outside the frame. (In a sense this is similar to Robert Rauschenberg's White Paintings which Cage characterized as 'airports for the lights, shadows, and particles'.[44]) Once, when someone left in the midst of a Cage concert, saying to the composer on the way out that there was no need to be at the concert since the same sounds could be heard in the street, Cage responded that that was precisely the point. The ultimate success for Cage would have been to make the concert hall obsolete because performance and life would be reunited for audiences. The frame, in other words, would be eliminated. Theatre would be eradicated.

But Cage was not necessarily advocating the elimination of performance. Rather, he was shifting the locus of creation, that is, framing. Once, when asked for a definition of the theatre, he responded: 'Anything that engages the eye and the ear.'[45] This sense of 'engagement' is equivalent to a frame: the observer selects something from the environment and extracts it – frames it – thereby transforming it into performance. (This may seem to bear some relation to sociological 'frame analysis', but Erving Goffman's system provided an explanation of how individuals organize information as they encounter the surrounding world and thereby extract meaning. Cage is suggesting the way in which an individual might transform aspects of the visual and aural environment into performance.) The radical implication of Cage's formulation is that the frame could be created by the spectator rather than by the performer as we normally assume. The 'performers' in Cage's *theatrum mundi* may not even be aware they are part of a performance. If theatre implies an intentionally created work of art, Cage provides a means whereby life can be transformed into art without the intention of the 'performers', thus once again eradicating all traditional notions of theatre and performance.

Post-modernism and the return of the frame

The history of art tends to be cyclical. Even before the height of the environmental movement in theatre in the early 1970s (which in the United States even briefly invaded the conservative realms of Broadway), a backlash had occurred. Robert Wilson and Richard Foreman, avatars of the avant-garde, had rejected the frameless theatre in favour of a radically framed one. Wilson's lavish theatre of images which seemed to be a living descendent of Alberti and his progeny, required the distancing effect of the proscenium. Richard Foreman's stages were a riot of frames ranging from the miniature baroque picture frames that comprised a larger literal frame around the stage to the famous strings that through their ostensible function served as metaphorical frames.

The frame gives the artist (director) total control over both the image and the spectator by keeping them within carefully delineated spaces on either side of the mediating window. Interestingly, the rise of the autocratic director coincided with the rise of modernist theatre, yet many of these same directors sought to dissolve the frame in order to incorporate or engage the audience. Ironically, post-modern design – a design that rejects the unity of the metanarrative, a design that is based upon rupture and incongruity – depends strongly on the presence of a frame. The pastiche of disparate elements of post-modern design requires the unifying structure of the stage in order to allow the spectator to apprehend the image as having any cogency. Thus, in the late twentieth century, it is opera that has become the site of the avant-garde, at least in regard to staging. The frame has reasserted itself with a vengeance, strongly encasing the post-modern pastiche of images, and erecting, once again, a window frame through which the audience perceives at a distance.

From the Symbolists of the 1880s onward to the onset of the post-modern backlash, the avant-garde in particular has continuously gnawed and hacked at the frame and the exclusivity of the stage. Most performance keeps the spectator outside the frame, thereby creating a subject–object relationship. Part of the modernist project has been the attempt to eradicate this dichotomy thereby rendering the subject and object part of a united entity.

Notes

1. Kenneth Macgowan and Robert Edmond Jones, *Continental Stagecraft* (New York: Harcourt, Brace, 1922), p.157.
2. See E. Barba and N. Savarese, *A Dictionary of Theatre Anthropology: The Secret Art of the Performer*, trans. Richard Fowler (London: Routledge, 1991), pp.9–10.
3. Guy Debord, *The Society of the Spectacle* (New York: Zone Books, 1994), p.13.
4. Debord, *Society of the Spectacle*, p.20.
5. See E. K. Chambers, *The English Folk Play* (Oxford: Oxford University Press, 1933), p.6, and *The Medieval Stage*, vol. I (Oxford: Oxford University Press, 1903), p.216.
6. Patrice Pavis, *Dictionary of the Theatre: Terms, Concepts, and Analysis*, trans. Christine Shantz (Toronto and Buffalo: University of Toronto Press, 1998), p.155.
7. Rudolph Arnheim, *Art and Visual Perception: A Psychology of the Creative Eye* (Berkeley and Los Angeles: University of California Press, 1974), p.239.
8. Leon Battista Alberti, *On Painting*, trans. Cecil Grayson (London: Penguin, 1991), p.54.
9. Arnheim, *Art and Visual Perception*, p.239.
10. Alberti, *On Painting*, p.65.
11. Christian Metz, *The Imaginary Signifier: Psychoanalysis and the Cinema*, trans. Celia Britton et al. (Bloomington: Indiana University Press, 1982), p.61. See also Martin Jay's essay, 'Scopic Regimes of Modernity', in Hal Foster, ed., *Vision and Visuality*, (New York: The New Press, 1988), pp.3–23.
12. Jay, 'Scopic Regimes of Modernity', pp.5–6.
13. Jay, 'Scopic Regimes of Modernity', p.5.
14. Alberti, *On Painting*, p.76.
15. Jay, 'Scopic Regimes of Modernity', p.9.
16. Jonathan Crary, *The Techniques of the Observer: On Vision and Modernity in the Nineteenth Century* (Cambridge: MIT Press, 1992), p.14. Because of the range of images and products within the realm of production he is investigating, and the social relations to these objects, Crary prefers the term 'observer'; but for a focus on theatre, I find the term 'spectator' more appropriate. See pp.5–6 for his definition of 'observer'.
17. Crary, *Techniques of the Observer*, pp.10–11.
18. Jean-Paul Sartre, *Being and Nothingness: A Phenomenological Essay on Ontology*, trans. Hazel E. Barnes (New York: Washington Square Press, 1956), pp.340 ff.
19. Sartre, *Being and Nothingness*, p.341.
20. Sartre, *Being and Nothingness*, p.342.
21. Roland Barthes, 'Baudelaire's Theater', in *A Barthes Reader*, ed. Susan Sontag (New York: Hill & Wang, 1998), p.75.
22. Maurice Maeterlinck, 'Menus propos – le theater', in Henri Dorra ed., *Symbolist Art Theories: A Critical Anthology*, (Berkeley and Los Angeles: University of California Press: 1994), p.145.
23. Quoted in Dorra, *Symbolist Art Theories*, p.143.
24. Frantisek Deak, *Symbolist Theater: The Formation of an Avant-Garde* (Baltimore, MD: Johns Hopkins University Press, 1993), pp.155–6.
25. Alfred Vallette, 'Le Théâtre du Peuple', *Mercure de France*, 19 (août 1896), p.383.

26. Alfred Jarry, 'Of the Futility of the Theatrical in the Theatre', in *Selected Works of Alfred Jarry*, ed. Roger Shattuck and Simon Watson Taylor (New York: Grove Press, 1965), pp.74–5.
27. Edward Gordon Craig, *The Theatre – Advancing* (Boston, MA: Little, Brown, 1919), p.45.
28. Charles Baudelaire, 'Correspondences', trans. in Dorra, *Symbolist Art Theories*, p.11.
29. Deak, *Symbolist Theater*, p.144.
30. Teodor de Wyzewa, 'Wagnerian Painting', in Dorra, *Symbolist Art Theories*, pp.148–9.
31. Pierre Quillard, 'The girl with cut-off hands', *The Drama Review*, 20:3 (September 1976): 123.
32. Svetlana Alpers, *The Art of Describing: Dutch Art in the Seventeenth Century* (Chicago: University of Chicago Press, 1984), p.xxv.
33. Jay, 'Scopic Regimes of Modernity', p.12.
34. Alfred Jarry, 'Preliminary Address at the First Performance of *Ubu Roi*, December 10, 1896', in *Selected Works of Alfred Jarry*, 77–8.
35. Alpers, *The Art of Describing*, p.44.
36. F. T. Marinetti, E. Settimelli and B. Corra, 'The Futurist Synthetic Theatre' [1915], in trans. R. W. Flint and Michael Kirby, *Futurist Performance* (New York: E. P. Dutton, 1971), p.197.
37. Marinetti, Settimelli and Corra, 'Futurist Synthetic Theatre', p.202.
38. Marinetti, Settimelli and Corra, 'Futurist Synthetic Theatre', p.199.
39. These Futurist events bear some resemblance to the actions advocated by Brazilian director Augusto Boal, but his events similarly staged in public spaces were intended to ultimately engage the spectators into discussion that would lead to an alteration of their life circumstances.
40. Martin Esslin, 'Max Reinhardt: High priest of theatricality', *The Drama Review*, 21:2 (June 1977): 10.
41. For a more detailed discussion of these projects, see Arnold Aronson, *The History and Theory of Environmental Scenography* (Ann Arbor: University of Michigan Research Press, 1981).
42. Antonin Artaud, *The Theater and Its Double*, trans. Mary Caroline Richards (New York: Grove Press, 1958), p.96.
43. 'Two theories of popular theatre', *Le Monde*, 21 October 1971, in René Hainuax and Yves Bonnat, *Stage Design Since 1960* (London: Harrap, 1972), p.8.
44. John Cage, 'On Robert Rauschenberg', *Silence* (Cambridge, MA: MIT Press, 1961), p.102.
45. Michael Kirby and Richard Schechner, 'An interview with John Cage', *Tulane Drama Review*, 10:2 (Winter 1965): 50.

3
Clown Shows: Anti-Theatricalist Theatricalism in Four Twentieth-Century Plays

Elinor Fuchs

Metatheatre is an old practice but a comparatively recent critical interest. It attained momentum among critics in the early 1960s, stirred partly by Lionel Abel's brief essays in *Metatheatre: A New View of Dramatic Form*. Abel claimed that a new dramatic 'form' had arisen in the English Renaissance and the Spanish Golden Age. '[T]ragedy would be replaced by metatheatre' in the theatres of Shakespeare and Calderon, Abel argued, after whom extended a lineage that stretched to Pirandello, Genet, Brecht and Beckett. These plays had not been recognized as a distinct form, Abel said, and had no name: 'I shall presume to designate them. I call them metaplays, works of metatheatre.'[1]

Though the study of Shakespeare's metadrama, along with its upper-caste cousin the dream play, has had a robust critical career, beginning even before Abel's large claim and continuing through the 1960s and 1970s, there has been little continuing effort to work out a general theory of metatheatrical dramatic form or to trace its development over time as a unified field.[2] An exception is Richard Hornby's essay, 'Varieties of the Metadramatic'. However Hornby's primary interest here is less critical than taxonomic.[3]

What explains this gap in criticism? Perhaps the modernist insight that all art is self-referential was thought to need no additional elaboration in the case of theatre. Perhaps the variety and ubiquity of metatheatrical motifs, appearing in, or with, tragedy, comedy, tragicomedy, pastoral and farce, has defeated inquiry. Perhaps the cult of Pirandello earlier in the century resulted in a corresponding pendulum swing. But at bottom, I suspect that further study has been blocked by a too literal devotion to Aristotelian categories of plot and character.

The present chapter seeks to reopen the question of metatheatre, or the theatricalist play as I prefer to call it.[4] For this discussion, I focus my interest on dramatic texts that are systemically theatricalist – that is, those which are constructed around incommensurate ontological 'worlds' – 'real' and theatricalized, or real and dream-like – and in which this incommensurability may be seen through many different dramatic 'elements' (I use Aristotle's term intentionally) of the dramatic structure, such as figure, action, language, mood, tone and landscape. I lay aside for this chapter the legion of examples that clutters discussions of theatricalism, in which various theatrical ruses of character or incident (such as disguises, lies, tricks, staged events) are organized by some figures at the expense of others, but in which the ontological base of the action is not in question.

The structurally theatricalist text can be fruitfully read not only from an Aristotelian, but from a Platonic perspective. Plato's understanding of truth and 'the Good' as given through a hierarchy of ontological levels is not a substitute for Aristotle's powerful analytic of reversal and recognition, but it offers a philosophical antecedent for the theatricalist play's parallel and sometimes multiple narrative registers. Under the sign of Plato, the 'soul' of the theatricalist dramatic work would be neither plot, as Aristotle argues, nor character as Hegel claims in his romantic revision of classic theory, but the relationship between or among ontological levels.

Given his settled anti-theatricalism, Plato's parable of the Cave in *The Republic*, Book VII, might seem an ironic source for the theatricalist play, yet it provides a concise and clarifying model. Staged in three scenes and an epilogue, its central drama consists of an ascending progress of landscapes that exchanges shadows cast upon the wall of a cave for the brilliance of the sun shining directly from the heavens. The progression is not simply scenic but spiritual and moral, for the same upward movement signifies the exchange of artifice for nature, mere appearance for truth, and error for the Good. While Plato is enough of a dramatist to offer a protagonist (the reluctant cave dweller released from his chains and forced to venture into the light), and a plot improved by a poignant, indeed almost tragic, conclusion (the traveller's return to the cave amidst the mockery and threats of its long-term denizens), in the telling it is still not the story of the traveller that most engages Plato; it is the light itself.

With its spatial division into opposed landscapes whose juxtaposition expresses an ontological, moral and performative hierarchy, the narrative of the cave models the very pattern of the classic theatricalist play. The palace and dungeon settings of *Life is a Dream*, court and forest of *A Midsummer Night's Dream* are variations on this polar structure. As in the allegory of the cave, these and other theatricalist plays multiply dramatic complexity by bringing different planes of reality into the same dramatic structure. Conflict in these structures is played out more between levels of representation than by individual figures, and is resolved by victory or defeat for a contending ontological principle (or perhaps a cheerful truce).

Yet, though theatricalist plays can be recognized by a certain repeating pattern, it may be misleading to call the theatricalist play a 'form', as Abel does, in the sense in which the term is usually understood, that is, as genre. Genres are traditionally defined by the Aristotelian criteria of plot structure and character type, while the pattern I am attempting to define is compatible with many different genres. Let us consider it, like pastoral, a mode.

Two examples from Shakespeare and Calderon, to whom Abel traces his own theme of metatheatre, will help to fill out this profile.[5] Read as a theatricalist play, *The Tempest* enacts stories, depicts figures and represents values from opposed ontological realms: the seen world of dream, magic and performance, and an unseen 'real' world of Milanese court intrigue. Distinctions between these worlds are expressed through 'site-specific' characters, objects and their significant alternative landscapes of mainland and island. The tools of theatrical creation in the play, Prospero's book and staff, have a special role in the ontological divide between mainland and island, 'real' and supernatural: unable to bridge these worlds, they will be drowned and buried in their own magic realm. It is not accidental that the 'real' world – the world of responsible governance for Prospero, adulthood and marriage for Miranda, obedience for the court, sobriety for the ship's crew, and of time and aging for them all – is the mainland, or that it is scenically unrepresented. The reality effect in the classical theatricalist play is enhanced by non-representation.

The layered dramaturgy of the theatricalist play becomes didactically schematic in Calderon's charming *auto, Great Theatre of the World*, a Christian version of the seventeenth chapter of the *Manual* by the Stoic Epictetus:

> Remember that you are an actor in a play, the character of which is determined by the Playwright; . . . if he wishes you to play the part of a beggar, remember to act even this role adroitly . . .[6]

The principal setting of the *Great Theatre* is the world-as-stage, where human life is written and directed by God. All human beings' identities are roles, their shelters settings, their possessions props, their clothing costumes.[7] From his perch on a golden globe above the world stage, God the Playwright, or *Autor*, watches his parade of figures enjoy or bemoan their alloted roles. As each, in turn, is surprised by Death, God determines their destinies of heavenly reward or fiery punishment. The enduring Real in this universe, these unwitting actors learn, is God and His everlasting order. God's domain – filled with angels above and demons below – remains largely unseen, as if to enact Paul's exhortation to the Corinthians: '[W]e do not look at the things which are seen, but at the things which are not seen. For the things which are seen *are* temporary, but the things which are not seen *are* eternal.'[8] Even Death is kept off stage, his authority magnified through his appearance only as a 'doleful Voice' summoning each figure to his or her inevitable stage exit (Calderon de la Barca, *Great Theatre of the World*, p.383).

Great Theatre of the World is a story of parallel if unequal realms, one visible but illusory and transitory, the other invisible yet infinite in time and space. Where Shakespeare returns his figures to the solidity of normative everyday experience, Calderon reverses polarities, exposing the everyday world as groundless and unreliable. Yet in both plays, in a doubling of theatrical illusion, it is the illusory world that comes into view; the credibility of the 'real world', whether defined by observed life or Christian Platonism, is reinforced by its absence from representation.[9]

To summarize, then, in the theatricalist play the dramaturgy of plot and character is subject to a prior condition, the dramaturgy of incommensurate ontological realms. These dramatic worlds relate to each other as a hierarchy of competing reals. The theatricalized plane is characteristically trumped by a plane representing a more constant real, whatever the ground of the real within the world of the play may be. In Lope's *Acting is Believing*, based loosely on the life of Genesius, the patron saint of actors, the leading actor of a theatre troupe is converted to a real faith in Jesus Christ in the course of performing the role of a believer. Enacting the role, he is summoned by an angel to a religious conviction beyond even his powers of performance, leading to much confusion about the 'script'. In the end, Genesius's stage martyrdom is exchanged for a real one off stage, and he is revealed, as in a vision, impaled.[10]

Even such a cursory examination of classic theatricalism reveals a curious phenomenon, the current of anti-theatricalism that runs through the plays. In each there is a leave-taking from theatre, and sometimes even *the* theatre, as in Lope, such that anti-theatricalism becomes a constituent element of theatricalist dramaturgy itself, its conscience and its ground. The theatricalist play, accompanied always by its anti-theatricalist other, can be seen as Plato's enduring gift to the theatre. The delight of theatre and the mist of dream are ultimately, sometimes sorrowfully, left behind for a turn, or a return, to an ontological 'gold standard', whether located on the plane of a Platonic ideal or the mundane real of lived life.

The classical model of the theatricalist play as a dyad of sign systems has survived surprisingly intact into and throughout the twentieth century, though it is sometimes invaded by the romantic theatricalist structure of collapsing frames created (not without the prior inspiration of Beaumont and Fielding) by Tieck in *Puss-in-Boots* and *The Topsy-Turvy World*. This classical model appears at the beginning of the century in Blok's lapidary *Fairground Booth*, and reappears in Pirandello, Beckett, Genet, Handke, Rosewicz, Peter Weiss, Heiner Müller, Adrienne Kennedy and Suzan-Lori Parks, to name some of its better known practitioners (and to omit several others, including the Evreinov of *The Chief Thing* and the Brecht of *A Man's a Man*, where it may be argued that theatricalist devices are mounted on a stable ontological foundation).

Traditionally, theatricalism has been the redoubt of metaphysics, ontology and epistemology in the theatre. The social and political became the province of realism. But increasingly in the twentieth century, theatricalism offered many playwrights a dramaturgical model that welcomed extreme irony and scepticism into representations of the material world. With theatricalist means, modern and contemporary playwrights have addressed many themes normally associated with realism – for instance, revolution, war, gender, race, fascism, AIDS – without incurring realism's obligations and limitations. For the balance of this chapter, as an approach to a theory of modern theatricalism, I will explore four modern theatricalist plays, seeking their similarities to and departures from the model of Renaissance and Spanish Golden Age theatricalism outlined above. I will devote particular attention to the role played in their structures by an implied anti-theatricalism.

Clown Shows 1 and 2: anti-theatricalism and terror

Performing figures appear in all theatricalist plays: authors, directors, playwrights, actors, spectators, stage managers. The clown/performer, famously used by Tieck in the figure of Hanswurst, is a modern familiar. He provides Genet's subtitle in *The Blacks: A Clown Show*,[11] weaves in and out of *Hamletmachine*,[12] is punned in the title of Handke's *Kaspar*,[13] is passed on from the gravedigger-clowns of *Hamlet* to the father-son digger/showman pair in Suzan-Lori Parks's *The America Play*.[14] The theatricalist play may be the clown's normal habitat, but each of these clown shows presents a divided world: the onstage *clownérie* is paralleled by an unseen dramatic site that, with one exception, is severely clownless. Each play suggests the possibility of a third realm as well, a utopian 'elsewhere'. It is to this third space, or (to enlist the film theory term fruitfully deployed by De Lauretis in *Technologies of Gender*, 'space-off'[15]) that the anti-theatrical has been removed.

In Genet and Müller, the clown's opposing world is a domain of revolution and terror that threatens to sweep away the decadent artifice of visible culture in an apocalyptic whirlwind. *The Blacks* and *Hamletmachine* take aim at post-war, post-colonialist European spectators, constructed as timid and corrupt, equally fearful of their own private racial projections as of their very public political failures. The terrors visited on this spectator are intensified theatrically through the device of non-representation that proved effective for classical theatricalism. In *The Blacks*, an unseen threat is juxtaposed against a plane of baroque theatrical artifice; in *Hamletmachine* an unseen threat plays against a tissue of on-stage theatricalist reference.

The visible plane in Genet is of course the ritual entertainment mounted on the premise of white racial phobia. Racism on stage becomes a demonstration in reverse of Genet's well-known anti-racialist frontispiece: 'But what exactly is a black? First of all, what's his colour?' If the basic theatrical gesture is 'standing-in', as Bruce Wilshire argues,[16] Genet piles up an Ossa-on-Pelion of vaudeville-like substitutions. The comical blonde wig and rouged white mask on the black male actor who stands in for the white female murder victim, the elaborate finery and ashen masks on the colonial 'court of justice', the shoe polish used to blacken 'black' skin, and the scenic centrepiece, the flower-decked catafalque of the white 'murder victim' later exposed as two chairs covered by a cloth: taken together these theatricalist signs of race and racial crime 'stand in' for the emptiness of negative racial stereotypes.

Cutting through the exaggerated display, declamatory rhetoric, and absurd fiction of the on-stage performance, however, is a deliberately non-theatrical text, whose setting is somewhere 'off'. In contrast to the 'fake elegance' (Genet, *The Blacks*, p.8) of his fellow performers, the figure Newport News, the on-stage representative of what seems to be an invisible black liberation movement, is barefoot and wears a plain woollen sweater. He moves slowly, speaks quietly and carries a revolver. He appears from time to time to bring terse reports from an unseen front: off stage a tribunal is meeting; a traitor to the group and its revolutionary cause is standing trial; if found guilty he will be executed. The theatricalist signals are familiar: in contrast to the risible clown act portraying blacks as apes dropped from trees, there exists a highly disciplined revolutionary movement; counterpoised to the vaudeville murder trial is a real court meting out inexorable justice. These two worlds play the visible against the invisible, the theatrical against the deadly serious anti-theatrical. The unrepresented world emits anti-theatrical signals of costume, speech and gesture; its refusal of represen-tation is itself an anti-theatrical stand. As a mark of its real-life authen-ticity, and as an antidote to theatre, it invokes real (not stage) blood. '[W]e've got to stop acting when we're among ourselves', says Newport News, 'we'll have to get used to taking responsibility for blood....' Archibald goes further: 'It's a matter of living blood, hot, supple, reeking blood, of blood that bleeds' (Genet, *The Blacks*, p.82). And later Newport News: 'Our aim is not only to corrode and dissolve the idea they'd like us to have of them, we must also fight them in their actual persons, in their flesh and blood'(p.112). It appears that terror is intended to be stirred in the white spectator by the gulf between the visible and off-stage actions: the mask of black degeneracy is used as camouflage for the true face of implacable black power. There is a final revelation, a final unmasking, or perhaps masking, but I must turn first to Heiner Müller in order to discuss the final moments of *The Blacks* and *Hamletmachine* together.

Though with less schematic order, *Hamletmachine* enacts a similar representational divide. *Hamlet* stands in for high-Enlightenment European culture, now in ruins. Its eponymous hero, the iconic theatri-calist protagonist, in ruins as well, invokes himself retrospectively: 'I was Hamlet' (Müller, *Hamletmachine*, p.53). This Hamlet wanders the Cold War landscape East and West, whose evil twins are Stalin and Coca-Cola. Himself a theatricalist figure, this Hamlet plays roles: now Ulrike Meinhof, now Emma Goldman, now Müller's first wife and always Ophelia. He is Lady Macbeth in reverse and would unsex himself: '*Face in his hands. I want to be a woman*' (p.55). His self-alienation reaches a pitch of theatricalist distancing: as the 'Actor Playing Hamlet' he bemoans his role: 'My drama doesn't happen anymore' (p.56). It is not by chance that Hamlet becomes the actor of himself precisely in scene 4, 'Pest in Buda/Battle for Greenland'. In nauseated self-disgust he divides into character and performer in the divided city of Budapest, and does so at the key moment of its greatest post-war East–West struggle, its failed revolution of 1956.

As in *The Blacks*, terror lurks beneath *Hamletmachine* as an alternate script. Its unseen action is recognized *as* an action only retrospectively, when at the end it breaks through the Hamlet figure's ennui and despair. Genet's revolutionary stealth tribunal is matched in Müller by a thunderbolt of revenge launched from the (then) 'third world'. The eruption achieves an abrupt reality effect, shocking the audience into an awareness of its true political situation – into life, as against the histrionics of theatre. In both plays, the grievances of an oppressed class, kept carefully off stage, suddenly become visible, violently changing the direction of the action. In Müller as in Genet, these point outside the text to real blood and death. 'When she walks through your bedrooms carrying butcher knives', comes the threat, 'you'll know the truth' (Müller, *Hamletmachine*, p.58).

Taking the traditional theatricalist role of the textual and experiential off-stage 'real', terror in these plays comes from an invisible elsewhere. In *The Blacks* this real-world disdains the gimcrackery of the represented action in order to 'spread panic by force and cunning' (Genet, *The Blacks*, p.112). A similar dramaturgical move appears in *Hamletmachine*. If Europe-as-Hamlet and Hamlet-as-Europe are on stage (however staged), the off-stage real is, not surprisingly, off-Europe, off-white and off-male. As in *The Task*, where the unmaskable 'real' of black skin guarantees the revolutionary commitment of the black Sasportas, so in *Hamletmachine* this off-stage world will persist until it destroys Europe's narcissistic self-performance: 'Long live hate and contempt, rebellion and death' cries its female messenger (p.58).

But…wait! On closer examination, the apparent gulf between on-stage artifice and off-stage 'real' breaks down. In a departure from classical theatricalism, the off-stage real worlds in both *The Blacks* and *Hamletmachine*, portending a revolutionary juggernaut of the dispossessed, may actually be performances in themselves, performances of a calculated dramaturgy of the real. These off-stage worlds insinuate themselves into representation not merely in the generic sense of partaking of the overall fiction of the dramatic text, but in a more assertive sense: they want to get into the act.

Near the end of *The Blacks*, the solidity of the imagined off-stage world is thrown into question with a peculiar stage direction announcing the traitor's execution: 'Suddenly a firecracker explodes off stage followed by several more. Sparks of fireworks are seen against the black velvet of the set' (pp.109–10). As we saw in the discussion both of classical theatricalism and of *The Blacks* as it developed, the unrepresented world had acquired the status of a polar 'real' through the cultivation of a kind of anti-theatricalism. Newport News, in his occasional, brief appearances, was an anti- or counter-theatrical figure as shown through costume, gait and speech. It may have been Genet's joke that he always exited 'stage left', never right, but where did we imagine him to go? What imaginative space does the revolutionary court and their prisoner inhabit?

Two-thirds through the play, Newport News arrives once more, but now stays on stage as the clown show veers off into a steaming, savage Africa of the European imagination. At the sight and sound of the firecrackers, he steps forward to report the conclusion of a trial he did not hear and to announce the execution he did not witness. Asked by his fellow black performers about the appearance of the new revolutionary leader who is the dead man's replacement, Newport News smiles. He is 'just as you imagine him' (p.112).

The outside reality has collapsed into the on-stage performance. The revolutionary movement has been reduced to the wings and the dressing rooms. The audience is signalled that the unrepresented action too is a mask, a false real. As Christopher Innes writes, going against the grain of most critical interpretation of *The Blacks*: '[T]he offstage events are overtly fake.'[17] But unlike Innes, I don't see the play as devouring itself in a nihilistic regress of stage attitudes. Genet throws the spectator back on her own problem of racial projection. The revolutionary black may be a mask from stage-left as the grotesquerie of the main plot is a mask from the right. But in what may be its purest anti-theatricalist gesture, the play holds back, because it cannot actually represent, the thing that accounts for its anguishing sense of menace, the deep ground of racial terror. Squirming uncomfortably in his seat, the white spectator protests he should not be murdered in his bed. He is left alone with his terror of terror, unable to choose between assigning it a basis in the outside world or in himself. Even the black spectator is challenged by the sudden groundlessness of the 'revolution'. The real presents itself, as Lacan says of his category of the Real, 'in the form of that which is *unassimilable* in it – in the form of the trauma, determining all that follows...'.[18]

Similarly, the implacable rejection of the Hamlet drama at the end of *Hamletmachine* does not turn against the artifice of drama itself, as it would seem it must, rejecting Europe and *Hamlet* together. Rather, the very rejection is itself a drama within the Western tradition, the drama of the avenger Elektra, who summons Lady Macbeth, Medea, the Manson gang and Conrad to her aid. The very setting – the speech from the 'heart of darkness' – provides an alternative to Europe, but an

alternative as constructed by fearful European fantasy. Spoken over the image of the mummified and silenced Ophelia, Elektra enters as a foil to the Hamlet plot, yet as a voice within it. Elektra's final chilling speech, with its threat of racial, sexual and class Armageddon, still appears to come out of the same hermeneutic circle that produced the Hamlet culture in the first place.

Walter Reich, editor of *Origins of Terrorism*, cites the State Department's definition of terrorism: 'Premeditated, politically-motivated violence perpetrated against non-combatant targets by subnational groups or clandestine state agents, *normally intended to influence an audience* (emphasis mine)'.[19] Even to the State Department, that is, terror places itself on the disputed boundary between representation and invisibility. Terror arises from the inability to guarantee the boundary. Lacan's Real stands on precisely this boundary. Žižek describes it as the 'hard kernel...which cannot be reduced to a universal play of illusory mirroring' within the symbolic order itself.[20]

In the language of theatricalism, then, the scenario of terror in the dramaturgy of Genet and Müller could be said to work in and on three stages: the on-stage illusion, the off-stage 'real' (subverting the on-stage illusion, it nevertheless avails itself of the language of theatrical representation) and, third, a Real real that holds power by virtue of its refusal to make an appearance, a deep backstage, as it were: the anti-theatricalist 'space-off'. The theatricalist structures of *The Blacks* and of *Hamletmachine* rely on this anti-theatricalist foundation; or to put it another way, rely on their ability to evoke an antitheatrical response in their audiences. The spectator's recognition of her own culpability, her own final unmasking, goes beyond substituting a representation of truth for a representation of artifice. These plays cultivate a true *dis-illusion*, a final understanding of the theatrical event that is deeply suspicious of the activity and metaphorics of theatre.

Clown Show 3: anti-theatricalist theatricalism as tragedy

The central figure of Peter Handke's *Kaspar* is based, as most readers will know, on the story of Kaspar Hauser, the 16-year-old German youth, possibly autistic, who stumbled into Nuremberg in 1828, starved and terrified, uneducated and without language, after years of apparent confinement. Both the figure of history and Handke's figure bear interesting comparison to Plato's man in the cave, to which I'll return. Some readers of the play see the plight (or criticize Handke for seeing the plight) of its central character as a figure out of Rousseau,[21] natural man forced to submit to a repressive acculturation. Others, while agreeing that the socializing operations of language are the villain of Handke's first full-length play, find no romance in the unsocialized condition of its central figure.

Handke points out that Kaspar is entirely a stage figure, and that the play should be read without psychological assumptions. *Kaspar* is not a story about a 'real person', but a theatrical demonstration of the alienating effect of language. Unquestionably Handke's *Kaspar* belongs in the long-standing tradition of the Austrian absorption with the problem of language, witnessed by Hofmannsthal's *Letter of Lord Chandos* of 1902, and in different ways by Freud, Karl Kraus, Thomas Bernhard and Wittgenstein, among others. It has thus been much discussed as a language play. However, the play may gain some specifically theatrical illumination when held up to the model I have been developing of the theatricalist tradition.

Despite Handke's prefatory organization of the action of the play into 16 phases, each organized around Kaspar's relationship to sentences, the opening images are coded with theatricalist signals. The stage can only be seen, Handke writes, 'as a representation of a stage'. Objects scattered on it tell no story, but 'are instantly recognizable as props'. Some of the props, for instance a shovel and a waste-basket, even bear the inscription 'STAGE'. The audience is signalled that they will 'witness an event that plays only on stage' (Handke, *Kaspar*, p.60–1).

In his first appearance, Kaspar stumbles through the divide in the curtain; it is a kind of birth, but also a version of an age-old clown and vaudeville routine. In his person, Kaspar himself is as theatrically coded as his surroundings. Wearing a pale mask expressing perpetual astonishment, he is suited out in a droll collection from the costume shop, 'a wide-brimmed hat with a band; a light-colored shirt with a closed collar; a colorful jacket with many (roughly seven) metal buttons; wide pants; clumsy shoes' (p.63). Upstage stands a closet with a number of doors. When they fall open, '[t]he audience sees that the closet contains several colorful theatrical costumes' (p.66).

The on-stage world of *Kaspar* is even more severely self-referential than the world of *The Blacks*. Though Genet signals at every moment that the scenario his figures enact is a theatrical fiction fashioned to the prejudices of the audience before it, Handke makes it clear that *Kaspar* exists without even the charade of 'real' characters who perform acts in the world. *Kaspar* is a theatrical lab slide, scoured clean of a past, future, or parallel external reference.

Handke's setting of his action on two planes, visible and invisible, fits the pattern of classic theatricalism. But just as the imaginative reach of his visible world is severely bounded by the actual theatre, so his 'off-stage' world is flattened and without dimension. Voices emanate from invisible speakers, a group of perhaps three that Handke calls the *Einsager*.[22] Their voices, Handke states in his introductory note, should be those which have a technical medium placed between themselves and the listeners:

> telephone voices, radio or television announcers' voices, the voice that tells the time on the phone, the voices of automatic answering services of all kinds...of announcers of train arrivals and departures...of language course records, of policemen as they speak through bullhorns at demonstrations, etc. etc.
>
> (Handke, *Kaspar*, p.59).

When the *Einsager* finally begin to speak in scene viii, Handke adds that their voices are 'without undertones or overtones', lacking 'the usual irony, humor, helpfulness, human warmth', as well as the 'the usual ominousness, dread, incorporeality or supernaturalness'. The best that they can offer is clarity: they are 'completely comprehensible' (p.59). The *Einsager* occupy the invisible position usually accorded the reality principle in the theatricalist scheme yet offer no hook to the realist imagination. Their very dimensionlessness is a key to Handke's suspicion of normative reality.

The interaction between the visible and invisible planes of the play proceeds in two large motions. The first describes a movement from visual and physical chaos to integration. As the clown Kaspar learns to manage his world through acceptable clichés taught by the *Einsager*, he learns how to adjust the stage picture into a representation of domestic realism. Spotlights guide him in the harmonious placement of objects, here a vase, there a stool. With wicked humour, Handke directs that Kaspar leave the stage and return with the prime insignia of bourgeois respectability (as I well remember from my grandmother's dining table), a plate of decorative waxed fruit. At a sign, a painting is lowered from the flies. 'What the painting represents is of no importance as long as it goes with the furnishings' Handke observes drily (p.87).

Everything must now 'go with' everything else. Kaspar finds matching clothes, as he matches action to sentence, thought to action. For a brief moment, on-stage and off-stage planes are aligned. After the *Einsager* announce that 'you are not allowed to think anything *different* from what you are saying' (p.101), they fall silent, so that even the visible and invisible planes of the action are seamlessly aligned. Kaspar will shortly announce his own Yahweh-like triumph of self-consolidation: 'I am the one I am' (p.102).

At just the moment that Kaspar organizes the stage picture into a harmonious semblance of a 'real' room, Handke offers the text's first direction calling for general stage lighting. 'The stage is festively lit' (p.88). Simultaneously, the *Einsager*, who have just previously instructed Kaspar that 'Living in a dark room only brings unnecessary thoughts' (p.87), celebrate the illumination of the stage. 'What is a nightmare in the dark is joyous certainty in the light', they say (p.88). In an ironic reversal on Plato's cave dweller who ventures above into the light of transparency and truth, Handke floods the stage (and his text) with light at the moment in the play that launches Kaspar's most trusting and thus most deluded relationship to the teachings of the *Einsager*. It is actually the moment of least transparency, leaving no light, as the expression goes, between Kaspar's mastery of the world and his idea of himself.

The moment is significant from a theatricalist point of view. Realism at every level, it seems to say – visual, psychological, behavioural, spiritual – consists of an alignment of effects such that nothing appears 'out of place'. With the triumphant 'I am the one I am', proclaiming that the visible 'I' perfectly matches the inner sense of 'I', the theatricalist tension must collapse, as in fact it does in the harmonious restorations of order at the end of many classic theatricalist plays. But Handke is critical of this state of realist conformity. The most theatrically 'worked' illusion, he suggests, is the one that appears least conscious of itself as theatre. Thus his scene of integration falls not at the end of the play, but as the central pivot on which to turn the 'reversal of fortune' that results in a far deeper chaos than the play began with. No sooner has Kaspar achieved self-recognition than a shadow falls: 'Why are there so many black worms falling about? *The stage becomes black*' (p.102). At the end of the first act, the doors of the theatrical-costume closet, which had finally remained closed as Kaspar gained control over his environment, subversively swing open. The illusion of the illusionist theater was short-lived. The theatricalist stage is restored.[23]

Like the infernal broom of the tale of the Sorcerer's Apprentice,[24] at first a magical being summoned into flesh, then an unstoppable, multiplying force bringing flood and chaos, Kaspar spawns a destructive chorus composed of masked doubles of himself. These 'screech, yodel, buzz, trumpet, draw snot into their noses, smack their lips, grunt, burp, ululate...squeak, bark, make the sounds of rain and storm, blow up bubble gum till it bursts, etc.' (pp.129–31). There have been many readings of Handke's metastatic Kaspars. One, for instance, speculates that they are the 'mass-produced' products of a society that 'moulds every human being into an identical form'; another, that they represent the repressive forces of totalitarianism.[25]

A theatricalist reading might focus first on the sheer proliferation of masks on the stage, taking note of Handke's stage direction that the Kaspars 'behave like crowds in crowd scenes in plays' (pp.139–40). But *Kaspar* departs from the classic theatricalist scenario in presenting no 'real world' to return or aspire to, and from modern variations in the absence of even an ironic reminder of a lost grounding principle. The division between on-stage learner and off-stage indoctrinators turns out to represent a social but not a 'truth' distinction, a distinction of authority, not ontology. Kaspar learns the authoritative language of the *Einsager*, but can it really be said that he is 'self'-alienated? Does (or did) Kaspar have a 'self' to alienate?

The first scenes of the play before the entrance of the *Einsager* discover Kaspar in possession of a single sentence, a *factotum* with which to negotiate the world: 'I want to be a person like somebody else was once' (p.65). It is the cry of the actor: I find myself by inhabiting a role. Kaspar is not an individual 'I' seeking an object of imitation; he is an actor/Everyman in the morality play of language, as he is Lacan's split subject: his 'I' is a function, in Kaspar's case, of a harsh symbolic order whose misleading constructive powers lead only to disintegration. He is like Lord Chandos, who loses 'completely the ability to think or to speak of anything coherently'. The very language the once successful writer Chandos must use

> crumbled in my mouth like mouldy fungi...For me everything disinte-grated into parts, those parts again into parts...Single words floated around me; they congealed into eyes which stared at me...whirlpools which gave me vertigo, and, reeling incessantly, led into the void.[26]

The actor/clown who had no choice but to enter a pre-socialized identity ends in a 'self'-engendered madness: 'I cannot rid myself of myself any more' (Handke, *Kaspar*, p.139). His final words, in the version translated by Michael Roloff, are of the theatre. Kaspar repeats Othello's anguished curse: 'Goats and monkeys' five times. As Lodovico asks on witnessing this scene, 'Are his wits safe? Is he not light of brain?' (*Othello*, IV.i).

There is no escape from the role-playing of the theatricalist mode on either the represented or unrepresented level of the play. It is this 'no exit' theatricalist strategy that makes the play unremittingly despairing and also enrages Handke's more materialist critics.[27] There is no reprieve from the circle of performance. Kaspar/Everyman is inescapably 'cast' in a pre-existing mold. His tragedy is not, as Linstead suggests, the loss of an 'unmediated relationship between the self and the world, consciousness and reality, inner world and outer world' (Linstead, *Outer World and Inner World*, p.51). Rather his is a deeper tragedy, in which there is not even a theoretical escape from the performance of self, but at the same time no escape from the despair the inescapability engenders, thus a tragedy of anti-theatricalist theatricalism. The sole language in which Lord Chandos might be able to write and think, he says, 'is neither Latin nor English, neither Italian nor Spanish, but a language none of whose words is known to me...' (pp.140–1). For Lord Chandos as for Kaspar, the chimera of authentic language and selfhood can be sought only in some recessed space-off. The 'real' for Kaspar is the Lacanian Real, that presses like a wound on representation, but can never enter it; for him, there is no available representation outside the shadows of Plato's cave.

Clown Show 4: anti-theatricalist theatricalism as comedy

Tragedy may pursue, but it never overtakes Suzan-Lori Parks's *The America Play*, where father and son, diggers by trade, are 'fakers' by calling. In a world that knows 'no effectual difference between continued affectation and reality', as Congreve's Scandal declares approvingly in *Love for Love*, performance is not indoctrination and loss, but invention and capital. Parks's 'Lesser Known' is a black gravedigger and Abe Lincoln lookalike who goes west to dig an 'exact replica' of the theme park that enchanted him back east on his honeymoon trip, the 'Great Hole of History'. In his replica, he performs a Lincoln assassination act, laughing and dropping dead, laughing and dropping dead, as visitors to the Hole pay a penny a shot to re-enact the scene at Ford's Theatre. Well what's a Lesser Known to do, asks Parks, if his history is 'unrecorded, dismembered, washed out'. Theatre is her answer: '[T]heatre, for me, is the perfect place to "make" history' (Parks, *The America Play*, p.4).

With a light-hearted enthusiasm for historical appropriation, Parks creates a play in the theatricalist mould where the represented world and its parallel unrepresented other are deliberately concordant: both are theme parks, sites of historical entertainment. Though the play is filled with ludicrous deference to the 'original' Great Hole, it is precisely the absence of an original that permits her 'Foundling Father' to step confidently into history. The represented and absent 'great holes' do not bear the relation of performance world to real world familiar from the classical theatricalist play. Rather they are both '[fake] *lieux de* [fake] *mémoire*', sites of mixed, sampled, reimagined, memory.[28] In such a world, the black gravedigger with his box of stage beards, one of which is blonde, can be a deadringer for Honest Abe.

In the second act, the imitation Great Hole is itself the site of an archeological dig. The Foundling Father's son Brazil, a gravedigger trained in the performance of mourning, digs for traces of his deceased father while his mother, Lucy, scans the air with a hearing trumpet for echoes from the past. Brazil triumphantly digs up a 'Tee-Vee' and a replica of George Washington's false teeth, unwittingly proving that 'history' is nothing but a collection of transient images and outright fakes. Like the other three 'clown shows' considered in this discussion, and this one most of all, *The America Play* reinscribes the divided dramatic scheme of traditional theatricalism only to undermine onto-logical difference between theatrical and real.

Parks creates a generous theatricalist landscape in *The America Play*. The basic dyad of her two performance parks is studded and festooned with subsidiary and surrounding representations – inset scenes from *This American Cousin*; Brazil's melodramatic funeral performances, plucked from nineteenth-century acting manuals; echoes, imitations, re-enactments, even the linguistic mirroring of chiasmus. Suffusing the play are traces of that most theatricalist of revenge tragedies *Hamlet*. In the first act, the Lesser Known compares himself to his 'Founding Father', playing satyr to Lincoln's Hyperion, while re-enacting the father's assassination in his own play within the play. In the second act, the *Hamlet* plot is revisited, a generation later. In an amusing parallel to the exhumation of the court fool Yorick, who like a loving father bore Prince Hamlet 'on his back a thousand times' (V.i.174), Brazil, a 'Clown'/Gravedigger himself, digs for traces of his father/clown. In this playful world, 'foundling' and 'lesser', the adjectives attached to Parks's central character, partly lose their tragic resonance.

Yet the very gesture of shrugging off a 'real' is grounded in nostalgia for it. In *The America Play*, the 'real' America is in a space-off of the imagination that neither Disney nor racism can invade. The quotation from Locke that is the play's frontispiece, 'In the beginning, all the world was America' (Parks, *The America Play*, p.159) locates precisely the anti-theatricalist problematic of the 'real' in Parks's theatricalist dramaturgy. In the beginning 'America' was an empty stage, on which all the stories might have been told differently, as Cixous says of the distortions of women's history. Thus, or so one might proceed with the metaphor, Parks sets her entire festive elaboration of performance in a framework of, and as a response to, the pre-theatrical. Still, 'in the beginning' can be read at least two ways, and the quotation also suggests the American capacity for self-creation, beginning, like theatre, again and again, generating endless versions underlain by no single truth.

* * *

I have argued that the structures of theatricalist plays are indebted to Plato's epistemology of ontological levels. Dramatic conflict in such plays arises from the contest between planes of representation depicting 'more real' and 'less real' ontologies. Through the 'more real' end of the ontological spectrum in these plays runs a buried vein of anti-theatricalism. To shift metaphors from mining to media, this anti-theatrical Real has moved off the representational screen and inhabits a felt but unseen 'space-off', giving rise to a vague but unrelievable distress. Whether dug into a hole or trapped on a stage, the figures who inhabit contemporary theatricalist plays, unlike their classical forebears, suspect 'the light' as yet one more illusion, but can't be sure, a dilemma shared by their audiences and played out in almost every practical arena of life. The modern theatre of theatricalist anti-theatricalism offers the stage image of this condition.

Notes

1. Lionel Abel, *Metatheatre* (New York: Hill & Wang, 1966), pp.61, 113.
2. See, for instance, Anne Barton, *Shakespeare and the Idea of the Play* (London: Chatto & Windus, 1962); James L. Calderwood, *Shakespearean Metadrama* (Minneapolis: Minnesota University Press, 1971); Robert Egan, *Drama Within Drama* (New York: Columbia University Press, 1975); Marjorie B. Garber, *Dream in Shakespeare: From Metaphor to Metamorphosis* (New Haven: Yale University Press, 1974); Sidney Homan, *When the Theater Turns to Itself* (Lewisburg: Bucknell, 1981); Robert J. Nelson, *Play Within a Play* (New Haven: Yale University Press 1958); and June Schlueter, *Metafictional Characters in Modern Drama* (New York: Columbia University Press, 1979).
3. Richard Hornby, *Drama, Metadrama, and Perception* (Lewisburg: Bucknell; London and Toronto: Associated University Presses, 1986).
4. There is no entirely satisfactory term for the self-reference in the dramatic text that is the subject of this chapter, for there is no term that reliably separates the theatrical self-consciousness of a Nora performing the Tarantella

within a solidly realistic framework from theatrical paradox as it functions in, for instance, *Six Characters in Search of an Author*. I have long been uncomfortable with the unnaturalizable Greek 'meta' as it is prefixed to 'theatre' in Abel, or to "drama", as in Calderwood and Hornby (see notes 2 and 3). For the purposes of this Chapter I revert to the homelier term 'Theatricalism', used extensively by Mordecai Gorelik in his 1940 *New Theatres for Old* (reprinted by Dutton, 1962), and by John Gassner, in *Producing the Play* (New York: The Dryden Press, 1953, p.354), and then in *Directions in Modern Theatre and Drama* (New York: Holt, Rinehart & Winston, 1966; see especially ch. 3, 'Theatricalism and Crisis', pp.133–91), an expanded version of his 1956 *Form and Idea in Modern Theatre*. However, I use 'Theatricalism' and the adjective 'theatricalist' more specifically than Gassner, who employed them interchangeably with such terms as presentational, non-illusionistic, stylized, formalist and simply theatrical.

5. One may question Abel's starting point in the Renaissance. See, for instance, Charles Segal's brilliant essay 'Metatragedy: Art, Illusion, Imitation', in *Dionysiac Poetics and Euripides' Bacchae* (Princeton and Guildford: Princeton University Press, 1982), pp.215–71.

6. See Lynda G. Christian's exemplary study, *Theatrum Mundi: The History of an Idea* (New York: Garland, 1987), pp.170–9.

7. Pedro Calderon de la Barca, *The Great Theatre of the World*, trans. Mack Hendricks Singleton, in *Masterpieces of the Spanish Golden Age*, ed. Angel Flores (New York: Holt, Rinehart & Winston, 1957).

8. 2 Corinthians, 4:18, *The Holy Bible*, New King James Version (Nashville: Thomas Nelson, 1982), p.1129.

9. This binary division of realms is not always so neat, even in classic theatricalism, as Beaumont's *The Knight of the Burning Pestle* amply demonstrates. Yet here, too, a foundational offstage geography of grocers' and barbers' shops supports the dizzying layers of adventure on the London stage.

10. Lope de Vega, *Acting is Believing*, trans. Michael D. McGaha (San Antonio: Trinity University Press, 1986).

11. Jean Genet, *The Blacks: A Clown Show* (New York: Grove, 1960).

12. Heiner Müller, *Hamletmachine*, in *Hamletmachine and Other Texts for the Stage*, trans. Carl Weber (New York: Performing Arts Journal Publications, 1984). See, for instance, 'Clown Number Two in the Spring of Communism' (p.53).

13. Peter Handke, *Kaspar*, in *Kaspar and other Plays*, trans. Michael Roloff (New York: Hill & Wang, 1969). Clown in German is *Kasper*; a *Kasperle* is the clown-figure Punch, and *Kasperletheater*, a Punch and Judy show.

14. Suzan-Lori Parks, *The America Play*, in *The America Play and Other Works* (New York: Theatre Communications Group, 1995).

15. Teresa de Lauretis, *Technologies of Gender* (Bloomington: Indiana University Press, 1987). See p.26 on 'space-off': 'the space not visible in the frame but inferable from what the frame makes visible'.

16. Bruce Wilshire, *Role Playing and Identity: The Limits of Theatre as Metaphor* (Bloomington: Indiana University Press, 1982). See especially ch. V, 'Variations on the Theatrical Theme of Standing In and Authorization'.

17. Christopher Innes, *Holy Theatre: Ritual and the Avant Garde* (Cambridge: Cambridge University Press, 1981), p.147.

18. Jacques Lacan, *The Four Fundamental Concepts of Psycho-Analysis*, ed. Jacques-Alain Miller, trans. Alan Sheridan (New York: W. W. Norton, 1981), p.55.
19. Walter Reich, 'Understanding Terrorist Behavior: the Limits and Opportunities of Psychological Inquiry', in Walter Reich, ed., *Origins of Terrorism* (Baltimore, MD: Johns Hopkins University Press. 1998), p.262.
20. Slavoj Žižek, *The Sublime Object of Ideology* (London: Verso, 1989), p.47.
21. See Robert Brustein's attack on *Kaspar* as cited in Amy Klatzkin, *Peter Handke: The First Five Plays* (Stanford: Stanford Honors Essay in Humanities, vol. XXIII, 1979), p.45.
22. The Michael Roloff translation keeps these figures within a theatrical frame of reference by translating 'Einsager' as 'Prompters'. While most commentators regard the word, literally translated as 'in-sayers' as an invention, Klatzkin observes that it is not a 'Handke invention at all. It is Austrian schoolboy slang for the classroom equivalent of a "kibbitzer"... [such as] a classmate who furtively gives you the answers you do not know, without the teacher's knowledge, if you are lucky' (*Peter Handke: The First Five Plays*, p.34)
23. The historical Kaspar Hauser himself had a similarly short-lived relationship to the light of education and socialization. Within five years of his discovery and reclamation, he was found mysteriously dead.
24. The tale, told by Lucian, inspired Goethe's ballad, *Der Zauberlehrling*, in turn the inspiration for the composer Paul Dukas's *L'Apprenti sorcier*.
25. See, for instance, Nicholas Hern, *Peter Handke: Theatre and Anti-Theatre* (London: Oswald Wolff, 1971), pp.68–9; and Richard Arthur Firda, *Peter Handke* (New York: Twayne, 1993), pp.24–5.
26. Hugo von Hoffmansthal, 'The Letter of Lord Chandos', in *Selected Prose*, trans. Mary Hottinger and Tania and James Stern, intro. Hermann Broch (New York: Pantheon, 1952), pp.133–5.
27. See Michael Linstead, *Outer World and Inner World: Socialisation and Emancipation in the Works of Peter Handke, 1964–1981* (Frankfurt am Main: Peter Lang, 1988).
28. Pierre Nora, *Realms of Memory: Rethinking the French Past*, trans. Arthur Goldhammer, ed. Lawrence D. Kritzman (New York: Columbia Unviersity Press, 1996). Many have questioned the translation of the French 'lieux' into the English 'realms'. I prefer 'sites', which includes, but is not limited to, actual place.

4
Anti-Theatricality in Twentieth-Century Opera

Herbert Lindenberger

An anti-theatrical opera would seem to be a contradiction in terms. Theatricality, after all, suggests an exaggerated perspective on what we take to be reality, a certain inauthenticity that, as Jonas Barish demonstrated in his magisterial book *The Antitheatrical Prejudice*, has been an issue within Western thought since its beginnings. The term *operatic* implies the exaggeration of a theatrical stance already assumed to be exaggerated. Thus, an opera that questions the nature and value of theatricality would seem to put enormous constraints on composers and performers, not to speak of audiences eager to experience the enactment of those high emotions that they would not dare to reveal in their everyday lives.

Yet many operas that we now see as central to the twentieth-century canon display an anti-theatricality similar to what Barish, in his final chapter, describes in such major dramatists of the century as Chekhov, Pirandello, Brecht and Beckett. Pirandello, as he puts it, poses 'a challenge to the theater as an expressive medium, a rebuke to its age-old claim to be able to instruct us about our true natures', while Beckett initiates 'a new radicalism' in which 'the tissue of plausible event is stripped away' and 'character is scraped down to the bone of consciousness'. For Barish, the revolutionary innovations of twentieth-century theatre have worked to 'burn down the ornate, overloaded theater of the past in the hope that a purified theater will rise from its ashes'.[1]

The task of the present essay is to demonstrate the differing ways that four operas cutting across the twentieth century – Debussy's *Pelléas et Mélisande* (1902), Schoenberg's *Moses und Aron* (1932), Stravinsky's *The Rake's Progress* (1951), and Messiaen's *Saint François d'Assise* (1983) – express an anti-theatricality analogous to what Barish explores in the drama of the same period. But unlike Barish, who considers modern drama in the light of a 2500-year debate about the theatre, I am principally concerned with the ways in which modernist works, whether spoken or musical, respond to what their creators and audiences would have viewed as peculiarly theatrical in the writing of the past. Thus, Brecht's use of a multitude of devices to break the theatrical illusion, or Beckett's insistent repetitions and his refusal to work toward what once counted as a dramatic resolution, play upon their audiences' knowledge and often too-willing acceptance of the conventions governing the so-called well-made play. In this form, whether the 'serious' drama of an Ibsen or the boulevard plays of a Scribe, the need for a constantly forward-moving plot and for characters who could pass for real-life persons provided a model that twentieth-century drama worked fervently to undo.

Similarly with opera. Just as the model for what counts as theatrical was rooted in the writing of the preceding century, so the model for what is peculiarly operatic derived from the works with which audiences have been most familiar, namely the canonical operas of the mid- and late nineteenth century. What we see as 'operatic' has, of course, changed in the course of history: what would have seemed operatic in the Venetian public theatres of the mid-seventeenth century is something quite different from what was deemed operatic in the heyday of *opera seria* during the eighteenth century.

For twentieth-century audiences, who until recent years rarely heard operas earlier than those of Mozart, the operatic canon occupied a relatively small segment of musical history. Despite differences in national styles, some key operas of the 1850s display an extreme of what subsequent opera-goers could perceive as operatic – in Italy, *Il trovatore* (1853); in Germany, *Tristan und Isolde* (1859); in France, *Faust* (1859). In *Il trovatore*, for example, we experience a melodramatic plot in which crises follow one another at a dizzying pace until the final catastrophe; an unrelenting extravagance of gesture, as in Leonora's putting a stop to the duel fought by her two would-be suitors or the gypsy's flamboyant narrative about her exchange of babies; and a frenzied piling up of the arias, duets and ensembles that take the formal conventions of early nineteenth-century opera to their limits. In *Tristan*, what we come to see as operatic derives from the large orchestra that defines and underlines the overwhelming emotions of the lovers; from the extraordinary length to which individual high points – the second-act love duet, Tristan's last-act feverish monologue – are sustained; from the sheer volume demanded of the voices throughout. In *Faust* the operatic manifests itself in the earnestness into which Goethe's theatrically self-conscious and sometimes comic text has been transformed; in the shamelessly sweet arias and duets assigned to the tenor and soprano; in the dramatic exuberance of its grand ensembles. If these and other operas of their time later seemed to hit a high-water mark of operatic theatricality, the final works by two of their composers show a clear retreat from this extreme.[2] In *Falstaff* (1893), for instance, Verdi allows arias and ensembles to be fragmented and truncated, as though questioning the authenticity with which he spoke out operatically some 40 years earlier. The most histrionic and also the most fully worked out aria, Ford's 'È sogno?', is actually a parody of the revenge arias endemic in earlier Italian opera. Indeed, *Falstaff* parodies such other elements of traditional opera as the wooing duet, the serenade and the conspiracy scene. Although parody is a common enough device within the comic genre to which *Falstaff* belongs, it is also significant that during the mid-nineteenth century comic opera had virtually ceased to exist in Italy. In its finale, *Falstaff*, like *Don Giovanni* (1787) a century before and like *The Rake's Progress* half a century later, draws its characters out of the action to allow them, like spectators in the theatre, to comment upon it.

Wagner's *Parsifal* tests the limits of nineteenth-century theatricality in ways that anticipate the anti-theatrical moves that I shall point out in operas of the next century. Note, for example, the sharp distinction between the 'secular' middle act, the only act in which audiences traditionally have applauded, and the two outer 'religious' acts, whose conclusions are acknowledged with awed silence. Wagner has carefully segregated what we are to view as theatrical and what supposedly transcends theatre.

In contrast to the two spiritual acts, *Parsifal*'s middle act is clearly the music drama's single operatic act. What we experience as operatic in this act – the flower maidens exercising their charms in Klingsor's magic garden, Kundry's role as love goddess – we are also to see as bogus – as dangerous and as inauthentic as anything that the anti-theatrical polemicists from Plato onwards, as Barish presents them in his book, found in earlier drama. The encounter between Parsifal and Kundry that should have brought the 'love' interest to a climax in Act Two becomes instead a proud repudiation of sexual love. Parsifal's loud exclamation, 'Amfortas! Die Wunde!', is an operatic gesture that also works to forestall the consummation of love. Indeed, once Parsifal has rejected Kundry's overtures, she loses her theatrical power and is gradually reduced, in the final part of the act, to the passive, virtually silent creature she becomes in the third act. Gurnemanz, the central figure of the two anti-theatrical acts of *Parsifal*, also has the longest role in this music drama, and, in view of his understated, unlyrical style, his is also the least 'operatic' role. His discourse remains relatively close to speech rhythms; when Wagner's characters in earlier music dramas – Loge, Mime and Beckmesser, for instance – speak this way, they are comic, ironic, grotesque, and they speak rapidly. But Gurnemanz speaks his lines slowly and with utter earnestness (he is, after all, the most knowing character of the opera) and only occasionally sings out to accompany the orchestra in one of the leitmotifs.

From the anti-theatricality of *Parsifal*'s Gurnemanz scenes it is a small but quite significant step to *Pelléas et Mélisande*. Wagner's approximation of speech rhythms, the frequent understatedness of both the words and the music, and the attempt to conjure up a sense of mystery unfamiliar within earlier opera – all these helped lay the groundwork for Debussy.

But the crucial element behind this most anti-theatrical of operas was the dramaturgy of the play by Maurice Maeterlinck (1892) from which Debussy drew his text. The play itself was an attempt to apply Symbolist theory to drama – with the result that, in his plays of the 1890s, the Symbolist disdain for explicitness and its advocacy of suggestiveness and understatement challenged the overt theatricality central to popular nineteenth-century drama.

Few dramatists have risen or fallen in esteem as fast as Maeterlinck. Little performed today, he lives on through Debussy's opera and, just as importantly, through his anti-theatrical legacy, which, as a recent book on Maeterlinck has argued, was picked up half a century after his heyday by dramatists such as Beckett, Ionesco and Pinter.[3] Note the following exchange from Maeterlinck's play as Golaud asks his child, Yniold, to observe his wife, Mélisande, through a window as she talks with his brother, Pelléas:

Golaud: What are they talking about?
Yniold: About me; always about me.
Golaud: And what are they saying about you?
Yniold: They're saying I'll be very big.
Golaud: How miserable for me! ... Don't Pelléas and Mommy ever talk about me when I'm not there?
Yniold: Yes, yes, Daddy.
Golaud: Oh! ... And what are they saying about me?
Yniold: They're saying I'll turn out to be as big as you.[4]

The inconsequentiality of this exchange, in which a jealous Golaud desperately seeks information about his wife's relations with his brother, is emblematic of the difficulties that audiences must have faced in making theatrical sense out of this play. The most urgent questions here receive typically childlike, *non sequitur* responses.

The music to which Debussy set these words reacts to earlier operatic discourse much as these lines react to earlier theatre.[5] Both the text and the music go against our usual expectations. In Debussy's setting of the lines before the ellipses, the orchestra creates a sinister effect to suggest Golaud's jealousy, which scarcely seems justified by Yniold's innocent reply that the lovers are discussing his future height. It builds to a climax that, it turns out, does little more than express Golaud's frustration that Yniold's replies tell him nothing.

My ellipses cover a speech of self-reproach by Golaud. When the questioning begins again, the orchestral response is minimal, with no climax, no strong emotions suggested. It is as though the new set of questions, though little different from the earlier ones, can no longer evoke emotion, not even frustration, but simply suggest a certain enervatedness in the dramatic action. The lines I have quoted are the same in both the play and the opera; for the play contained all the elements that Debussy needed to achieve the anti-theatrical effects he sought. The elusiveness for which this opera is celebrated (or, by some listeners, condemned) is located most conspicuously in its heroine. Mélisande's elusiveness is not simply an aspect of the *fatalité* that she shares with a multitude of her contemporaries in literature, opera, painting and dance. Knowing as little as we do about her (where is she from? what motivates her? what causes her death?) is necessary for the aura of untheatricality that both Maeterlinck and Debussy sought to achieve. Endowing her with better-defined contours or placing her actions within a cause-and-effect sequence would have given her a conventional theatricality that it was her creators' need to avoid at all costs.

A synopsis of the play or the opera would not in itself reveal its anti-theatrical quality. In fact, the story would look like a typical nineteenth-century opera plot about adultery and revenge on the part of the wronged mate. We are unaware of its unconventional quality until we read the actual dialogue or listen to the music. This quality is particularly evident if we compare the final love scene (Act 4, scene 4) between Pelléas and Mélisande, culminating as it does in Golaud's killing of his rival, with its implied model, the love duet of *Tristan und Isolde*, which too is interrupted by the jealous husband's appearance and the mortal wounding of the illicit lover.

Whereas Wagner's scene builds steadily, inexorably toward its grand climax, with the lovers singing in unison as it nears its end, Debussy's remains for the most part restrained, with occasional moments of agitation and passion punctuating the quiet atmosphere. His lovers' acknowledgment of their love, quite in contrast to Wagner's high-volume declarations, is spoken virtually in a whisper, with minimal orchestral accompaniment. And whereas Wagner's lovers, oblivious of Brangaene's warnings, are taken by surprise by the husband's entrance, Debussy's become aware of Golaud lurking nearby in the forest and then remain passive as he kills his brother and wounds his wife. While Wagner's love-night culminates in a long series of recriminations, Debussy's ends abruptly after Golaud's action, to be followed by the anticlimactic final act, at the beginning of which we learn – in an undermining of cause-and-effect relationships typical of Maeterlinck and Debussy – that Mélisande's wound was not in itself serious enough to kill her. Few if any last acts in opera are as anticlimactic as that of *Pelléas*, but then few climactic scenes are as restrained as the love duet immediately preceding it.

Even a century after its première, *Pelléas et Mélisande* has not fully acclimated itself for opera-goers. My own experience attending many productions of *Pelléas* over the years has taught me to avoid conversing during intermissions with fellow subscribers, for the latter, having come to the theatre with expectations nurtured by the standard repertory, often complain that everything they treasure about opera – full-throated song, high drama, forward-thrusting music – is missing here.

When Mélisande, almost midway through the opera, sings from the balcony about her long hair ('Mes longs cheveux descendent...'[6]), we think we have finally been granted an aria. Yet in the context of any earlier nineteenth-century opera her song would not even seem like an aria – indeed, it would scarcely compel an audience's attention. As Debussy was reported saying long before he even conceived this opera, 'In the opera house they sing *too much*. One should *sing* only when it is worthwhile and hold moving lyrical expression in reserve.'[7] The mode of vocal discourse that Debussy invented for this, his only completed opera, was, of course, a deliberate attempt to undo what he took to be an overwrought, antiquated operatic language. As he put it in his brief statement, 'Why I Wrote *Pelléas*', 'I ... tried to obey a law of beauty that seems notably ignored when it comes to dramatic music: the characters of this opera try to sing like real people, and not in an arbitrary language made up of worn-out clichés. That is why the reproach has been made concerning my so-called taste for monotonous declamation, where nothing seems melodic.'[8] Earlier in this note Debussy, after noting his own 'passionate pilgrimages to Bayreuth' in his youth, had complained of Wagner as 'a great collector of formulae' (*Debussy on Music*, p.74). What has made *Pelléas* difficult for opera-goers ever since its première is precisely its avoidance of easy formulae, whether Wagnerian or Italian.

The anti-theatrical quality of Debussy's declamation appears 'undramatic' only when measured by what its audiences were most familiar with. It is significant, for instance, that the first performances of Monteverdi's operas since the seventeenth century took place within two years after the première of *Pelléas et Mélisande* and that the critic Louis Laloy, a fervent Debussy admirer, wrote that 'the criticisms aimed at the *Orfeo*...resemble those aimed at *Pelléas*. The two works should displease the same spirits.'[9] Moreover, French opera before the nineteenth century had been marked by a mode of discourse far closer to speech than to the mode that had characterized Italian opera since the eighteenth century and that also dominated opera in France during the nineteenth. What we see as anti-theatrical, as I have been arguing, is what challenges and violates the theatrical conventions with which we are most immediately familiar.

The anti-theatricality of Schoenberg's *Moses und Aron* takes a quite different form from that of *Pelléas*. Its non-tonal method is not in itself an indication of anti-theatricality. After all, vocal music, including opera, was a central concern for Schoenberg and his followers. Schoenberg's first operatic venture, the mini-opera *Erwartung* (1909), composed directly after his break with tonality, seems thoroughly theatrical despite its iconoclastic musical technique. Atonal music, both during its free phase and after Schoenberg had developed the 12-tone method in the early 1920s, lent itself particularly well to creating strong theatrical effects, especially the depiction of extreme psychological states, as in the sustained hysteria of *Erwartung* or the visions and the violence portrayed in the title character of Alban Berg's *Wozzeck* (1925).

A similar theatricality distinguishes *Moses und Aron*, which in one sense looks like the most theatrical of major twentieth-century operas. Although Schoenberg was never able to set the final act of the libretto he had himself written, the work as it stands is a grand-scale post-Wagnerian music drama with a huge orchestra, large choruses, dances and spectacular scenic effects, above all in the scene depicting the Hebrews worshipping the Golden Calf.

To cite only a few of the opportunities that *Moses und Aron* has granted its stage directors and scenic designers, this scene includes such elements as a group of old men killing themselves before the Calf; the crazed crowd of worshippers killing a youth who, in the name of the

Hebrew God, challenges polytheism; a drunken dance; four naked maidens who are embraced by priests as the latter are about to knife them to death as sacrifices; and, to bring this scene to a climactic end, an action in which the men tear off their clothes, denude the women and stage an orgy at the altar. No Hollywood Biblical extravaganza is likely to outdo Schoenberg's script.

And yet the extreme theatricality that Schoenberg realizes in this opera is thoroughly challenged by the role that Moses undertakes. As in *Parsifal*, the anti-theatrical is defined for us through the presence of strongly theatrical elements. While *Parsifal* is divided between overtly theatrical and anti-theatrical scenes, *Moses und Aron* presents its two antithetical figures at once, sometimes, indeed, in duet with one another. These two figures are depicted from the beginning as representing contradictory views about theatrical performance. Whereas Aron is willing to grant the unruly crowd its desire to participate in the ceremonies associated with its traditional gods, Moses stands resolutely for the interdiction against such rituals imposed upon them by the monotheistic God whose message he is trying to convey. Schoenberg, in this opera, is in fact dramatizing that long-standing conflict about representation within the Judeo-Christian tradition that Jonas Barish's book has portrayed.

For Moses, the one God must remain unrepresentable: indeed, the word *'unvorstellbar'* ('unrepresentable'), echoing innumerable times in his speeches, is doubtless the most memorable word in the opera. But Moses is also depicted from the outset as a man without verbal skills, and he depends upon his slickly articulate brother to convey his message to the crowd. In the second act, once Moses has ascended Mount Sinai to receive the Ten Commandments, Aron finds himself having to deal with the crowd, and he allows it to go its own, theatrically inclined way by enacting its traditional polytheistic rituals. Aron has already demonstrated his theatrical ways in the first act when, to impress the crowd, he temporarily transformed Moses's staff into a serpent and cured his brother's leprous hand.

The conflict between the brothers manifests itself in musical terms through the sharply contrasting modes of vocal discourse associated with each. Whereas Aron's role is assigned to a tenor who sings his lines in a smoothly lyrical manner, Moses's part is not even sung but is uttered in a mode called *Sprechstimme* that Schoenberg had devised early in his atonal period. Although musical pitches are recorded for the singer, these notes are uttered in a way much closer to speech than to song. Moreover, the contrast we hear between Moses's austere, harsh bass voice and Aron's slick tenor, with both of them often singing in duet, dramatizes the opera's essential conflict at every point in the most conspicuous manner possible. At the end of the second act, which is as far as Schoenberg got in the musical setting of his three-act text, Moses returns from the mountain to condemn Aron's and the crowd's conduct in uncompromising terms. The opera thus culminates in a thorough repudiation of the theatricality we have been witnessing throughout.

The debate about theatricality central to *Moses und Aron* can be interpreted allegorically in at least two ways – the first political, the second aesthetic. In view of the fact that Schoenberg was working on his opera in Berlin during the later 1920s and early 1930s, any listener – indeed, any reader of the libretto – finds it difficult not to connect Aron's manipulation of the anarchic crowd with Hitler's similar endeavours during these, the crucial years in his rise to power. When we hear these words spoken by Aron to please the crowd after its demand for its older gods, it is difficult to resist detecting their resemblance to Hitler's rhetoric:

> I'm returning your gods to you
> and you to them,
> as you have demanded...
> You are providing the content,
> I shall give it a form:
> common, visible, graspable
> eternalized in gold...
> You will be happy.[10]

Moses und Aron also invites a second set of political meanings. During the mid-1920s, before he had written the opera's libretto, Schoenberg wrote a non-musical drama, *Der biblische Weg*, in which two modern embodiments of Moses and Aron appear as conflicting sides of a single figure, a scarcely veiled portrait of Theodor Herzl, the founder of Zionism. The play itself is a highly theatrical representation of the political difficulties that Herzl encountered through his inability to reconcile the 'theatrical' needs of everyday political dealings with his 'untheatrical' need to maintain his integrity.

But Schoenberg's opera suggests still another set of meanings, this one within the realm of aesthetics. As the leader of the Central European musical avant-garde, Schoenberg, like his older contemporary Sigmund Freud, felt a keen identification with Moses. From Schoenberg's point of view, the break with tonality and the later development of the 12-tone scale were inevitable stages in the history of musical form. Like Moses, he viewed himself as chosen to lead others into new and unfamiliar territory. And also like Moses, he saw himself as a lonely figure, one who was in fact persecuted by those unwilling to undergo the hardships (for Moses, life in the desert; for Schoenberg, hearing difficult music in the concert hall) that he demanded of them. Within Schoenberg's imaginative world, audiences were all too ready to turn to the Arons of contemporary music, that is, toward the traditionally tonal, more readily digestible composers who could offer them the easy listening of a quick musical fix. Only by enduring the untheatrical rigours he demanded of them could audiences hope to enter the musical promised land.

The untheatricality we experience in Stravinsky's *The Rake's Progress* is quite different in kind from that of either *Pelléas et Mélisande* or *Moses und Aron*. Whereas the latter two operas expect their audiences to accept the aesthetic illusion they create, Stravinsky's encourages audiences to distance themselves from the on-stage action. For Stravinsky and his librettists, W. H. Auden and Chester Kallman, *The Rake's Progress* project provided an opportunity self-consciously to re-examine the conventions of opera, in both their verbal and musical aspects. Enjoyable though the resulting music and the stage action may be, the opera's creators have made it impossible for a viewer simply to sit back unthinkingly. The opera's untheatricality thus lies in the fact that, in keeping us from being trapped by the stage illusion, it forces us to think seriously about the history and nature of operatic conventions.

To be sure, many earlier operas undermined the aesthetic illusion and played explicitly with convention. Stravinsky's epilogue, in which the characters return to comment on their actions, was, as I mentioned earlier, anticipated by *Don Giovanni* and *Falstaff*. Offenbach's and Gilbert and Sullivan's operettas provide innumerable spoofs of easily recognizable operatic conventions. And the Strauss–Hofmannsthal *Ariadne auf Naxos* (1916) juxtaposes *opera seria* with *commedia dell'arte* to expose the limitations and the underlying meanings of each of these forms.

But *The Rake's Progress* pursues its examination of the past with a seriousness and a rigour unique in the history of opera. For all its toying with stage illusion, *Ariadne auf Naxos* culminates in the most thoroughgoingly imaginable illusion, in which the once-despairing heroine is rescued by a hero with whom she engages in an ecstatic and unashamedly operatic love duet. Moreover, Stravinsky had made the examination of the musical past central to many compositions of his neoclassical period, for example, *Pulcinella* (1920), which reworks Pergolesi and his contemporaries, and *Le baiser de la fée* (1928), a rewriting of various Tchaikovsky pieces.

The Rake's Progress is the last major work of this period. Unlike the pieces I mention above, it re-examines not a single composer or period, but rather the nature of opera. Not that Stravinsky directly evokes the Wagnerian tradition, which remains present for us through its deliberate absence. For *The Rake's Progress* resolutely brackets this tradition, against which he polemicized throughout his career, to pursue the form and conventions of the pre-Wagnerian number opera, with its predictable succession of recitatives, cavatinas, cabalettas and larger ensembles.[11] Those familiar with the operatic past keep hearing snippets from earlier number operas – or, at least, they think they hear something familiar, for Stravinsky has hidden his traces and also distorted his sources with telling dissonances. As he himself later reported, during the planning stage of the opera he and Auden 'attended a two-piano performance of *Così fan tutte* together – an omen, perhaps, for the *Rake* is deeply involved in *Così*'.[12]

But *The Rake's Progress* is also deeply involved in the whole history of opera, from its beginnings through at least Verdi. As an early commentator on this work put it: 'The whole genre of opera itself serves as model'[13] and allusions to the operatic past have proved readily discernible.[14] Since Auden and Kallman happened to be avid opera listeners, the whole project displays a thorough knowingness about the medium built in from the beginning. Note, for instance, the disposition of the various roles, which follows the system of early to mid-nineteenth-century Italian opera: the rash tenor lover (Tom Rakewell); his bland lyric-soprano beloved (Anne Trulove); the bass patriarchal father (Trulove); the baritone villain (Nick Shadow); the mezzo-soprano pushy other woman (Baba). And note the genealogy of Nick Shadow, who looks back to the devil figure in the various Faust/Mephistopheles operas as well as to the multiple villains of *Les Contes d'Hoffmann* (1881).

The *Rake's* closeness to operatic tradition lies not only in its larger plan but, above all, in its individual segments. For example, Anne Trulove's long and elaborate solo scene at the end of the first act parallels Violetta's similar scene closing the first act of *La traviata*.[15] In each case the librettists have rigorously organized their material to make the plot fit the conventions governing a soprano's Act 1 aria: the opening recitative that defines the character's dilemma; the ensuing andante, in which she seems to have made up her mind; the *tempo di mezzo*, in which she displays some second thoughts about her earlier resolution; and, finally, the glittering, showpiece cabaletta, where she makes her resolution once and for all (for Violetta, to maintain her freedom; for Anne, to go after Tom in London). Both the music and the words, 'I go, I go to him'

(Stravinsky, *The Rake's Progress*, pp.127–9), of this last section have the characteristic forward thrust of the Italian cabaletta. In each scene, moreover, the character is temporarily rendered indecisive by an external voice (for Violetta, her lover's; for Anne, her father's). And each cabaletta, after a good bit of florid singing, culminates in a triumphant high C (or, in the case of *La traviata*, an E flat for those sopranos brave enough to try).

Despite the high artifice of *The Rake's Progress*, Stravinsky provides a number of moments in which we are at least briefly taken in by the illusions and even moved – above all in the madhouse scene as Anne sings a simple lullaby to her dying, demented lover (pp.383–5). But as soon as this scene ends, the composer cunningly breaks the illusion with the epilogue.

Audiences unfamiliar with opera may well take *The Rake's Progress*, with its auctioning off of the bearded 'other woman' and its bordello and madhouse scenes, as a thoroughly theatrical romp. But its theatricality is so overt and outrageous that it also forces us to reflect upon what this is all about – as, indeed, its characters do in the epilogue. The ironic distance that it encourages was, in fact, present already in the caricatured poses of the Hogarth series of paintings upon which the libretto is based. After Stravinsky happened to see these paintings in Chicago during a touring exhibition in 1947, he recognized that he now had the subject for what was to be his only full-length opera. And he must doubtless have sensed a kinship between Hogarth's sense of irony and his own.

If *The Rake's Progress* achieves its untheatricality by encouraging us to rethink the very nature of theatricality, Messiaen's *Saint François d'Assise* makes no bones about its refusal even to appear to be theatrical. Until the Paris Opéra's director, Rolf Liebermann, persuaded the composer in 1975 to undertake this project, nobody, including Messiaen himself, would have imagined an opera coming out of this pious figure, whose *oeuvre* consisted mainly of keyboard and instrumental work, much of it of a specifically religious nature.

Messiaen himself acknowledged the implausibility of his becoming an opera composer. For one thing, he did not feel he possessed the gift for operatic composition. Nor was he interested in the medium from a theatrical point of view. Indeed, according to his own account, he accepted the invitation only after Liebermann ordered him to 'write an opera for the Opéra de Paris' in the presence of the then-president of France, Georges Pompidou, during a state dinner.[16] Messiaen's statements on opera generally express disdain – of fans 'who wait for the tenor's high B-flat' and of others who 'come only for the spectacle' (p.208).

The majority of operas, for him, fall into two categories: those 'that are good theater and bad music and those that are good music and bad theater' (Messiaen, *Music and Colour*, p.208).

But Messiaen also showed immense respect for a select few operas whose music he revered and which he analysed regularly in his classes – most notably, to judge from references in his writing, *Pelléas et Mélisande, Tristan und Isolde, Boris Godunov* and *Wozzeck*. Indeed, the first of these played a special role in his life, for, as he declared in an interview shortly before his death, studying the score of *Pelléas* at age 10 made him decide to become a composer;[17]; as he had put it in an earlier interview, *Pelléas* had the effect of 'a revelation, love at first sight... That was probably the most decisive influence I've received – and it's also an opera, isn't it?'[18] It is significant that this most untheatrical of composers should be shaped by so anti-theatrical an opera – to the point that he jokes about whether it really is an opera in the first place!

But once Messiaen had consented to write an opera, he was careful to set limits on its theatricality. Composing a saint's life – and particularly one whose story, unlike those of saints who suffered martyrdom, lacked sensational elements – inhibited any temptation to be overly dramatic. To avoid undue artifice, Messiaen based his libretto on the known sources about Francis's life and, as much as possible, on the saint's own writings; the *Canticle of the Sun*, for example, is quoted nearly in full, though it is spread out among several scenes. In addition, Messiaen sought to avoid many operatic conventions: 'There's no overture', he boasted, 'no interludes between the various scenes, no symphonic numbers that can be played separately...there are neither arias nor vocal ensembles.'[19] He viewed the chorus as the only traditional operatic convention that he retained. And much of the opera's verbal content consists of theological discussion, prayer and the enunciation of exempla.

Messiaen's fear of ordinary theatricality motivated him to discard some well-known episodes from St Francis's life. For example, Francis's meeting with St Clare found no place in the opera because of posthumous rumours of 'a love affair between the two saints' (Messiaen, *Form and Color*, p.213). Francis's conflict with his father was omitted for fear of setting up an Oedipal drama ('I loathe psychoanalysis', Messiaen says [p.213]). The saint's taming of the Wolf of Gubbio, a central element in Franciscan iconography, could not be accommodated because the animal might look as ridiculous on stage as the 'grotesque dragon in *Siegfried*' (p.213), and his dispute with Assisi town officials was unsatisfactory because it would have necessitated 'other characters with period costumes' (p.215). The closest Messiaen came to introducing an operatic villain ('sin isn't interesting, dirt isn't interesting' [p.213]) is the unpleasant, bureaucratically minded Frère Élie. So what was left in the story to shape an opera? Certainly some famous incidents passed the composer's rigorous screening test – for example, St Francis's curing of the leper, his communication with the birds, and his receiving the stigmata. Still, by ordinary operatic or theatrical standards *Saint François d'Assise* is conspicuously short on incidents. It is a slow-progressing spectacle with some four hours of music (not counting its two intermissions) in eight scenes, each one of them built around a single incident involving relatively few characters, with the saint present in all but one.

Messiaen concocted a form of musical discourse unlike that of any earlier opera. Instead of singing arias the characters chant in a declamatory style, which, though influenced by the speech rhythms of *Boris Godunov* and *Pelléas*, creates a thoroughly original effect because of the relative slowness of the music and, even more important, because the orchestra remains subdued during the speeches. Orchestral and choral commentary, instead of accompanying the characters' declamation, tends to occur between phrases and speeches. Messiaen's declamatory style, moreover, evokes a medieval modal world, which, as one commentator puts it, creates a 'contrast between archaic musical converse among the characters and continuous surprise from the orchestra'.[20] Much of this orchestral commentary consists of birdsongs that Messiaen transcribed and that are central to much of his other music. But the birdsongs have a special function in *Saint François d'Assise*, not only in the scene with the birds, which includes both a 'small' and a 'grand' concert of the birds, but also in defining the characters of the opera. Each character is, in fact, associated with one or more particular birds. During the two so-called '*concerts d'oiseaux*' Messiaen even labels his birds and their respective countries of origin in his score.[21] Through the often strange sounds of these birdsongs, together with the huge chorus and orchestra Messiaen demands for the opera, the composer creates a powerful sonic experience that achieves its own, unique form of theatricality. Moreover, the unfamiliar instruments he insists upon – three Ondes Martenot, the Geophone, and all manner of exotic percussion devices – may well cause listeners to re-evaluate what precisely they mean by the term 'theatricality'. Within the terms of this chapter, the characters' slow and stately dialogue, like the *Sprechstimme* in which Schoenberg's Moses speaks, can be viewed as an anti-theatrical extreme against which the loud and dissonant orchestral outbursts, similarly to those of Schoenberg, define their theatricality by means of the sharp contrast they offer between opposing modes of discourse.

And despite Messiaen's disdain for ordinary theatre, he expresses pride in what at one point he even called the 'theatricality' of the leper scene,[22] which, after St Francis has kissed the leper, culminates in the latter's 'jumping and dancing like a madman'.[23] Since this moment of high action comes at the end of a slowly developing, half-hour-long scene, the dramaturgy that Messiaen is practising in this work is one that contrasts conspicuously with the high-pitched drama characteristic of nineteenth-century opera.

But so also does the dramaturgy of the other three works I have discussed in detail. Both Debussy and Messiaen, for instance, despite a leisureliness that seems to defy an earlier concept of theatricality, create hypnotic effects for their audiences that define a new mode of theatricality. (Hypnosis, by its very nature, demands a slowing down.) Schoenberg, by confronting theatrical and anti-theatrical characters within a single work, and Stravinsky, by inviting his audience to join him in anatomizing the conventions of earlier opera, force us to reconsider what theatricality is all about in the first place.

The anti-theatricality I have located in these four works should not obscure the fact that many great twentieth-century operas remain securely within a traditional theatrical mode. Certainly the operas of Puccini and Strauss, who, though born in the mid-nineteenth century, composed most of their operas during the twentieth, seem theatrical to the core – this despite Strauss's occasionally exposing the theatrical illusion, as in *Ariadne auf Naxos* and in his final opera, *Capriccio* (1942). Alban Berg's two operas, however innovative their musical style, perpetuate the dramatic method of post-Wagnerian music drama. Benjamin Britten moved directly from his grand-operatic *Peter Grimes* (1945) to his small-scale, anti-theatrical chamber opera *The Rape of Lucretia* (1946), whose static quality (with a corresponding paucity of dramatic action in which even the rape scene remains understated) is guaranteed by the fact that the roles of the two narrators are about as long as those of the characters within the story. And again, like many anti-theatrical operas, and certainly including the Schoenberg and Messiaen operas I have discussed above, *The Rape of Lucretia* invokes a religious aura – in this instance, Christian stoicism – to establish its distance from ordinary theatricality.

Many twentieth-century operas have manifested a similarly static quality – to the point that critics often call them 'oratorio-like'. One thinks, for instance, of John Adams's *The Death of Klinghoffer* (1991) but also, for that matter, of *Saint François d'Assise*. And one might note that

Schoenberg first conceived *Moses und Aron* as an oratorio, but was persuaded by his publisher to use the material for an opera instead. 'Opera' and 'oratorio', moreover, have been used as opposing terms since the early eighteenth century. Though Handel's oratorios today seem at least as 'operatic' as his *opere serie* (some, like *Samson* and *Semele*, even achieving success on the stage), they defined themselves in their time by means of their contrast with opera – religious rather than secular, bourgeois rather than aristocratic, native rather than foreign. From the point of view of the present article, it is significant that, in the course of the twentieth century, the opera–oratorio dichotomy no longer seems as absolute as before, that, in fact, seemingly static, oratorio-like operas have proved their power on the stage.

Within the final quarter of the twentieth century, a number of musical dramas (whether or not one chooses to call them operas) explored the possibilities of anti-theatricality even more radically than the four on which this article has focused. For example, Philip Glass's *Einstein on the Beach* (1976) and Steve Reich's *The Cave* (1993), through their avoidance of operatic vocal style, their use of electronic synthe-sizers, and the minimalist technique that frustrates a listener's desire for musical closure, challenge their audiences as to whether even to label them 'opera' in the first place.[24]

The past quarter-century has also, above all in Europe, been the age of so-called directorial opera, in which celebrity directors such as Patrice Chéreau, Harry Kupfer and Peter Sellars have radically rethought (some would even say dismembered) a good bit of the traditional canon. Through the unexpected visual effects they project – for example, a medieval potentate in black tie, or TV monitors displaying multiple images of a character singing her aria downstage – or through the changes in décor that they have instituted, most notoriously, perhaps, introducing the Rhine Maidens as prostitutes tending a dam during Wagner's own time or Don Giovanni operating among gangs in the South Bronx, they have, in effect, 'anti-theatricalized' works whose unself-conscious theatri-cality had never before been in doubt.

By now it should be clear that the term *anti-theatricality* I have used to characterize some significant twentieth-century operas is not monolithic in meaning but covers a range of stances – the slow, hypnotic approach of *Pelléas et Mélisande* and *Saint François d'Assise*; the outrageous staginess of *The Rake's Progress*, which forces audiences to think about the nature of operatic convention; and the stark dichotomy of anti-theatrical and theatrical discourses that marks the titular figures of *Moses und Aron*. Yet, in their differing ways, all these stances depend upon their audiences' recognition that these operas have broken with the unselfconscious theatricality that marked most operas of the preceding century.

It may well be that these twentieth-century forms of anti-theatricality have worked to initiate a new mode of theatricality quite different from the nineteenth-century form against which it originally defined itself. After all, today's audiences, at least in the major operatic centres, retain little if any memory of the melodramatic acting and staging routines that once dominated operatic interpretation. Can it be that works such as *Saint François d'Assise* or *Einstein on the Beach*, or post-modern reinterpretations of *Il trovatore* or *Die Meistersinger*, will emerge as exemplars of operatic norms? And will the dichotomy between the theatrical and the anti-theatrical upon which this essay is predicated soon come to seem irrelevant?

Notes

1. Jonas Barish, *The Antitheatrical Prejudice* (Berkeley: University of California Press, 1981), pp.453, 457, 464.
2. My use of *Falstaff* and *Parsifal*, in the following pages, as transitions from a highly theatrical nineteenth-century mode to a more muted twentieth-century one was suggested by Linda and Michael Hutcheon's essay on Verdi's and Wagner's late style ('Tutto nel mondo è burla: Rethinking Late Style in Verdi (and Wagner)', *Verdi 2001: Atti del convegno internazionale di studi*, ed. Fabrizio della Seta, Roberta Montemorra Marvin and Marco Marica (Florence: Olschki, 2003), pp.905–28.
3. See Patrick McGuinness, *Maurice Maeterlinck and the Making of Modern Theatre* (Oxford: Oxford University Press, 2000), pp.86–7, 155, 161, 170, 198–203, 213–16, 226, 228–9, 234–5.
4. Maurice Maeterlinck, *Théâtre* (Paris: Bibliothèque-Charpentier), 2(1929), pp.83–5. Translations here and throughout this chapter are my own.
5. Claude Debussy, *Pelléas et Mélisande* (New York: Dover, 1985), pp.227–30.
6. Debussy, *Pelléas and Mélisande*, pp.153–4.
7. Quoted in Robert Orledge, *Debussy and the Theatre* (Cambridge: Cambridge University Press, 1982), p.49 (emphasis Debussy's).
8. *Debussy on Music*, comp. François Lesure, ed. and trans. Richard Langham Smith (New York: Knopf, 1977), p.75.
9. Louis Laloy, 'Schola Cantorum – 26 février', *La Revue musicale*, 15 March 1904: 170.
10. Arnold Schoenberg, *Moses und Aron* (Mainz: Schott, 2000), pp.189–94.
11. See Igor Stravinsky and Robert Craft, *Memories and Commentaries* (Berkeley: University of California Press, 1960), pp.167–76.
12. Stravinsky and Craft, *Memories and Commentaries*, p.158.
13. Harald Kaufmann, 'Ausverkauf der alten Oper: Notizen zu Strawinsky (1961)', *Bertolt Brecht/Kurt Weill*, Die Dreigroschenoper; *Igor Strawinsky*, The Rake's Progress: *Texte, Materialien, Kommentare*, ed. Attila Csampai and Dietmar Holland (Hamburg: Rowohlt, 1987), p.290.

14. Kaufmann, 'Ausverkauf der alten Oper', pp.292–5, and Paul Griffiths, *Igor Stravinsky: The Rake's Progress* (Cambridge: Cambridge University Press, 1982), pp.96–8.

15. Igor Stravinsky, *The Rake's Progress* (London: Boosey and Hawkes, 1951), pp.112–30; Guiseppe Verdi, *La traviata*, ed. Fabrizio della Seta (Chicago: University of Chicago Press, 1996), pp.80–7.

16. Oliver Messiaen, *Music and Color: Conversations with Claude Samuel*, trans. E. Thomas Glaso (Portland, OR: Amadeus Press, 1986), p.207.

17. See Jean-Christophe Marti, ' "It's a Secret of Love": An Interview with Olivier Messiaen', trans. Stewart Spencer, liner notes, *Saint François d'Assise* (Deutsche Grammophon, 1999), pp.24–5.

18. Messiaen, *Music and Color*, pp.110–11.

19. Messiaen, *Music and Color*, p.223.

20. Paul Griffiths, '*Saint François d'Assise*', *The Messiaen Companion*, ed. Peter Hill (London: Faber, 1995), p.505.

21. Olivier Messiaen, *Saint François d'Assise* (Paris: Alphonse Leduc, 1988–92), vol.6, pp.183–98, 282–318).

22. Messiaen, *Music and Color*, p.209.

23. Messiaen, *Saint François d'Assise*, vol.3, p.129.

24. There were, of course, some notable experiments in anti-theatrical opera during the first half of the twentieth century, many of them collaborations between major modernist writers, designers and composers. One thinks, for instance, of the Satie/Cocteau/Picasso *Parade* (1917), the Thomson/Stein *Four Saints in Three Acts* (1933), and the Poulenc/Apollinaire *Les Mamelles de Tirésias* (1947). What distinguishes these works from more recent anti-theatrical experiments is that the former tended to be of a more occasional and 'scandalous' nature, while the latter can often get performed in opera houses – indeed, are sometimes even commissioned by opera companies. For detailed discussions of the three works mentioned above, see Daniel Albright, *Untwisting the Serpent: Modernism in Music, Literature, and Other Arts* (Chicago: University of Chicago Press, 2000), pp.185–97, 311–63, 297–308.

5

'All the Frame's a Stage': (Anti-)Theatricality and Cinematic Modernism

Charlie Keil

> The history of cinema is often treated as the history of its emancipation from theatrical models...Movies are regarded as advancing from theatrical stasis to cinematic fluidity, from theatrical artificiality to cinematic naturalness and immediateness. But this view is far too simple.[1]

Susan Sontag's suspicion of attempts to see film's relation to theatre as a steady evolutionary movement toward the cinematic should encourage us to question exactly how theatricality has operated as a term in cinema's ongoing self-definition. In what follows, I will provide one possible history of theatricality's relevance to cinema's aesthetic development, designed to counter the flawed model Sontag criticizes. In its place, I substitute a history of three parts, wherein theatre's usefulness to film undergoes noticeable changes, mirrored in shifting theoretical responses to cinema as an artform. Though I would argue the nature of cinema's relationship to theatre emerges as dialectical, this has not prevented film's ultimate definition of theatricality from blurring into the anti-theatrical – the legacy of enduring strains of modernist ambition which have shaped cinema's sense of aesthetic autonomy.

From 'photoplay' to 'photogénie': defining cinema as anti-theatrical

As a medium developed in the late nineteenth century, cinema was first promoted and enjoyed as a technological novelty, a hybrid of screen-based entertainment and the experimental study of motion. Within its first decade of existence, as it gravitated more consistently toward story-telling, film found itself aligned less with the likes of magic lantern shows and x-rays and more with traditional narrative forms. None cast a greater shadow over cinema's emergence as an independent mode of representation than the theatre. By 1907, when cinema was on the cusp of becoming industrially stable and culturally pervasive, questions of self-definition became more evident, fuelled by the nascent trade press, itself devoted to securing social respectability and economic viability for motion pictures. Theatre typically loomed large in any attempts at establishing an aesthetic identity for the fledgeling medium. Some of the earliest names coined for cinema – such as 'photoplay' and 'the silent stage' – convey this indebtedness to theatre.[2] In part, the constant invocation of the theatre merely recognized the evident similarities between the two forms: both typically involved actors engaged in the enactment of stories. But cinema also aimed to appropriate the cultural cachet accorded its predecessor, a motive which fuelled the film industry's pursuit of a variety of legitimating strategies, including manufacturers hiring theatrically trained talent in earnest by 1908 and Adoph Zukor choosing the name 'Famous Players in Famous Plays' for the company he formed to produce early features several years later.

Yet emulation of the theatre came at a price. First, by comparing itself to the stage, cinema risked seeming like nothing more than a diminished imitator. (Note how even the term 'the silent stage' hints at film's relative deficiency.) Second, slavish copying of theatre's methods would do little to establish cinema's unique formal capacities and thus proved ineffective in making a case for film as art. Numerous champions of cinema sensed this dilemma and offered various ways to address it. One was to celebrate cinema's differences from theatre as attributes which canny filmmakers could exploit for aesthetic gain. From the outset, cinema had distinguished itself as a medium capable of harnessing the activities and settings of everyday life, as evidenced by the popularity of the *actualité*. As filmmakers gravitated toward story-telling, they could continue to find ways to incorporate cinema's penchant for capturing the outside world, a world largely unavailable to theatrical modes of presentation. Accordingly, as early as 1911 one finds that commentators such as Hanford C. Judson advocate abandoning the shopworn artifice of the theatre in favour of the inherent realism of cinema:

> The proper work of the photoplay is to give life as life really is, at its chosen, dramatic moments, and I believe that we shall find that all the well-known theatrical makeshifts, so effective on the stage, will be less effective in a photoplay than the simplicity of every-day life is.

Photoplay producers will find that they will have to discover new and original tricks of their own.[3]

Judson's comments invite comparison to the position adopted by later theorists of cinema's ontology, such as André Bazin, who advocated for a particular, realist aesthetic based on cinema's roots in photography. (Bazin, a figure I will return to later, would also argue famously, and, in seemingly paradoxical fashion, that cinema best served theatre by reproducing drama in its textual integrity.) Yet this was not the only way to distinguish film from theatre. The other, increasingly popular, approach involved focusing on the ways in which cinema was *not* reality, which became a way of accounting for its art-making capacity; these, in turn, would prove to be distinct from the defining features of other, similar media. Collectively, film's unique features would constitute the basis for a cinematic art that would be distinct from both reality *and* theatrical artifice.

In many ways, despite Judson's claims, cinema was less like the phenomenal world than theatre. The latter featured flesh-and-blood beings enacting stories in real time, employing their actual voices and impressing audiences with their three-dimensional corporeality. Cinema, on the other hand, lacked colour (aside from the stylized effects afforded by tinting and toning) and sound (save for the accompaniment provided within the exhibition context, which only underlined the aural deficiency within the text itself), possessed only two dimensions (being a projected image on a flat screen), and was always already absent, the recorded events having taken place at a time earlier than the moment when viewers perceive the images in projected form. These attributes, often regarded as liabilities by those intent on seeing cinema as an impoverished version of the dramatic stage, served as the foundation of an aesthetic which would shape appreciation of cinema up until the advent of sound. This aesthetic would also fuel initial efforts by cinema's advocates to link the medium with early twentieth-century modernist tendencies which stressed promotion (and, ideally, self-conscious exploration) of the distinct formal properties of selected modes of artistic expression.

Cultivation of cinema's unique potential for artistry, then, finally depended upon its distinctiveness from other arts, particularly theatre, insofar as theatre came to represent a false goal for cinema, its inappropriateness as a model signalled by the castigation of misguided filmic drama as 'stagey' or 'theatrical'. By the time the medium had reached an undisputed point of aesthetic maturity in the silent period, theorists and critics celebrated those examples of cinematic art which epitomized formal autonomy. The stylistic markers of a silent cinematic modernism were the elements deriving specifically from the resources of the medium: shot scale, mobile framing and editing. Collectively, these features of style would help to banish any vestiges of theatricality: cinema was not bound to a single space, nor an integral timeframe; performance was a malleable component, subject as it was to the fragmentary powers of montage and the distorting potential of the camera lens; and the spectatorial position afforded by cinema had moved far from that of the fixed theatrical viewer located outside the depicted spectacle to the endlessly fluid and mobile viewer floating on the periphery of the ongoing action. One of the salient shifts within cinematic practice from film's initial years to this later stage involves the transformation of narrational norms to ensure increased spectatorial involvement. Kristin Thompson has characterized this shift in the following terms:

> In the shift from primitive to classical film practice, the spectator's implicit spatial relation to the action changed significantly. During the primitive period, the camera usually remained at a distance from the action, *framing it in a way that suggested a stage seen by a spectator in a theater seat* [my emphasis] ... But the omnipresent narration of the classical cinema situates the spectator at the optimum viewpoint in each shot. Staging, composition, and editing combine to move that viewpoint instantly as the action shifts. There arose the enduring ... image of the spectator as invisible onlooker present on the scene; filmmakers and theorists have invoked this idea to the present day in explaining ... virtually any standard technique.[4]

Theorists' concern with spectatorial activity fuelled the privileging of formal devices which aided in the consecration of film as an autonomous art. Accordingly, the close-up signalled the shifting of a viewer's attention for Hugo Münsterberg, just as camera angles secured 'the emotional identification of the spectator with the characters in the film' according to Béla Balázs, and the mobile camera emulated the very workings of subjectivity for Rudolf Arnheim.[5] Arnheim, in particular, devoted much of his writing to enumerating the ways in which cinema channelled its formal particularities toward unique artistic expression, which often led him to contrast film's effects and capacities with those of the theatre. Film's muteness was for Arnheim one of the medium's crucial defining features; unlike theatre, which was totally reliant on the spoken word, cinema could direct the attention of its spectator visually:

> Perhaps the point has never been made explicitly – and it seems significant that it occurs to very few theatergoers – how unnatural, how stylized, all stage art is because the actors never stop talking. Every action is overlaid and clothed with words... That this method of presenting an event is not a matter of course will be clearly realized only after seeing from a good silent film how the action proceeds quite easily without any use of words at all... In a film... little events... are exactly of the same type as the 'macroscopic' ones, those represented by the human actors. And hence arises a most satisfactory homogeneity.[6]

As long as cinema remained silent, critical valuation and artistic practice worked in tandem to ensure that modernist experimentation involved the elevation of inherently 'cinematic' features of the medium. The development of montage's capacity to create rhythm, engender a sense of disorientation, or even forge connections of a conceptual nature cemented the definition of silent film art as medium-specific and inherently anti-theatrical. Film's 'liberation' from the space-time continuum served as the foundation for most creative uses of editing and firmly aligned silent-era film-making predicated on the innovative resources of cutting with the modernist play, with stream of consciousness in the novel, or the collapsing of perspectival space in fine art.

While self-styled experimental cinema did not entirely abandon association with theatre during the mature silent era (as the *succès d'estime* of German Expressionist film-making demonstrates), disdain for the limitations of theatre was a commonly adopted position. The French Impressionist critics-cum-filmmakers readily embraced music and dance as forms to be emulated, but expressed only scorn for dramatic models. Germaine Dulac, for example, believed that any allegiance to theatre would represent a deviation from cinema's ideal aesthetic course:

> [T]he fundamental error which dominated the first scenarios, [was that they] were imbued with the preconception that a dramatic action could not develop otherwise than in the manner of a novel or a play, that is, by means of specific events rather than by means of suggestiveness of expression... And from this comes the stagnation of the cinema. From this comes the fact that the seventh art, an

ample, magnificent and new mode of expression, seems in most of its productions to be stricken with sterility, and fills us with disillusionment and sometimes with bitterness.[7]

The Impressionists developed the concept of photogénie to convey the essence of cinema, its capacity to both capture and transform the spirit of the objects recorded by the camera. The imagistic and rhythmic potential of cinema distanced it significantly from the literal-minded confines of the theatre. In their valorization of montage, the Soviet advocates of cinematic specificity were even more committed in their opposition to the stage, with Lev Kuleshov declaring 'there is no doubt that theatre and theatre workers bring nothing but harm to cinema', and Abram Room claiming 'theatre is "seeming" whereas cinema is "being"'.[8] By 1927, Adrian Piotrovsky was convinced that theatre's only hope was to become 'cinefied', so clearly superior were the newer medium's techniques and its embodiment of an aesthetic dialectic.[9] Theoretical consensus clearly held that a cinematic anti-theatricality would ensure the medium's continued aesthetic development.

Hopes for cinema's ongoing success as a modernist medium of seemingly boundless potential, especially when contrasted to the shop-worn aesthetics of the theatre, ground to a halt with the introduction of pre-recorded sound in the late 1920s. Avant-garde film-making activity virtually ceased in production centres such as France, and critical enthusiasm for film's aesthetic capacity abated dramatically, in recognition of the diminished prospects for the same degree of artistic experimentation as had been evident in the late silent period. As Alan Williams has pointed out:

> In Europe, the coming of sound brought relative stylistic uniformity to a diverse set of textual strategies produced by a remarkable variety of art movements, tendencies, and stubborn individualists...Ambitious European producers no longer were obliged to remain in the 'art cinema' niche of their own markets, and production capital migrated to where rates of return were the highest. This, perhaps acting in tandem with the greater 'inertia' and semantic independence of images with synchronous sound, would have all but doomed both the radical avant-garde and the commercially oriented 'art cinema' in Europe...[10]

The modified realism of Hollywood's classical style became the international norm, and critics despaired of sound cinema ever approximating the degree of stylistic expressiveness the late silent era had achieved. In particular, the excessive talkiness of early sound pictures, the importation of stage-trained personnel, and the abundance of filmed properties derived from theatrical material indicated to many that the introduction of sound would chain film to theatre in a manner which could only ensure aesthetic paralysis and spell an end to cinema's modernist ambitions.

The realist aesthetic and a new version of theatricality

> Now that the screen can welcome other kinds of theatre besides comedy without betraying them, there is no reason to suppose that it cannot likewise give the theatre new life, employing certain of the stage's new techniques. Film cannot be, indeed must not be, as we have seen, simply a paradoxical modality of theatre production... not only is theatre on film from now on aesthetically founded in truth and fact, not only do we know that henceforth there are no plays that cannot be brought to the screen, whatever their style, provided one can visualize a reconversion of stage space in accordance with the data. But it may also be that the only possible modern theatrical production of certain classics would be on the screen.[11]

André Bazin's relentless promotion of a realist aesthetic in a body of influential film criticism and theory developed throughout the decade following World War II helped redefine how cinema could contend with sound and remain art. For our purposes, Bazin's theory gains particular significance in its implicit capacity to isolate the very features of film style which align it most obviously with theatre – the long take, deep focus and staging in depth – and place them at the centre of a preferred aesthetic which serves as the basis for a new form of modernist cinema. While theorists of an earlier era had despaired in the face of sound's influence on cinematic style, seeing the increased capacity for realism as a blow against retention of a medium-specific aesthetic programme, Bazin argued the opposite. Believing cinema's roots in photography dictated that its primary goal be to record reality with as much fidelity as technology permitted, Bazin welcomed the introduction of sound. Additionally, he found in figures such as Jean Renoir and Orson Welles the ideal practitioners of a stylistic approach which wedded respect for cinema's ontology with a style promoting both increased spectatorial freedom and an 'ambiguity of expression' derived directly from observation of the real world in all its complexity.

That the films of Renoir and Welles often seemed 'theatrical' insofar as their deep spaces, their frontally oriented compositions and their extended, unedited shots recalled the stage much more than the average sound-era classical film posed no problems for Bazin. He prized their fluidity of integral action which preserved the spatio-temporal continuity of the phenomenal world and provided for the spectator the opportunity to engage with each image's inherent multiplicity of meanings. It is precisely this quality which allows us to view these films as privileged examples of a resurgent modernist strain in sound cinema – a modernism dependent precisely on the films' modified theatricality. No longer a stigma, the association with theatre represents liberation from the interpretative dictates of Hollywood classical *découpage* and staging. When Welles presents a scene in a single take using deep focus and relatively static framing, as he does in the celebrated kitchen-table scene from *The Magnificent Ambersons*, the effect is not, for Bazin, a replication of outdated stagecraft, but rather a vigorous engagement with the resources of a medium designed to relay the intensity of an action's unfolding without interruption or premeditation. Only then can a variety of meanings – true ambiguity – emerge out of the cinema. Similarly, Renoir allows a variety of interrelated actions to weave themselves in and out of a space – such as the halls and rooms of the château in *Rules of the Game* – without cutting for emphasis or even, when possible, transition from one space to the next. Such a strategy preserves the complexity of the events on view and refuses to interpret the significance of these events and their interconnection for the viewer.

That both Welles and Renoir signalled their recognition of theatre's influence on their cinematic art only confirmed the medium's renewed importance in redefining how cinematic modernism could incorporate the legacy of the stage. As Bazin said of Welles: 'It is no chance matter that some of the best filmmakers are also the best stage directors. Welles...did not come to cinema out of cynicism...[instead, cinema is for him and others like him] only a complementary form of theatre, the chance to produce theatre precisely as they see and feel it.'[12] Welles's background in theatre led him to trust his actors to sustain the force of their performances throughout a long take at the same time that it aided him in staging intricate actions within striking deep-space compositions. Though *Citizen Kane* is often championed precisely because it seems so deliriously and self-consciously 'cinematic', one should not neglect the dimension of the film that trades on Welles's theatrical heritage. More specifically, the film's long take/deep focus aesthetic refuses the breakdown of dramatic space classical film-making depends upon. Often eschewing the foundational cutting patterns constitutive of continuity editing – shot/counter-shot, matches on action and the like – Welles gravitates toward the single composition in depth for many of *Kane*'s bravura shots. Accordingly, a significant number of the film's most memorable moments, and those which involve pivotal dramatic confrontations, are constructed as actions staged in depth, occasionally employing three distinct planes of dramatic space. Such a strategy sustains dramatic tension because the actors remain within one another's physical presence. And, as in the theatre, one is permitted to view the interactions among these pertinent *dramatis personae*, with no cut-aways for reaction shots or emotional heightening through the selective employment of close-ups. Most importantly, in Bazinian terms, the spatial field within which character interaction occurs remains intact throughout such scenes.

As much as *Kane*'s deep focus technique was a function of the combined resources of particular technologies (improvements in lighting, lenses and film stock), artistic innovation (both Welles and his cinematographer Gregg Toland went to great lengths to ensure that others would be aware of their efforts to secure the effects achieved) and resistance to prevailing Hollywood norms, it aided in the promotion of performance and staging as central to the film's production of complex meanings.[13] The integral dramatic space on view was matched by an integrity of performance: no longer were the actions of the actors chopped up into manageable chunks of screen time altered by shifting camera positions and changes to shot scale. The 'optimum viewpoint' Kristin Thompson attributes to the spectatorial position afforded by classical editing patterns has been supplanted by a more stable vantage point in *Kane* which privileges an unbroken set of actions performed before an unmoving camera. At least for the duration of any single static long take, the spectator retains the same perspective on the action depicted, confronting directly the meanings put forward by people and objects displayed within an image of unsurpassed depth. This emphatic theatricality was the key to *Kane*'s modernism; as Bazin puts it, 'it is no exaggeration to say that *Citizen Kane* is unthinkable shot in any other way but in depth. The uncertainty in which we find ourselves as to the spiritual key or the interpretation we should put on the film is built into the very design of the image.'[14] The expressly theatrical aesthetic of *Kane* became a formal demonstration of its concern with the inscrutable nature of human behaviour. The film's central question – what is the basis for our knowledge of others? – finds itself reinforced perpetually by long takes shot in depth which offer the viewer the opportunity for scrutiny without supplying the comfort of answers. Welles's version of a realist aesthetic offered a theatricality in the service of a renewed cinematic modernism.

Welles's post-war film work engaged explicitly with theatre in his adaptations of Shakespeare, beginning with *Macbeth* in 1948; Jean Renoir's thematic engagement with the world of theatre also seemed to increase as his career progressed, most explicitly in *Le Carrosse d'or, French Can-Can* and *Eléna et les hommes*. But theatricality, understood both as technique and subject, emerges in both *Rules of the Game* and *Grand Illusion* as well, films central to Bazin's contention that the sound-era realism emerging in Renoir's efforts of the 1930s was realizing cinema's aesthetic goals more fully than ever before. In *Rules of the Game*, for example, the narrative action climaxes during an evening of festivities at the Marquis's château, La Colinère, the film's main setting. Everyone has gathered to watch an evening of theatrical divertissements, musical numbers performed on a stage established in the château's main room. Soon however, the action spills from the performing space to the rooms and corridors beyond, with many of the participants remaining in costume and Renoir's roving camera creating links between the space of the public stage and that of the adjoining private rooms. In fact, his aesthetic approach refuses to accept the two spaces as separate: doors are constantly flung open to reveal spaces extending into deeper spatial fields, exposing actions previously shielded from the view of others (and of us as viewers). As the ever-growing group of involved parties snakes through a series of interlinked rooms, the acts on stage become (con)fused with the actions occurring elsewhere, and the diegetic audience for the fête also becomes host to the antics of those caught up in various romantic intrigues. By the end, all space has become performative space, and the guests can no longer distinguish between staged entertainments and impassioned real-life pursuits. At a pivotal point the Marquis instructs his major domo to 'stop this farce' and the usually unflappable servant can only respond in frustration, 'which one?'.

Renoir's invocation of theatricality gains force precisely because his method reflects a knowing absorption of theatrical technique at the same time that it extends its spatio-temporal foundations. The added element is the persistently moving camera, which not only follows characters and links actions, but establishes the film's frame as endlessly mobile and fluid, much as the parameters of the château's diegetic performance space keep increasing until every locale invites being understood in such terms. Thus, the château's checkerboard floor directs characters to follow pre-established pathways; the maid Lisette's mock resistance to the seductive advances of Marceau emerges as a dance staged around a kitchen table; and the terrace and its steps serve as the impromptu stage for both Octave's failed attempt at assuming the role of conductor and the Marquis' address to his guests following the shooting of André. At the same time that Renoir's moving camera extends the frame of the screen to indicate activity extending past its borders (in Bazinian terms, the filmic equivalent of a phenomenal world without any boundaries beyond its capacity to be seen/shown), that same camera blurs the distinctions between the world on and off the stage: both are contained within an expansive frame determined to strain its own limits. The modernist paradox of *Rules of the Game* is that it uses a realist aesthetic to reinforce the inherent artificiality of the world it explores and defines as real. Though Renoir's films would serve as a touchstone for a later generation of cinematic modernists, the approach to realism and theatricality in these post-war works would differ substantially. The art cinema of the 1950s and 1960s viewed the illusory nature of realism as an opportunity to embrace theatricality as a privileged way of highlighting cinema's very constructedness, leading film far from Bazin's ideal.

The reflexive turn: theatricality in the art cinema

> I am also interested in the theatrical aspect. Already in *Le Petit Soldat*, where I was trying to discover the concrete, I noticed that the closer I came to the concrete, the closer I came to the theatre... I'd like to film *Six Characters in Search of an Author* to show through cinema what theatre is. By being realistic one discovers the theatre, and by being theatrical... These are the boxes of *Le Carrosse d'or*: behind the theatre there is life, and behind life, the theatre. I started from the imaginary and discovered reality; but behind reality, there is again imagination.[15]

Jean-Luc Godard's recasting of theatricality as a form of realism which only reveals another theatricality again takes its inspiration from Renoir's reflexive musings on these relationships in *Le Carosse d'or* and finds its ultimate manifestation in the desire to film a modernist, self-referential play to reveal theatre's essence through cinema. The idea that art, in all its difficulty, may be the only knowable form of reality propels modernist art's insistent interrogation of its own structures, but such thinking distances cinematic art's role from the realist goals articulated by Bazin. Nonetheless, Bazin's valorization of both *Citizen Kane* and *Rules of the Game* had stressed the challenges they pose to the viewer, understood within the context of their emphasis on a realist aesthetic, but one which leaves open the possibility of complexity and multiple meanings.[16] That realist aesthetic found extended demonstration in the post-war films of the Italian neorealists, a body of work Bazin analysed continually, discerning in it the ideal fusion of form and content. The neorealists' devotion to an unvarnished exploration of the social realities of war-torn Italy might seem to offer little to the resurgence of cinematic modernism; on the contrary, the episodic plots and open-ended conclusions of films such as *Bicycle Thieves* and *Umberto D* provided a model for the elliptical treatment of narrative structures which would become a hallmark of a major strain of post-war cinematic modernism, the European art film.[17] The art cinema incorporated the central planks of Bazin's aesthetic – deep focus, long takes, mobile framing and depth staging – while also rediscovering the potential of montage, used now to fragment the temporal order of narratives, disrupt coherent representation of space, and convey the vagaries of human psychology.

In many ways, the comprehensive stylistic self-consciousness of the art cinema recalled the medium-specific experimentation of the late silent era. But the thoroughgoing reflexivity of many of the art cinema's most canonical works reveals the influence of a post-war model of modernism, heavily indebted to Clement Greenberg's notions of how the modernist medium strives to define the limits of its own form. Not only should the modernist film foreground those features of cinematic practice which define it as a medium, but it should do so to demonstrate the process by which film becomes art. In this way, every modernist film's subject is the manner in which it comes to create itself, a subject realizable only in a self-conscious examination of the very fundamentals of film form employed. The purest exemplum would be the structural film, which rigorously subjects an isolated aspect of film technique (such as framing) to a systematic and exhaustive battery of variations, resulting in such celebrated monuments of 1960s-era experimental cinema as *Wavelength, Serene Velocity* and *T, O, U, C, H, I, N, G*. Within the context of the narrative art cinema, the ideal modernist gesture would be to fashion a film which reveals itself to be a meditation on its own troubled existence, leading to the *mise-en-abîme* structure of Fellini's *8½* or Bergman's *Persona*, films that become compendia of their directors' previously demonstrated concerns and styles.[18]

But the privileging of such autobiographical reflexivity suggests that the only route for the modernist art film lay in intensive cinematic self-examination. This was only half of the equation. If modernism's ultimate goal was for a given art form to revel in its ability to know itself, this could be achieved as much through an oppositional invocation of accepted norms as through sustained internal analysis. This translated into modernist films deliberately plundering cinema's past to critically examine the underlying logic of appropriated genre conventions, as in Godard's borrowing from film noir and the crime film in *À Bout de souffle* and *Bande à part* and the musical (replete with colour and widescreen) in *Une Femme est une femme*. But it also meant systematically defying the accepted formal norms associated with classical cinema, resulting in the self-conscious employment of the long take (Antonioni, Janscó), narrationally overt camera movements (Resnais), jump cuts (Bertolucci and many of the French New Wave directors), and stylized use of colour and other elements of the *mise-en-scène* (Fellini). Finally, establishing itself as the most protean of art forms, modernist cinema engaged with other artistic traditions, from painting (Antonioni and De Chirico) to the novel (Resnais and the *noveau roman*) to theatre (Bergman and the chamber drama). As David Bordwell has noted, this strain within art cinema was in keeping with tendencies evident within modernist art generally:

> Many critics and theorists accordingly came to see the modernist work in any medium as critically engaging with other works and traditions. The serial musical work attacked orthodox tonality; the *nouveau roman* dismantled the detective story and the psychological novel. Modernism was to be art about art – its premises, patterns, and procedures.[19]

For this reason, theatricality proved useful as a deliberate strategy within the modernist filmmaker's aesthetic arsenal. First, self-conscious appropriation of methods aligned with another medium only verified the modernist auteur's knowledge of the limits of film's specificity. In other words, invoking theatricality bespoke a knowing citation of representational means outside of the traditional lexicon of film-making practice. Enhanced frontality, fixity of framing and artificial compositions signalled a modernist willingness to flout accepted standards of the 'cinematic', paradoxically proving modernism's ability to best shape an operative definition of the same. Second, if the project of modernism (and even more that of its ideologically motivated variant, political modernism) was to challenge the illusionism of conventional cinema, what better way than through the anti-illusionistic properties of a provocatively artificial theatricality? Unlike the theatrically inflected compositions of Welles, which still traded on depth and invited Bazinian comparisons to the ambiguity provided by phenomenal reality, the modernist tableau refused any such parallels. Here was a mode of presentation which could only be understood as deliberately referring to the constructedness of the theatrical world, hence dispelling any sense of the illusionistic engagement offered by the cinema of verisimilitude while also defining cinematic representation as equally constructed into the bargain.

Insofar as the theatricality of modernist cinema was often predicated on a deliberate flatness of the image, it could also recall the static long shots, or tableaux, of early cinema, famously described as the Primitive Mode of Representation by one of the period's champions, Noël Burch. So modernist employment of a deliberate theatricality not only defied the illusionism of later cinematic developments, but reflected on the centrality of 'the interplay of surface and depth' to initial modes of film-making. As Bordwell points out, in Burch's view, 'the distant and external framings...offer a quasi-Brechtian disengagement...And if Pollock's Abstract Expressionism came to be called "all-over painting", we might call the PMR's use of the frame "all-over staging", since Burch considers it a protomodernist strategy.'[20] Ironically, then, the modernist cinema of the post-war era returns us to a consideration of the relationship between theatre and early film with which we began. In both instances, the link between the two functioned to elevate the aesthetic reputation of cinema; by the time of post-war modernism, however, any allusion to theatrical technique arrives heavily coded. Referencing of theatricality demands recognition as an anti-illusionist strategy loaded with ideological significance and designed to be understood as a complex validation of cinema's power.

This is not the place to investigate the manner in which cinema's invocation of theatricality might encourage a reductive understanding of theatre's techniques and effects. Any cinematic misconstrual of the full aesthetic force of theatricality pales in the face of film's insistence on finding such a misconstrual both formally and politically useful. One could argue that the effectiveness of modernist cinema's enlistment of theatricality was to forever cast it as a form of anti-theatricality at the same time. The legacy of that paradox continues to make itself felt today, even as the context of post-modernism has ostensibly caused modernist strategies to lose their capacity to shock (also leading to a corresponding loss in art's power). For proof, one need look no further than the recent examples of *Moulin Rouge* and *Dogville*, two films whose radically different approaches to a stylized *mise-en-scène* can only reveal current gestures toward theatricality as deliberately, even proudly, empty. In such instances, the emptiness proves contagious, indicating that the post-modern variation on filmic anti-theatricality may well be a concomitant impulse to see the cinematic as equally barren. The pervasive citation of the cinematic in media-savvy forms (ultimately all designed as advertising) points to the final irony: if theatricality loses its power to designate cinematic plenitude, cinema must now function in theatre's stead, becoming the post-modern era's privileged marker of outmoded aesthetics.

Notes

1. Susan Sontag, 'Theatre and Film' [1966], in *Styles of Radical Will* (New York: Dell Publishing, 1981), p.100.
2. For more on the relevance of the names chosen for cinema in its formative years, see Lee Grieveson, *Policing Cinema: Movies and Censorship in Early Twentieth-Century America* (Berkeley: University of California Press, 2004), pp.1–6.
3. Hanford C. Judson, 'What Gets Over', *Moving Picture World*, 15 April 1911. I discuss the attitude of the trade press toward theatre (represented by the comments of Judson and others) at greater length in *Early American Cinema in Transition: Story, Style, and Filmmaking, 1907–1913* (Madison: University of Wisconsin Press, 2001), pp.39–44.
4. Kristin Thompson, 'Classical Narrative Space and the Spectator's Attention', in *The Classical Hollywood Cinema: Film Style and Mode of Production to 1960*, co-authored with David Bordwell and Janet Staiger (New York: Columbia University Press, 1985), p.214.
5. Hugo Münsterberg, *The Film: A Psychological Study*, 1916 (New York: Dover Publications, 1970), pp.36–8; Béla Belázs, *Theory of the Film: Character and Growth of a New Art*, 1952 (New York: Dover Publications, 1970), p.92; Rudolf Arnheim, *Film as Art*, 1933 (Berkeley: University of California Press, 1957), p.112.
6. Arnheim, *Film as Art*, p.84–5.
7. Germaine Dulac, 'From 'Visual and Anti-Visual Films'', 1928, in P. Adams Sitney, ed., *The Avant-Garde Film: A Reader of Theory and Criticism* (New York: New York University Press, 1978), p.33.
8. Lev Kuleshov, 'Cinema as the Fixing of Theatrical Action', 1922, in *The Film Factory: Russian and Soviet Cinema Documents, 1896–1939*, ed. Richard Taylor and Ian Christie (New York: Routledge, 1994), p.66; Abram Room, 'Cinema and Theatre', 1925, in *The Film Factory*, p.128.

9. Adrian Piotrovksy, 'The Cinefication of Theatre – Some General Points', in Taylor and Christie, *The Film Factory*, p.180.

10. Alan Williams, 'Historical and Theoretical Issues in the Coming of Recorded Sound to the Cinema', in Rick Altman, ed., *Sound Theory/Sound Practice* (New York: Routledge, 1992), pp.135–7.

11. André Bazin, 'Theatre and Cinema – Part Two', 1951, *What Is Cinema? Volume One*, ed. Hugh Gray (Berkeley: University of California Press, 1967), pp.121–3.

12. Bazin, 'Theatre and Cinema – Part Two', pp.123–4.

13. For an informative overview of how the efforts of Welles and Toland were represented and received within the Hollywood craft community, see David Bordwell, 'Deep Focus Cinematography', in *The Classical Hollywood Cinema*, pp.345–9.

14. André Bazin, 'The Evolution of the Language of Cinema', *What Is Cinema? Volume One*, p.36.

15. Jean-Luc Godard, interview, *Cahiers du Cinéma*, 138 (December 1962); rpt. and translated in *Godard on Godard*, trans. and ed. Tom Milne (New York: Da Capo Press, 1986), p.181.

16. For a representative example, see André Bazin, 'The French Renoir', 1958, *Jean Renoir*, ed. François Truffaut (New York: Simon & Schuster, 1986), pp.82–3.

17. For a representative study of the links between neorealism and the art cinema, wherein a film such as Rosselini's *Voyage to Italy* becomes a key transitional text, see Robert Kolker's *The Altering Eye: Contemporary International Cinema* (New York: Oxford University Press, 1983).

18. For one such reading, see Christian Metz, 'Mirror Construction in Fellini's 8½', in *Film Language: A Semiotics of the Cinema* (New York: Oxford University Press, 1974), pp.228–34.

19. David Bordwell, *On the History of Film Style* (Cambridge, MA: Harvard University Press, 1997), p.86.

20. Bordwell, *On the History of Film Style*, p.105.

Part II
Materials

6
Anti-Theatricality and the Limits of Naturalism

Kirk Williams

In the broadest and most transhistorical sense, the anti-theatrical prejudice can be seen as a trope whereby the long-standing Western anxiety about secondariness or supplementarity finds cultural expression. This metaphysical problematic leads by implication to other familiar moral hierarchies, most notably the binarisms that set essence against appearance, feminine against masculine, writing against speech, fiction against truth. For the anti-theatrical polemicist, theatre stands in for the ambiguities and indeterminacy of history itself, metaphorically invoking, as Jonas Barish so eloquently puts it, 'a whole shoal of evils, of varying shapes and sizes, from the social sea'.[1] The reading of anti-theatrical discourse in the Western tradition that Barish gives us reveals the startling paradox that anti-theatricality is ultimately not about the theatre and always about something else: the stage is inevitably a mere symptom for some other, less effable social or metaphysical malady. The case 'against' the theatre is fascinating precisely because it stages such a broad spectrum of transhistorical anxieties in historically and culturally specific terms, such that anti-theatrical diatribes often come to powerfully dramatize conflicts and antipathies that are essentially local and radically contingent.[2]

Barish notes that the anti-theatrical stance is, by its very nature, riddled with contradiction and ambivalence, owing in part to the epistemological privilege accorded the visual and specular throughout Western history: even as it is dangerously seductive and misleading, feminizing and excessive, the theatre also partakes of the immediacy of the Event (as opposed to the mediacy of narrative) and the truth of empirical observation. It is precisely because it promises to be the most 'real' of all the arts that its factitiousness must be attacked so vigorously. Theatre practitioners have long been aware of and even thematized this particular anti-theatrical charge. Dramas going back to Euripides's *Bacchae* have meditated on the power and perils of theatrical performance and often rely for their dramatic effect on the spectator's anxiety about the shifting nature of images. Western theatre has been concerned with its enabling conditions from its very beginning, and for this reason the stage itself is often the best and most persuasive setting for an exploration of its own moral failings and ontological dangers. Anti-theatricality is, in short, a trope specific to, and even parasitically dependent upon, theatrical representation. One might argue that it is the *raison d'être* of the theatre itself.

A particularly stunning example of 'anti-theatrical' theatricality is evinced by the first of the self-proclaimed 'modern' theatrical movements in Germany: the Naturalist movement of the closing decades of the nineteenth century. Naturalist sensibilities appeared relatively late in Germany, more than a decade after Zola's pioneering work in France and Ibsen's first Naturalist experiments in the theatre.[3] Yet the Germans made up for their belatedness by attempting to articulate and put into practice a far more systematic programme of Naturalist aesthetics than any of its earlier practitioners in other countries. Beginning with the literary criticism of the Hart brothers and refined in the theoretical essays of Otto Brahm, Max Halbe, Michael Georg Conrad, Arno Holz and Johannes Schlaf, among others, German dramaturgical discourse articulated a rigorous aesthetic agenda that dramatists like Gerhart Hauptmann and the group of theatre practitioners assembled by Brahm, first at the Freie Bühne (The Free Stage) and later at the Deutsches Theater, worked to implement.[4] The German Naturalists saw themselves in opposition to an idealist tradition that had – rightly or wrongly – come to be associated with social and aesthetic conservatism. Their explicit objective was to completely remove the barrier separating theatre from life, to create an illusion so powerful that it would render the theatrical medium absolutely transparent. One must experience theatre as one experiences life itself, argued Arno Holz, seeing in the events on-stage 'a slice of life as if one is peering through a window' ('Evolution des Dramas', p.227).[5] The point is to replace theatrical artifice with 'a near-perfect reality, in other words, to drive the "Theatre" gradually from the theatre' ('Vorwart', p.138). In place of traditional theatricality the Naturalists substituted scientific accuracy of observation, the precise recording of minutiae, the recording of life as it occurs 'second-by-second'.[6] Here was an aesthetics that celebrated the social reality that ostensibly resides in the detailed and particular circumstances of quotidian existence. In focusing so relentlessly upon material specificity as an irreducible locus of meaning, Naturalist theatre takes a stand against subjective interpretation; leaving very little to the imagination, it seems to reject metaphor utterly, embracing in its stead the metonymic 'truth' that seems to reside in detail.[7] This concern brings together material existence and psychic life as never before, resulting in what one might call a kind of 'hystericization' of the stage space, a notion I will return to presently.

The Naturalists' aesthetics were a function of their social objectives; the abjuration of theatricality and the presentation of 'reality' on the stage was meant to herald and bring about more truthful communal interactions and a less 'theatrical' structure of social subjectivity.[8] Yet this aesthetic strategy ultimately compromises the Naturalists' allegedly progressive social goals. Even as it positions itself against material excess and social pretension, Naturalist theatre indulges in excesses of its own in the form of precisely detailed stage directions, localized settings and meticulous character descriptions that seek to limit or even foreclose interpretive licence on the part of actors, directors and audience.[9] Such a generic strategy works against any metaphoric or allegorical reading: it is, in part, a quest for absolute transparency of meaning. However much characters may attempt to disguise their origins or motives, to fashion themselves in particular ways, their true nature inevitably reveals itself to the audience in explicitly physical terms.[10] If truth is empirically obvious, and all performative gestures or strategies are doomed to failure, then social or economic re-invention is equally impossible. By locating 'truth' in a body that is unable to dissimulate, to hide its corrupt nature or origins, Naturalist aesthetics work against any true democratization of value, any possibility that economic change will bring about a new ethics and a new social order. Even as Naturalism 'uncovers' the economic and political circumstances that create collective misery, its anti-theatrical insistence upon transparency undercuts any genuine social subversiveness. In short, the anti-theatricality that sustains Naturalist theatre neutralizes its political efficacy.

Naturalism in the theatre is not about social change; it is, first and foremost, an aesthetic statement, an oppositional genre that invokes social conditions allegorically. Refusing metaphor within the performance event itself, Naturalism embraces it in a larger metatheatrical sense. The real struggle is neither economic nor political, despite the fact that these issues figure largely in so many German Naturalist works. Rather, the struggle is for new modes of representation, new aesthetic strategies that seek to usurp the privilege of the old, to create new hierarchies without really calling hierarchy itself into question. For all the controversy it generated in its day, Naturalism as aesthetic strategy is profoundly conservative and deeply antipathetic to change. In this brief chapter, I would like to explore this idea in the context of two plays by Gerhart Hauptmann, the most prominent of the German Naturalist dramatists. It is not my intention to 'discredit' either naturalism or Hauptmann, but rather to uncover some of the contradictions or points of impossibility that result from the anti-theatrical assumptions that subtend both dramas. The two plays are Hauptmann's earliest dramatic work, *Before Daybreak*, and his most famous (or infamous) naturalist drama, *The Weavers*. The former is by most accounts a prototypical Naturalist drama, while the latter attempts to push the boundaries of the genre, substituting class for character and a quasi-operatic leitmotiv – the persistent *Dreissiger's Song* – for traditional dramatic unities.[11]

Before Daybreak was controversial in its day, surpassed in controversy only by *The Weavers*, a work derived from a historical uprising of oppressed and starving weavers against the exploitation of the manufacturers and which ends in a kind of Dionysian frenzy as the military moves in to crush the rioting workers.[12] By contrast, *Before Daybreak* is a more restrained work, set in the claustrophobic interior of the Hoffman-Krause farm; although Hauptmann subtitled it 'A Social Drama', it is more obviously a psychological one in that it unfolds on the uncanny borderline between psychic and social life. The characters are less sociological types than symptoms of a social malaise. The libidinal excesses of the rural *arrivistes* are set against the pompous asceticism of the outsider Loth and the pernicious and cruel scientifism of Doctor Schimmelpfennig; caught between them is the tragic figure of Helen Krause, unable to transcend her origins but tortured by the explicitly literary romanticism that will eventually be her undoing. Despite its emphasis on the private sphere, the play is not without economic resonance: it encodes the traditional Naturalist opposition between those who produce (the absent miners) and those who exploit and consume (the main characters in the play). The Hoffman-Krause family made a fortune when coal was discovered on its Silesian farm, and the land now lies virtually dormant (the apples in the orchard, we are told, either rot or are stolen by the hungry miners) while the family drinks itself to death. The free-thinking and utopian idealist Loth is equally useless: he arrives at the farm to borrow money for his grand vision of a better world, but is incapable of any real action. From our historical vantage point he is clearly a protofascist obsessed with genetic hygiene; his social reformist tendencies have their etiology in an obsessive need for purification of all kinds, and in an aggressive scopophilia that masquerades as scientific objectivity. Traditional dramatic criticism has attempted to accord Loth a moral or at least epistemological authority, and has consistently been troubled by the play's ending, in which Loth abandons Helen and his erstwhile social vision when confronted with Schimmelpfennig's 'medical' assessment of the family's hereditary disease, alcoholism.[13] In fact, the play offers no locus of distanced objectivity, despite its adherence to the familiar anthropological device whereby a seemingly objective outsider opens the dramatic question and unveils the truth through observation. True to its title, *Before Daybreak* is a play about waiting, waiting for enlightenment, waiting for the light of reason to illuminate and finally dismantle the manifold hypocrisies and theatrical self-delusions that sustain the stagnant and miserable existence of the characters. Loth's arrival would seem to bring this waiting to an end. Instead, Loth himself is interiorized by the relentlessly oppressive environment; his amorous desire for Helen Krause ultimately nullifies his exteriority and unmasks him as a pompous hypocrite.

Trapped in this suffocating environment governed by desire and deceit, the characters in *Before Daybreak* circulate aimlessly in a dark and airless realm more infernal than any mineshaft. In keeping with the Naturalist 'formula,' the male characters find their attempt at self-fashioning undone by circumstance, but are nonetheless incapable of moving beyond it. This is typical Naturalist fare, of course, and fully in keeping with the anti-theatrical assumptions that sustain the genre. It can also stand as real social criticism in that Loth, Hoffman and Schimmelpfennig are all presented as educated men capable of rational thought and at least some degree of self-awareness. Judged according to the secular theology of naturalism, they represent reason's failure to govern the will, and are consequently consigned to the dramatic purgatory of moral stasis. In other words, their failings are inseparable from the historical moment they inhabit, and their stasis bespeaks, among other things, a failure of intellectual vision in a time of rapid industrialization and economic change. Were this play to concern these characters only, we might see it as the 'social drama' Hauptmann claimed to write.

The women in the play tell a different story, however; here the Naturalist's anti-theatrical impulse finds its clearest and least 'social' expression. From the moment they appear on stage, their pathology is written on their bodies, written, that is, in the form of very explicit stage directions that leave little to chance. Mrs Krause is described as a 'peasant woman', dressed 'no better than a washerwoman', her face is 'hard, sensual, nasty' (Hauptman, *Before Daybreak*, p.15).[14] Her next appearance has her 'dreadfully overdressed', a crude and ignorant peasant obviously pretending to be a *grande dame* (p.29). Her companion, Mrs Spiller, betrays her corporeality literally with every breath,[15] while Helen Krause, arguably the most sympathetic character in the play, enters with a book in her hand, but 'cannot quite hide the fact that she is a country girl' (p.16). Although her reading would seem to lift her above the level of her coarse and appetitive family, we are meant to see it as yet another sort of excess, the idle and implicitly libidinal pleasure of a woman with 'unusually abundant hair' and a 'too plump body' (p.16). The other important female character, Martha Hoffman, never appears on stage, although she is listed among the *dramatis personae*. About to give birth, she is reduced to an inarticulate sound from off stage, the 'moaning of the woman in labour' (p.86).[16] This most corporealizing of events casts its shadow over the play as a whole: the birth of stillborn child will be the drama's only obvious metaphor, a figural reminder that these characters have no future, no hope of transcending the material circumstances in which they find themselves.

The irreducible corporeality of these women derives, of course, from a long-standing historical tradition whereby women are paradoxically associated with both dissimulation and transparency. Duplicitous by virtue of her secondariness, woman represents the temptation of the erotic, the lure of worldly materiality, the spectre of spiritual death. This association is so enduring, so theologically sanctioned that its structural basis has been effaced: in short, it appears to be a 'natural' and inarguable fact. Not surprisingly, then, woman is also uniquely capable of representing absolutes such as truth, justice and so on, albeit only in allegorical terms. Hauptmann's reliance on these mythic structures is obvious: his female characters appear as mere types. Mrs Krause is the monstrous, garrulous hag so familiar from anti-feminist lore of the Middle Ages, her 'sidekick', Mrs Spiller, a caricature of the witch-midwife, while Helen Krause is a figure familiar to any reader of nineteenth-century novels: the simple country girl seduced and ruined not by the handsome and urbane stranger, Loth, but by literature itself. She commits suicide off stage in the wake of Loth's abrupt departure, an act with particular significance in light of the fact that she had been reading the similarly plotted *Sorrows of Young Werther*.

Although all these women are obvious fictional types, their mythic origins serve to naturalize their representation such that they seem to present irreducible truths about the human condition, truths that fine clothes and an even finer library cannot camouflage. The postlapsarian environment of the Krause farm, an unweeded garden in which everything of value has gone to seed and rot, is a degenerate world of absolute supplementarity. Nowhere is this more apparent than in these poor performers, these women who would be more than they are, but can only demonstrate their failure to 'be' more than inert bodies governed by an appetitive nature, by unbridled desire. They are the locus of the play's anti-theatrical agenda, and, consequently, the site of its socio-political failure. Both more and less human than the three 'rational' male characters, the women remind us that the question of anti-theatricality is first and foremost the question of the subject *per se*, and as such, it is an ethical as well as an aesthetic question. Anti-theatrical discourse assumes, of course, that there is an empirically verifiable subject of that discourse, or, to put it more bluntly, that it is possible to see a coherent, autonomous 'self' behind the seductive veils of theatrical dissimulation. Naturalism claims this self as the elusive object of its dramatic quest; although the world it evokes is a dark and cruel place, a world of shadows and veils, it implicitly assumes that all theatrical lies can be subjected to the light of reason, that the metaphysical 'daybreak' that Hauptmann's title promises will come, heralded by a new theatre that has the moral strength to act against its own best aesthetic interests. It also assumes that this enlightenment will be the impetus for real social and political change: seeing ourselves as we are, we will recoil in horror and be morally compelled to bring about a better, post-theatrical world inhabited by ethical beings who are governed by a refined and clearly directed will, rather than by mere appetite. Clearly this post-theatrical fantasy has had its converts historically, most notably in the Soviet realists who took naturalism to its (illogical) extreme. The irony of this post-theatrical theatre is that it can never be more than a return to allegory. Naturalism at its limit can only allegorize its own impossibility, thus proving that the theatre is never more theatrical, more metaphorical, than when it attempts to transcend its own conditions of representation.

Thus, the inevitable feminizing of the theatrical (a notion so culturally embedded that it is almost a tautology) pushes Naturalist drama back into mere allegory; traditionally, this has been called the 'epic' mode that inhabits, or perhaps infects, the genre. Although it is certainly possible for an epic, allegorically structured drama to commit to social change,[17] Hauptmann's play betrays a fatal complicity with the hypoc-risies it seeks to demolish. Relying as it does on gendered archetypes, as well on the irreducibility of the body as a locus of truth and transparency, *Before Daybreak* tries to have it both ways, that is, to see the feminized body as a site of excess and theatrical degeneracy, while simultaneously holding fast to the scientific belief in empirical observation as the foun-dation of social progress and ethical action. Here we see the clash between literary and scientific theology, that is, between the belief in mythic (and therefore static) archetypes and the newer faith in evolution and progress. This is, of course, simply the old conflict between fate and free will, providential and actual time. For Hauptmann, the feminine and feminized characters are irredeemably bound to the material and the libidinal. Their bodies are inert and unmetaphorizable, incapable of reason or even will. The male characters, on the other hand, have failed to use the reason they were given, have allowed appetite and weak will to paralyse them morally and psychologically. They are bound by circumstance and environment, rather than a corrupt materialized 'nature'. They are, in short, the intended subject of Naturalist political discourse, while the women are non-subjects, static and unchanging proof that theatricality is a futile strategy for self-reinvention.

Before Daybreak, like many plays of the genre, is a drama at odds with itself politically and ethically. In its effort to transcend masquerade and social performance, it must necessarily rely on binary metaphysical oppositions that effectively naturalize and materialize the very conditions it would claim to be 'social'. It is progressive in its social criticism, but absolutely regressive in its representational strategies. Interestingly, this conflict is played out at the thematic level in the character of the erstwhile reformer, Loth. Convinced that the world can be improved by scientific methods and determined to explore and ameliorate the living conditions of the exploited miners, he ultimately recoils in horror when confronted with the 'fact' of Helen's fallen nature: the Krause family's hereditary weakness for alcohol. So, too, the play itself sets out to expose the corrupt effects of industrialization on a once-idealized bucolic landscape, but ultimately retreats from this progressive agenda, choosing instead to focus on the representational equivalent of genetic inevitability, namely the belief in the immutable nature of the theatricalized and feminized body.

This binary opposition between environmentally determined male characters and their naturally corrupt feminine/feminized counterparts is, I must emphasize, a structural distinction. I make this point because Hauptmann's later and most well known work, *The Weavers*, relies on a different, yet no less absolute distinction between those who consume, the factory owners, and those who are consumed, the weavers themselves. Like *Before Daybreak*, *The Weavers* makes much of the issue of ingestion and digestion, although in the latter play the social problem of hunger takes on a mythic significance: the weavers' revolutionary anthem labels the manufacturer Dreissiger and his kind as 'cannibals', while the starving workers are forced to eat pet dogs, carrion and even the textiles themselves in an attempt to stay alive. The cannibalism motif may seem to be simply a powerful political metaphor for the exploitative relationship between producers and consumers, slaves and masters. Here, as in *Before Daybreak*, however, there is an obvious attempt to refuse the 'retreat' into metaphoricity. Like all Naturalist dramas, *The Weavers* is at odds with metaphor, which, like the theatre itself, has long been associated with rhetorical excess, with duplicity, with a tropological turn away from the real. Of course, this anti-metaphoric agenda remains more of a mystical quest than an actual dramaturgical strategy, but it nonetheless informs the play at every level. When, for example, the manufacturer Dreissiger attempts to claim that it is he, rather than the weavers, who has the greatest cross to bear, he does so in terms of a metaphor that can only be taken literally. 'And who doesn't try to blame everything on the manufacturer', he laments, 'who wouldn't want to suck his blood and live off him? No, No! if only you could stand in my shoes [literally: be in my skin] for once, you would be fed up soon enough' (Hauptmann, *The Weavers*, p.345). The irony is unambiguous: could the starving weavers be Dreissiger, they would, if nothing else, not be famished (the German phrase is 'genug satt kriegen', which translates literally as 'to have had enough to eat').

The weavers, like the women in *Before Daybreak*, seem to be both more and less human than the other characters. Their hunger and misery have transformed their bodies such that they appear to be by turns animalistic, like the great bear-like Ansorge, or 'gnomelike', as the suppliant weavers are described in the opening scene, or, in the case of the young women, pale, ethereal and ghostly, as if they had already moved beyond this world and into the next (p.325). They are both absolutely earthbound, in the manner of 'gnomes' and animals, and otherworldly, sublime objects whose bodies are barely there at all. Hunger and overwork have reduced – or elevated – them to this state; they are no longer subjects in any real sense, but rather objects too numerous to be of any real value in and of themselves. There is a surreal, almost hagiographical quality to the drama that undercuts its socio-political impact, and its historical specificity; again, like *Before Daybreak*, it takes Naturalism to its epic/allegorical conclusion, ending not with a moment of moral clarity, but rather with a martyrdom that can only seem superfluous and decontextualized, a moment of sublime irrelevance.

Despite this epic/allegorical turn, *The Weavers* situates itself quite unambiguously within the anti-idealist tradition of Naturalist drama. Subtitled 'A Play of the 1840s', it makes a claim on the particular and the historically contingent in evoking an actual weavers' uprising during a time of widespread political tumult. If the weavers themselves are defined solely in terms of their corporeality – or lack thereof – so, too, their physical environment is necessarily overdetermined, cluttered with small and seemingly gratuitous objects. This sort of setting, which is typical of Naturalist drama, obviously represents an effort to grasp the contingent, material reality of a situation by establishing what Roland Barthes has labelled a 'reality effect'.[18] Although this term is somewhat anachronistic in the current critical climate, it does represent an effort to come to terms with the problem of the real and 'true' within any generically closed signifying system, which takes us back yet again to the problem of theatrical anti-theatricality. The fetishization of detail in Naturalist drama speaks to the metaphysical problematic I have been discussing here – the desire to return to the real through a paradoxical emphasis on the supplementary – as well as to the more 'material' question of history in relation to fiction, of the historicity or 'truth' of the dramatic text itself.

Based loosely on an actual historical event, *The Weavers* takes pains to recreate the actual conditions in which the weavers lived and worked. It does this by surrounding, one might even say burying, the weavers themselves in detail. In the stage directions at the opening of Act 2, the room in which the Baumert family toils is described as narrow and low-ceilinged, the bodies of the weavers are so etched with misery that they are themselves texts, corporeal histories of economic oppression: Mother Baumert's face is

> emaciated to the skeletal, with wrinkles and creases etched upon bloodless skin, with sunken eyes made red and watery from wool dust, smoke and labour by candlelight, a long, goitrous throat with folds and tendons, a breast covered by kerchiefs and rags.
>
> (Hauptmann, *The Weavers*, p.351)

She is practically a corpse, the room in which she sits, long and shallow, not unlike a coffin. Reduced to near inanimacy, the Baumerts seem to exist outside representation; their misery is absolute, static, and finally extra-historical. Encrypted and desiccated, they are incapable of dissimulation; they are truly anti-theatrical in that they are, for all intents and purposes, dead bodies. Like some archaeological site awaiting excavation, the 'tomb' is littered with objects that situate them historically: 'garish pictures of saints', drying rags, 'useless trash', battered cooking utensils and the tools of their trade nearly crowd them out of the small space. The room has a life that the bloodless bodies of its inhabitants seem to lack, and the multiplication of objects, so particular, contingent and gratuitous, seems to tell the story that the characters cannot. The setting is not unlike the body of the hysteric, who, silenced by trauma and entombed in repression, nonetheless 'speaks' symptomatically. The contrast between the abject, corpse-like bodies of the weavers, and the excessive material details of their context returns us to the tensions and paradoxes that characterized Hauptmann's earlier work. If the bodies of the weavers represent (metaphorically, of course) a refusal of metaphor and the theatrical excesses it implies, this prodigality of contextual detail constitutes a hysterical return of the repressed, a compensatory supplement that is meant, paradoxically, to create an atmosphere of truth and transparency. Instead, the effect is that of an airless, crowded tomb, littered with archaeological artifacts and with dead bodies awaiting reanimation. And this points to what *The Weavers* is really about: it is a drama about a dead culture, re-awakened by the theatre, a culture which then suffers a 'second death' as Slavoj Žižek puts it, a death necessitated by the anti-theatrical bias of Naturalism itself.[19] The historical "truth" about the weavers' revolt, that it was a failure, and that this failure ultimately portended the displacement of the weavers themselves through industrial mechanization, is simply the context for a decidedly allegorical affirmation of the moral significance of Naturalist drama and its anti-theatrical agenda.

The Weavers is a drama that can be seen to operate on two levels which are ideologically at odds. Historically and thematically, the weavers are sacrificed to the greed of the manufacturers; their revolt is a noble but futile attempt to reclaim their humanity in the face of an economic system that has eaten away at their dignity and buried them in misery. This is the stuff of tragedy, complete with a cathartic moment of transcendence at the end, when the death of the pious Old Hilse transforms the drama into a sacred history, a political martyrology. Aesthetically, something quite different emerges. The weavers are already dead, both culturally and economically (from the historical standpoint of the playwright, this is certainly true); they are silenced, encrypted, all but forgotten. Enter Moritz Jager, the generically necessary 'outsider', who, unlike Loth in *Before Daybreak*, has a clear relation to the dramatist himself. Jager introduces the Baumerts to the inflammatory song known alternately as *Blood Justice* or *Dreissiger's Song*, which effectively reanimates the family and finally the weavers as a whole.[20] The song creates a sense of class consciousness that allows the weavers to re-imagine themselves in literary/dramatic terms. This political anthem moves the weavers to action precisely because it inscribes them within a pre-existing narrative that casts them as sublime victims of a demonic nemesis: it sentimentalizes and theatricalizes their plight by moving it to unambiguous and reductive moral terrain. Much is gained through this textualizing strategy, but much is lost as well. The weavers finally find the courage to rise up against the manufacturer Dreissiger, but in the process they lose their moral and aesthetic purity: the song lures them away from the absolute and into the realm of desire (as opposed to simple need) and excess. In other words, they are seduced by a theatrical vision of themselves that ultimately leads them away from truth and into the feminine realm of fiction. Given the anti-theatrical agenda of Naturalism as a genre, this turn away from originary purity – however static and grim that purity may have been – can only lead to destruction.

This moralistic turn at the metadramatic level explains some of the seemingly gratuitous details and characters introduced in the third act, which immediately follows the recital of the song in the second. Act 3 is set in a local tavern, owned by the genial Welzel and populated by various local types: a farmer, a forester, a cabinetmaker, and the requisite outsider, a traveling salesman, as well as Welzel's wife and pretty adolescent daughter, who sits embroidering. As so often, the tavern setting offers itself as a social microcosm and, in this case, as a *petit bourgeois* alternative to the dark and desperate world of the weavers. Here the community gives a different view of the weavers and their situation, a view tinged with the smug and self-exonerating criticism that the privileged so often level at the less fortunate. The salesman notes the seeming contradiction between the journalistic obsession with the weavers' misery, and their excessive, even festive funeral rituals; the local carpenter elaborates on the weavers' 'unreasonable' and 'exaggerated' notion of funereal rites, adding that he himself is 'all for respectfulness in children, but not so that the mourning survivors are oppressed with debts for the rest of their lives' (p.385). For the first time, the audience sees characters closer to their own class, and while they certainly are not presented as sympathetic or even justified in their criticism of the impoverished weavers, these bourgeois, 'respectable' people shift the terms of the discourse in important ways. The previous acts have shown only the abject need of the weavers as a class; here they come to be associated with theatrical, even carnivalesque funerals, with boasting, sarcastic retorts and self-dramatizing exaggeration. Several young weavers enter sporting tattoos that inscribe their anger upon their bodies and mark them as a class – yet another sign that they have 'fallen' into the supplementary, into the theatrical realm of desire. Their very bodies now bear the trace of textuality: the song has politicized them and given them class consciousness, but it has also tainted them by moving them beyond mere need and into the realm of desire, into representation. Once they have fallen away from the pure, putatively extra-semiotic state of near inanimacy, they lose their moral superiority and become effectively feminized. They are now metonymically linked to the innkeeper's pretty daughter Anna, who aspires to better herself by making a grand marriage. Anna's social aspirations are a bourgeois mirror of the weavers' economic demands, her idle stitchery a frivolous parallel to their labour, in that it is a purely excessive and theatrical act of no economic value.

Here, as in *Before Daybreak*, we see the mythic and fundamentally depoliticizing aspects of naturalism as a genre. If the Krause farm is a post-lapsarian realm of pathological excess, *The Weavers* is yet another quasi-theological narrative, another story about the fall into desire, or, in this case, ideology. *Dreissiger's Song* marks the emergence of a collective consciousness for the weavers; interpellated by the simple oppositions and demand for justice in the anthem, they now see themselves in a new light – the implicitly deceptive light of ideological 'truth'. Hauptmann does not condemn this ideological epiphany absolutely, but he does associate it with a turn to the theatrical, a turn which is also a move away from truth, purity and clarity. It is not that the weavers fall into a state of false consciousness; it is rather that, for the Naturalist, any kind of consciousness partakes of falseness. From a Freudian perspective, Naturalist drama is governed by the death drive, which, as many psychoanalytic critics have suggested, brings the psychic and the aesthetic into potentially fatal conflict. Freud explained (or attempted to explain) the death drive in terms of the organism's desire to 'return to inanimacy'; this desire is displaced libidinally, repeatedly 'acted out' or symptomatized through various erotic and theatrical pathologies such as sadism and masochism.[21]

For those of us who prefer to think in historical terms, it makes more sense to see naturalism as a return to the metaphysical and theological conflicts that have both threatened and motivated drama since its inception. The tension between reason and passion that has informed anti-theatrical diatribes since Plato finds a comfortable place in the Naturalist universe, a place founded on binary oppositions and traditional metaphysical hierarchies. The rotting orchards of the Krause farm, the forbidden song and its effects in *The Weavers* both reflect Hauptmann's anti-theatrical bias, a bias that implicitly condemns political consciousness as a form of ideological seduction, a misrecognition, if a necessary one. For the weavers themselves, this seduction reanimates them, but it also

opens the door to ritualistic excesses. At the end of the play the Dionysian frenzy of the rioting weavers is set against the pious minimalism of
Old Hilse, a character who exists simply to remind the audience that
the other weavers have indeed fallen away from pure presence. Ideological
self-awareness has feminized them – in the last act it is the shrewish and
garrulous Luise who speaks for them – and has led them away from the
truth. When Hilse's blind wife cries out for her son Gottlieb, who has
joined the weavers at the last minute in an attempt to save Luise, her
husband replies that he is now 'with the devil' (p.479). His defection
takes on mythic significance; in these final moments, the play becomes
a kind of reverse hagiographical narrative. 'Gottlieb' has indeed gone
to the devil, and with him the weavers themselves, whose 'conversion'
has led them to a second death, a spiritual end that is finally more
horrible than the living death they had endured before the uprising.

What emerges from this analysis is a somewhat different picture of
naturalism as a 'social' or political genre. However much Naturalist
drama sought to reveal, expose and scrutinize social and political injus-
tices, it also worked to 'naturalize' them such that they are seen to be
not only inevitable, but symptomatic of a world fallen into theatricality
and dissimulation. Despite its emphasis on the scientific and empirical,
naturalism relies on mythic structures and assumptions that can only
subvert any humanist notion of social progress; owing to its moral
commitment to anti-theatricality, moreover, it betrays an ethical
ambivalence that confounds any stable meaning or closure. Hauptmann's
early dramas, which many have called prototypically Naturalist, seem
to look in these two directions. They look forward into a future in
which those who produce are not relegated to an infernal world
governed by a tyrannical class of non-productive consumers, which is
another way of saying that they have a materialist agenda that is at least
potentially revolutionary in the Marxist sense. On the other hand, they
look backward into the mythic past as the locus of irreducible truths
about human nature, drawing on structures that are as conservative as
they are inexorable. In attempting to make sense of this ambivalence,
we might profitably begin to think about naturalism as a liminal genre
that situates itself, however inadvertently, on the borderline between
science and myth. Rather than condemning Naturalist drama as a
manifestly flawed and even failed attempt at social criticism, I would
like to think of it as a profoundly ethical genre, in that it confronts the
question of subjectivity and ethical action, and ultimately leaves the
question open. It neither celebrates theatricality, as some theorists are
wont to do these days, nor does it dismiss it absolutely, as positivists

and puritans have attempted to do throughout history. Instead, it stages the question of subjectivity – the ethical question, in other words – in terms of the 'problem' of theatricality. This is an old question that must, in an ethical sense, be posed again and again in new contexts. This repetition does not negate its historical urgency, or its epistemological significance. If anything, it serves to remind us that there are some issues that are both transhistorical in their persistence, yet absolutely contingent and temporal in their form. And addressing these issues, these contradictions is, after all, what drama has always done best.

Notes

1. Jonas Barish, *The Anti-theatrical Prejudice* (Berkeley: University of California Press, 1981), p.85.
2. Barish observes at the very beginning of his seminal work on anti-theatricality that the prejudice against the stage is in fact 'more than a prejudice' against a particular cultural activity precisely because it inevitably leads beyond the performance event itself to fundamental questions of epistemology, ontology and deontology; it reflects 'something permanent about the way we think of ourselves and our lives' (Barish, *The Anti-theatrical Prejudice*, p.2).
3. For a detailed history of German naturalism in English, see John Osborne, *Gerhart Hauptmann and the Naturalist Drama*, 2nd edn (Amsterdam: Harwood Academic Publishers, 1998).
4. The major manifestos and other assorted theoretical statements of German Naturalism are collected in Manfred Brauneck and Christine Müller, eds, *Naturalismus: Manifeste und Dokumente Zur deutschen Literatur 1880–1900* (Stuttgart: Metzler, 1987).
5. All translations from German originals are my own.
6. Concepts included in what came to be known as 'Sekundenstil', practiced most notably by Holz and Schlaf. Arno Holz, 'Evolution des dramas', in *Dieneue Wortkunst: Eine Zusammenfassung ihrer ersten grundlegenden Dokumente*, 1st edn (Berlin: Dietz, 1925), pp.211–484, and 'Vorwart', in *Sozialaristokraten: Komödie*, ed. Theo Meyer (Stuttgart: Reclam, 1980).
7. Heinrich Hart (*Gesammelte Werke*, ed. Julius Hart, vol. 3, Berlin: Fleischel, 1907) saw this privileging of detail as naturalism's most radical innovation and contribution: 'The old kind of art could only say of the falling leaf that it sinks to the ground in a spiralling movement. The new art describes this process second by second; it describes how the leaf appears red on one side, a shadowy grey on the other, and how a second later this is reversed; it describes how the leaf first falls vertically, then is blown to one side, then falls vertically again' (p.69). The aesthetic privilege that naturalism accords the detail is, as Walter Benjamin and others have noted, a reflection of the nineteenth-century's anxiety about the secularization of society, the rise of consumerism, and what we might call the post-classical 'invention' of the everyday.
8. The social aspirations behind Naturalist aesthetics were evident from the very beginning of the movement; see for example the essay by Ernst Henriet

Lehnsmann, 'Die Kunst und der Sozialismus', in Brauneck and Müller, *Naturalismus*, pp.23–32.

9. A tendency that certainly raised the ire of shrewd theatre observers at the time; Karl Frenzel, theatre critic for the important *Nationalzeitung*, for example, ironically noted at the première of Hauptmann's *Before Daybreak*: 'What a pity that [the director] forgot the main item from the second act set – the dung-fork with the crowing cock on it' (quoted in Michael Patterson, *The Revolution in German Theatre, 1900–1933*, Boston, MA: Routledge, 1981, p.33).

10. Women, in particular, who affect the dress and manner of their betters are often described as hard, shallow or crude despite their fine camouflage; their attempts at 'dissimulation' are inevitably betrayed by their own bodies. This characteristic of Naturalist drama will be explored in more detail later in this chapter.

11. For an overview of the main critical arguments surrounding *Before Daybreak* and *The Weavers* in English, see John Osborne, *Gerhart Hauptmann and the Naturalist Drama*, 2nd edn, (Amsterdam: Harwood Academic Publishers, 1998), pp.87–99, 135–48.

12. *The Weavers* premièred at the Deutsches Theatre on 25 September 1894; after viewing the performance, Kaiser Wilhelm II cancelled his subscription and withdrew his support for the theatre while the police immediately prohibited any further public performances, a ban that continued until after the turn of the century.

13. See, for example, Werner Bellman's essay, 'Gerhart Hauptmann: *Vor Sonnenaufgang*, Naturalismus – soziales Drama – Tendenzdichting', *Dramen des Naturalismus*, Interpretation (Stuttgart: Reclam, 1988), pp.7–46.

14. All page references are to the *Centenar Ausgabe* of Hauptmann's work. Gerhart Hauptmann, *Sämttiche Werke: Centenar Ausgabe*, ed. Hans-Egon Hass, vol. 1, (Frankfurt: Propyläen, 1966).

15. 'Mrs Spiller appears shortly after Mrs Krause. She is small, lop-sided, and decked out in the cast-off garments of Mrs Krause ... Her breathing is always accompanied with a quiet moan which is perceptible whenever she speaks as a soft *mmm*' (p.30).

16. This stage direction, surely one of the most notorious in the German theatrical tradition, generated a genuine scandal at the play's première as an enraged spectator, a certain Dr Kastan, stood up at this point in the performance and offered Schimmelpfennig a pair of forceps.

17. Most notably in the case of Brecht, whose anti-theatrical impulses manifested themselves quite differently from those of the Naturalists.

18. Roland Barthes, 'L'effet de éel', *Communications II* (1968): 84–9.

19. Slavoj Žižek, *The Subline Object of Ideology* (London: Verso, 1989), pp.131–49.

20. The concluding words of the song at the end of the second act (p.377):

It doesn't help to beg or pray
For naught is all complaint
"If you don't like it, go away
Go starve yourselves"

. . .

Now think about the despair
And the misery of these poor people
Who do not have enough to eat
Is there no pity anymore?

Pity, Hah! A beautiful feeling
Foreign to you cannibals
Everybody knows your goal:
To have our skins and shirts.

21. Sigmund Freud, *Beyond the Pleasure Principle*, trans. and ed. James Strachey (New York: Norton, 1961), pp.52–78.

7
Deploying/Destroying the Primitivist Body in Hurston and Brecht

Elin Diamond

In April 1928, several months into her second folklore-collecting expedition, Zora Neale Hurston wrote to Langston Hughes:

> Did I tell you before I left about the new, the *real* Negro art theatre I plan? Well I shall, or rather *we* shall act out the folk tales, however short, with the abrupt angularity and naivete of the primitive 'bama nigger.[1]

Hurston wrote in the self-reflexive code of black intellectuals. As a scientifically sanctioned label for bodies of colour at the bottom rung of the evolutionary ladder, the 'primitive' was, by the late 1920s, an over-determined keyword for colonial subject, ethnological object, modernist fetish and, subsuming all three, the most recognizable commodity in the marketplace of international modernism. Langston Hughes, Hurston's intellectual coeval, would have decoded her satire easily. 'Angular' was a common descriptor for the energized abstraction of African masks and movements (Hurston would use the same term in her 'Characteristics of Negro Expression'), while 'primitive 'bama nigger[s]' were the cherished informants of her anthropological research, the working-class black Southerners who, not without irony themselves, taught her folk-tales, songs, dances and root magic, and allowed themselves to be 'salvaged' in her books, essays and plays.

Hurston's *real* Negro art theatre was meant perhaps as a dismissal of the struggling Negro Art Theatre, one of many amateur groups in Harlem in the 1920s that produced middle-class melodramas and classical plays in an effort to align African-American performance to bourgeois culture. What Hurston proposed instead was both witty and iconoclastic, an 'art theatre' that, like the performance events of the European avant-garde, sought to destroy and redefine reigning ideas of art and of theatre. Over a decade earlier F. T. Marinetti famously imagined a 'variety theatre' that was 'naturally anti-academic, primitive, and naive... with powerful caricatures... abysses of the ridiculous... delicious impalpable ironies'.[2] Marinetti's futurist rhetoric is typically ostentatious yet Variety's destruction of 'the Solemn, the Sacred, the Serious, and the Sublime' anticipates the anarchic humour of Hurston's revues and sketches of 1931.[3] And Hurston echoes the defiant spirit of the Dada artist-performers of the Cabaret Voltaire (1916) when she tells Hughes that they themselves (not professional actors) should 'act out' her folk materials.

No doubt Hurston was raising a laugh, reminding Hughes of her impromptu ventriloquizing of rural southerners at Harlem rent parties. Yet behind the image of two sophisticated self-created urbanites re-enacting the Alabama man's 'abrupt angularity and naivete' lies a complex proposition about theatre and theatre-making. Like all dramatic modernists, Hurston detested the gate-keeping bourgeois theatre establishment, what Bertolt Brecht would call 'the apparatus', the function of which was to promote comfortable – that is, profitable – middle-brow entertainment. But unlike the dada and surrealist practitioners, Hurston and Brecht did not reject representation. They *had* mimetic objects – for Hurston, that sly vernacular Everyman, the 'primitive 'bama nigger', for Brecht the working-class 'children of the scientific age'. The question for Hurston, as for Brecht, was how to develop a technique of representation in contradistinction to the tired conventions of bourgeois Naturalism, that could articulate the subtle dynamism of working-class life – for Hurston, the experience of blacks 'farthest down'. If Hurston thought the primitive 'bama man's abrupt angularity' was 'natural' to him, she also thought it was detachable from him – a characteristic that could and should be 'acted out'.[4] This chapter looks at two early dramatic experiments, Hurston's *Color Struck* (1925) and Brecht's *Drums in the Night (Trommeln in der Nacht,* 1922), and examines the paradoxical decision, taken by both writers, to reveal social life by dipping into the slough of modernism's most dubious mass-cultural discourse – raucous, colourizing, dehumanizing primitivism.

As is well known, primitivism sits on a pile of simple ahistorical essentialisms: dark-skinned peoples are, or are deep down, drum-beating, irrational, excessively embodied children of nature. To the 'civilized' eye, the primitive signifies an enticing and inferior otherness, a projection of white culture's repressed libidinal forces. In *The Elementary Forms of the Religious Life* (1912), French sociologist Emile Durkheim described aboriginal rites as orgiastic passions 'free from all control...violent gestures, cries, veritable howls, and deafening noises of every sort' (*affranchies de tout controle...gestes violents, veritables hurlements, bruits assourdissants de toute sorte*).[5] Sophisticated moderns like anthropologist Zora Neale Hurston frequently used the term 'primitive' to denote unsophisticated social development ('Primitive minds...are quick to anger' ('Research', *ZNH*, p.689); 'The primitive man exchanges descriptive words' ('Characteristics', *ZNH*, p.830). However, primiti*vism* is inseparable from the long history of colonialism. As Ronald Bush notes: 'Europe had been conquering people for four centuries and had used representations of subjected peoples to mediate its repressed desires. But at the end of the nineteenth century, this appropriation accelerated at a rate that was rivaled only by the pace of political expansionism and technological and social change' (Barkan and Bush, *The Primitive Project*, p.9). From the colonial expositions and anthropological encounters at the turn of the century to *Der Blaue Reiter* (1912) and the Cabaret Voltaire, to *art nègre* and the Harlem 'jungle' cabarets of the 1920s, non-Western, but particularly African and African-American, art, music and dance typified modernist daring and consumerist chic. How, then, link primitivism to the nuances and complexities of experience? The primitivist sign, like the processes of commodity exchange, *occludes* particularity. And yet in *Color Struck* and *Drums in the Night*, Hurston and Brecht worked close to the abyss of primitivism as a means of rethinking and representing the contradictions of modern sociality.

That primitivism was a pervasive aesthetic language used by playwrights of vastly different dispositions might be just another of modernism's transatlantic curiosities. Constellating the work of Zora Neale Hurston (1891–1960) with that of her contemporary Bertolt Brecht (1898–1956), however, requires some discussion. If Hurston's literary brilliance and artistic ambitions were, like Brecht's, recognized early, she was an American black woman coming of age in the virulently racist early decades of the twentieth century, and possessed none of his cultural or actual capital. He died lionized, if still politically suspect; she died penniless, her four novels, autobiography and two anthropological texts out of print and forgotten. Yet in the early 1920s, both were theatrical innovators, seeking to mine commodity culture as an antidote to settled bourgeois and, in Hurston's case, racist traditions of theatrical practice. Hurston's *Color Struck* and Brecht's *Drums in the Night* predate their authors' immersion in social science (Boasian anthropology and Marxist sociology respectively) and were thus, I am suggesting, more porous to primitivist fashion. In both plays, a sexual melodrama collides with primitivist signifiers that, instead of mystifying social existence, paradoxically become the means by which the audience is asked to understand it. Yet such understanding can only be oblique, a compromise between destructive tendencies. The primitivist body, once deployed on stage, will not willingly exit or cede space to a body of social particulars.

As a general principle, performance presents an arresting encounter of body and discourse. In stage space the performer's body is meaningful only through sedimented discourses – theatrical and cultural conventions of gender, genre, race, nationality, among others. In the 1920s, primitivism was one of those 'other' cultural discourses that for a time stamped all theatrical languages with its exoticism and allure. Performance can never erase the conventions that give it meaning, but it can put them in play. Primitivism occupies pariah status in current cultural criticism, even as it did for Harlem Renaissance intellectuals who condemned the tendency of New Negro writers to reduce 'Negro life' to the 'meretricious themes of jazz', the 'primitivism of cabaret and jungle'.[6]

But Hurston and Brecht embraced primitivism, put it in play, borrowed its prurient energy to assault bourgeois aesthetic traditions that equated psychological depth in characterization with social truth. In this, their early work could be constellated with avant-gardists on the margins of legitimate theatre before and after World War I, who attacked realism's psychological interiority by exploding the body (Artaud's *Un Jet de Sang*, 1925), by turning brains into straw (Kokoschka's *Sphinx and Strawman*, 1907) or anuses (Jarry's *Ubu Roi*, 1896). However, in the rabidly capitalistic and racist 1920s, 'the pervasive condition of off-centeredness', as James Clifford puts it, required something more than the spectacular distortions of avant-garde provocations.[7] Hurston and Brecht deflected psychology, not by suppressing all traces of mimetic meaning-making (characters, conflict, narrative telos) but by reorienting the axis of body and discourse. Their dramaturgy stressed 'powers of expression' (sensuous corporeality in performance) – over 'powers of representation' (textual and theatrical coherence), but while these slippery terms may help distinguish avant-garde from modernist drama, Hurston and Brecht worked rather to extend the reach of mimetic art to embody the new experiences of modernity.[8] Primitivism, the most coded of discourses – instantly recognizable as both embodied commodity and the means of commodification – deployed and destroyed, unleashed and negated the 'natural' black body of popular and high cultural exchange. Paradoxically, in primitivism, the least experimental of discourses, Hurston's and

Brecht's early dramas reassert experiment's etymolgical link to experience.[9]

* * *

Zora Neale Hurston arrived in New York City in 1925 with a play in her pocket. Possibly her first play, *Color Struck* (1925) is an edgy translation, one of many early attempts to work into words and gestures certain life experiences remembered from the all-black town of Eatonville, Florida, where she lived until her mother's death in 1904. *Color Struck* was given second prize at an awards dinner for the Urban League's *Opportunity: A Journal of Negro Life*, where Hurston was toasted along with a veritable Who's Who of Harlem Renaissance literati (and many future 'Niggerati'). But the play seems never to have been produced.[10] In this it joins most of the estimated 20 plays, including her 'concerts', that Hurston wrote and which saw no or short-lived production. And yet the correct destination for the folklore collected in Eatonville, Polk County, New Orleans, Miami, and later the Bahamas and Haiti, was, she felt, the theatre, or should have been, since the 'poise for drama' ('Characteristics', *ZNH* 830) among working-class blacks produced 'the greatest cultural wealth of the continent.' Material for 'the real Negro theatre', Hurston claimed, lay where no one was looking for it, in her 'native village' and other newly industrialized communities of the South. As Hurston tells it, and as so many scholars have repeated, she knew the folklore of Eatonville but 'wore it like a tight chemise', unable to see it as a distinct resource, until 'the spyglass of anthropology' gave her the ability to discern from the flow of experience what she and other anthropologists called the 'characteristic' gestures, phrases and practices of black Southerners.[11]

The spyglass was, of course, given to her at Barnard in 1925, in classes with the leading anthropologist Franz Boas. Early in his career Boas had rejected the evolutionary model of physical anthropology and the racialist science it fostered. While Boas and his student Melvin Herskovitz insisted that Hurston learn to measure heads, Boas had more sensitive instruments of scientific discovery. Customs, traditions and lore, gathered through judicious fieldwork, were to be analysed and evaluated in relation to the totality of participants, not to a putative European standard. Focusing on a well-defined geographical territory, the Boasian anthropologist discerned the linguistic patterns that groups of people shared in common, whilst understanding these patterns as historically contingent, subject to encounter and, thus, diffusion and adaptation.

Hurston's encounter with Boas was providential for both. If he gave her ballast and techniques – techniques she sometimes found onerous – she was the ultimate participant-observer, able to offer him data to support his theory that American black culture derived from the dissemination and retention of African practices. As Boas evidently believed folk-tale collection was already fairly advanced, he instructed Hurston to attend to how experience became embodied form: 'pay attention, not so much to content, but rather to the form of diction, movements, and so on... [the] habitual movements in telling tales, or in ordinary conversation.'[12]

   Color Struck was probably written during Hurston's intermittent years at Howard University (1921–4), before coming to New York. After the *Opportunity* contest in 1925, Hurston revised the play and resubmitted it to *Opportunity* in 1926 where it won an honourable mention. It was finally published in November 1926 in the first (and only) edition of *Fire!!*, a journal devoted to 'the proletariat rather than the bourgeoisie'.[13] Like Eulalie Spence, Georgia Douglas Johnson, Willis Richardson, May Miller and many others, Hurston was responding to the call from Montgomery Gregory and Alain Locke for native dramas that would render the reality of black life without demeaning sentimentality. According to Kathy Perkins, 'native drama' in the Harlem Renaissance referred to race or propaganda plays that explored racial oppression, and to folk plays that offered 'realistic' but entertaining portraits of vernacular culture in the rural South.[14] That early twentieth-century drama about American Negroes be 'realistic' is an understandable requirement – how else counteract almost a century of American minstrelsy with its roster of degrading stereotypes? Still, the notion of a realistic folk play should give pause. The eminent domain of the folk play, in the oft-cited dicta of Johann Gottfried von Herder's concept of the *Volk*, was the antithesis of a realist aesthetic, at least as Western drama defines that term. For Herder the authentic late eighteenth-century German was the peasant, the mythic repository of the 'characteristic language, folk literature, and myth' of a nation.[15] The sources of the peasant personality lay not in legislated 'rights' (a discourse that produced, from Diderot through Ibsen, the individuated characters we know in dramatic realism) but in the community. Barbara Kirshenblatt-Gimblett traces the Herderian *Volkskunde* concept through the nineteenth-century British notion of the 'salvage' of artefacts of the disappearing past, to the exuberant collection of Boas and his students, noting that 'folklore...understood as oral tradition...continues to be in the present without being fully of the present'.[16] As Richard Dorson puts it, 'from its initial conceptualization, folklore has suggested the outlines of a hidden, forgotten backward culture'.[17] In his own contributions to his celebrated anthology, *The New Negro* (1925), Alain Locke saw this backwardness as corrigible by New Negro artists. 'No sane observer, no matter how sympathetic...would contend that the great masses are articulate as yet', but New Negro writers could carry 'the folk gift to the altitudes of art'.[18]

New Negro intellectuals writing folk plays reinforced their characters' inarticulateness, not only through 'realistic' vernacular but also through plots and settings that, as in Georgia Douglas Johnson's *Plumes*, show characters full of dogged intention, ensnared by persistent superstition – in other words, the clear inferiors to their creators and probable spectators. Hurston, who actually knew the people such dramas characterized, found another way. Instead of pitting a supposedly authentic folk culture against the primitivism that pervaded commercial Harlem, from the jungle décor of its jazz clubs to the African masks and sculptures that filled the flats of wealthy white patrons, Hurston embraced the contradictions. *Color Struck*, a play in four brief scenes, is a deliberate modernist hybrid. It opens in 1900 with, as Hurston writes in stage directions, '*a happy lot of Negroes boarding a train in Jacksonville Florida, headed for a cakewalking contest in St. Augustine*'.[19] Hurston has them dressed '*in their gaudy tawdry best*', an image dangerously close to minstrelsy, yet she places them explicitly inside a 'Jim Crow railway car', a pointed juxtaposition, as Sandra Richards notes: 'For possible spectators who shared the class background of the semi-urban, working-class characters on stage, for African American readers of *Opportunity* magazine, the indignities of travelling Jim Crow were well known, so that it would be immediately understood that the frivolity of the travellers is happening within a circumscribed space of racism.'[20]

Our attention is drawn to a drama of intra-racial suspicion arising between Emmaline and John, the representative cakewalkers from Jacksonville. Jealous of John's kindness toward Effie, a mulatto woman, and certain that he cannot love her darker skin, Emma picks fights during the ride and, as scene 2 moves into scene 3, refuses to cakewalk, forcing John to choose Effie and thus to confirm her suspicions. In the final fourth scene, set 20 years later (in the 'present'), John, who had relocated to Philadelphia, returns, now widowed, to Jacksonville to find and finally marry Emma. Significantly, Hurston places Emma in a 'one-room shack in an alley', a typical locale of folk plays, although 'in the alley' suggests the poor section of an urban, not a rural, environment. Emma has now produced a mulatto daughter of her own, whom John readily accepts. She leaves to fetch a doctor to tend to the dying child but, suddenly colour struck again, rushes back to find John bending over the girl. She forces him out of her life once again, leaving him to intone the folkloric moral appropriate to the scene's setting: 'So this is the woman I've been wearing over my heart like a rose for twenty years! She so despises her own skin that she can't believe any one else could love it!' (Hurston, *Color Struck*, p.102).

Dialectically skewing this moralism, though, is *Color Struck*'s most 'characteristic' feature: a cakewalk scene that splits the play down the middle, destroying the coherence of the realistic folk play:

Scene III – Dance Hall (*draped in Spanish moss*)
Master of Ceremonies: Couples to de floor! Stan' back, ladies an' gentlemen – give 'em plenty room.
(*Music changes to 'Way Down in Georgia'. Orchestra sings. Effie takes the arm that John offers her and they parade to the other end of the hall. She takes her place. John goes back upstage to the platform, takes off his silk hat in a graceful sweep as he bows deeply to Effie. She lifts her skirts and curtsies to the floor. Both smile broadly. They advance toward each other, meet midway, then, arm in arm, begin to 'strut'. John falters as he faces her, but recovers promptly and is perfection in his style. (Seven to nine minutes to curtain. Fervor of spectators grows until all are taking part in some way – either hand-clapping or singing the words. At curtain they have reached frenzy.*)

QUICK CURTAIN
(*It stays down a few seconds to indicate ending of contest and goes up again on John and Effie being declared winners by judges.*)
Master (on platform, with John and Effie on the floor before him): By unanimous decision de cake goes to de couple from Jacksonville!
(Hurston, *Color Struck*, p.97)

Hurston frames the spectacular contest by deliberately unframing it. A performance of '7 to 9' minutes undermines the illusion of continuous dramatic time, opening up an ambiguous temporality saturated with communal energy and, inescapably, primitivist coloration. Derived from slave parodies of the European quadrilles danced by plantation owners, and from competitions sponsored by slave owners, the cakewalk is a rhythmic high-stepping, back-arching strut, more parade step than dance. Descendants of the formerly enslaved, Hurston's cakewalkers are drawn together from different cities in Florida and, performing only for themselves, present an image of relaxed, self-pleasuring cohesion. Yet historical and cultural echoes of homegrown American primitivism abound: Hurston's happy lot of Negroes perform minstrelsy gestures so generic that Hurston fails to give one instigator a name:

> ONE OF THE MEN: (*standing, lifting his 'plug' in a grand manner*) Howdy do, Miss Effie, you'se lookin' jes lak a rose...[L]emme scorch you to a seat.
>
> (Hurston, *Color Struck*, p.90)

This overweening dandy, long a resident of minstrelsy skits, is later called Dinky. He repeats his grandiloquent 'scorching', this time in tight proximity to Hurston's standard English: '...*Joe Clarke is escorted into the next room by Dinky*', a linguistic montage that not only limns the action but also raises the satiric temperature for readers of *Fire!!* (p.94). The palmetto leaves and Spanish moss decorating the dance hall in *Color Struck* are other Janus-faced signs, recalling both the familiar flora of Hurston's native state and the gross caricatures of 'plantation' settings in the third acts of minstrel shows and of 'chocolate' revues of the 1920s (*Plantation Revue*, 1922, and its imitators).[21] Indeed Hurston's cakewalk scene, set in 1900, is timed to recall the era of transition when the cakewalk appeared to leave minstrelsy's burlesque houses for more respectable venues. The Jubilee Spectacle and Cakewalk in Madison Square Garden, 1892, was followed by Will Marion Cook and Paul Lawrence Dunbar's *Clorindy, or the Origin of the Cakewalk*, the first all-black show to play at a major theatre (the Casino) in New York, and, in one of the many proleptic moments of *art nègre*, at the Nouveau Cirque in Paris, 1904. Jean Cocteau rapturously described the 'abrupt angularity' of cakewalkers M. et Mme Elks:

> They danced: skinny, crooked, beribboned, glittering with sequins, hats raked over their eyes...knees higher than their thrust-out chins, hands twirling flexible canes...They danced, they glided, they reared, they kicked, *they broke themselves in two, three, four...* and behind them the whole city, the whole of Europe, began dancing [my italics].[22]

In 1906, Claude Debussy made the quintessentially modernist, that is, primitivist gesture, with his composition *Golliwog's Cakewalk*. Yet sheet music for the 'The Coon's Paradise' 1905 reflects pure minstrelsy. As Michael North notes, the cover 'shows a cakewalking couple between a chicken stealer and a card game', standard fare of minstrelsy skits.[23] A final testament to the ambivalent nature of cakewalk performances will have to stand for many. In 1925, when *Color Struck* won second prize in the *Opportunity* contest, the shrewd and gifted Josephine Baker began earning serious money in *La Revue Nègre* in Paris by galloping on stage on all fours, wearing minstrelsy tatters and very little else, manoeuvring her audience into a 'frenzy' against a plantation backdrop of Spanish moss. *Color Struck*'s cakewalk – its black bodies in frenzied dance – placed within an all-black context, yet destined for performance before, inevitably, mixed audiences – destroys the integrity of the vernacular folk play in order to open it to the complexity of black cultural production in the 1920s. Rather than seal off the 'authentic' folk from acts tainted by primitivism and minstrelsy, Hurston puts in view, and demands apprehension of, black culture's multiple, intertwining legacies. Clearly Hurston sought to show that newly urbanized black Southerners in 1900 deeply enjoyed the old cakewalk, admired skilful execution, revelled in what drew them together, and thought not at all about Parisian aesthetes or minstrelsy *ordure*. Unlike primitivist spectacles, produced and consumed in the main by sophisticated audiences hungry to recover the 'barbarian's innocence . . . [and] natural goodness' (Watkins, *Pyramids at the Louvre*, p.68), Hurston exhibits a fractious social group *before* they congeal into the 'frenzy' of performance.

Yet Hurston also underscores the density of the scene with the image of the isolated on-stage spectator. Emma is designated not only to show the show (*'she flings the curtain wide open'*) but to offer an emblematic counterweight to the folkloric moral that condemns her to lifelong isolation (*'John:* She so despises her own skin . . .'). In John's and the folk play's logic, Emma has crippled herself by internalizing colour codes imposed by whites during slavery; thus she *'shrinks into the Spanish moss'* as the performance begins, and sits *'motionless'* – in direct contrast to the communal dynamism of the strutters. But Emma's emphatic lines before drawing the curtain speak to a social condition as pervasive as Jim Crow. 'Oh, them half whites, they gets everything, they gets everything everybody else wants! The men, the jobs – everything! The whole world's got a sign on it. Wanted: Light colored. Us blacks was made for cobble stones.' In text after text, Hurston agreed. '. . . why was it the yellow-skinned people among us had so much prestige . . . The lighter the girl, the more money and prestige she was apt to marry.'[24] Casting her concerts in 1931 Hurston would seek darker-skinned women for ensemble roles, a direct rebuff to the practice of hiring 'octoroon chorus girls' in Harlem's elite jazz clubs in the 1920s.[25] In the temporal arc of the play – 1900 to the 'present' of 1925 – Hurston satirizes her bourgeois contemporaries, black and white, past and present, who might scoff at Emma's ignorance but who reproduce the attitudes and conditions that torment her. Yet if she supplied a final stage image of torment – Emmaline alone, rocking repetitively and 'sobbing' in the darkness beside the corpse of her mulatto child – Hurston was no fan of the 'sobbing school of Negrohood' ('How It Feels To Be Colored Me', *ZNH*, p.827).

The hero of *Color Struck* is not Emmaline but the play's fractured hybrid form, its refusal to represent the 'real' of black social life either in folk-play form or in the shape of primitivist spectacle. Indeed, Hurston's manipulation of dramatic style is aggressively dialectical and destructive. She deploys the modernist sign of signs – the 'primitive' dancing black body – to destroy the sanctimony of the folk play and yet when Emma '*buries her face*' in the Spanish moss, the sign of countless minstrelsy and black revue settings, she devalues the primitivist sign, tarnishes its aura, just as Emma's apostrophic yell ('Oh, them half-whites! . . .') destroys the sublimity of the primitivist body decorating the long history of the cakewalk show. Hurston's aesthetic destructions play out, and also *play against*, the avant-garde's energetic disregard of representation. Her aim is not to deny mimesis but to remake it, her quarry the still unregistered experiences of semi-urban working-class southern blacks as they were viewed, and necessarily misrecognized, by northern sophisticates. Clearly for Hurston, black modernity – like folklore itself – was 'still in the making'. *Color Struck's* representation of black experience lies neither in the image of the isolated woman nor in the group of oblivious revellers but, as in the modernist aesthetic Hurston's drama reflected and reshaped, in their unstable montage-like friction.

* * *

In 1926, Josephine Baker, after conquering Paris, moved on to Berlin. Regarded as a 'figure of German expressionism [and] of German primitivism', one observer remarked, 'Miss Baker dance[s] with extreme grotesque artistry and pure style, like an Egyptian or archaic figure.'[26] Unique though she was, the German intelligentsia had prepared itself for over a decade to appreciate her. Although most discussions of the importation of African artefacts centres on Paris, primitivism swept through Germany in the years before World War I. The almanac of the Munich-based Expressionist group *Der Blaue Reiter*, edited by Franz Marc and Wassily Kandinsky, was a stunning example of the complexity of the confrontation between Western art and its colonial 'others'. Reproductions of paintings by Picasso, Matisse, Cezanne, Marc and Gauguin appeared alongside stone sculpture from Mexico, a Brazilian mask, a mask from Gabon and sculpture from the Cameroons. The almanac itself represented the modernist curio cabinet, the non-Western work on view not merely to suggest a 'primal' energy and natural innocence, but, as Glenn Watkins puts it, 'to provide a new orientation and promote fresh perspectives among the seemingly dissimilar' (Watkins, *Pyramids at the Louvre*, p.75). Of course nothing was said about imperialism. In the 1890s, during the great European land grab of West Africa, Germany staked its claim to what is now Togo, the Cameroons and Namibia (in the west) and Tanzania (in the east), colonies that were stripped from Germany at its defeat in World War I.

Five years earlier, in the Blaue Reiter era, daring scholars like Carl Einstein sought to legitimate the German-African connection. Yet his *Negerplastik* (1915), one of the first serious works on African sculpture, deployed a scholarly version of familiar primitivist discourse. Einstein bemoaned the negative effects of secularization and modernization in the West, the loss of common ground and a binding style, which, he felt, the African artefacts retained.[27] In 1915 Richard Huelsenbeck read his 'negro poems' in Berlin and by 1918 had opened dada's German front, Club Dada. In this period, as Brecht was working on his first plays, travelling frequently between Munich and his native Augsburg, he may have read accounts of Richard Huelsenbeck's first dada lecture in January 1918, which extolled the happy primitivism of the Cabaret Voltaire and its next incarnation, the Galerie Dada, (July 1916–May 1917): 'Together we made a beautiful negro music with rattles, wooden drumsticks, and many primitive instruments.' Huelsenbeck himself chanted 'authentic' Negro poems into the night, ending in shouts of 'Umba, umba'. It was 'a witches' sabbath such as you cannot imagine, a hurrying and scurrying from morning till evening, an intoxication of drums and tom-toms, an ecstasy of tap and Cubist dances'.[28] Tap dancing, made famous in minstrelsy tours of the continent, looked Cubist, that is, angular, to Huelsenbeck and the total effect was a primitivist 'witches' sabbath' guaranteed to revivify the limp, routinized European body. By the late teens of the decade an avant-garde invocation of 'drums in the night' was chic.

Brecht's play of that title was long a political embarrassment to him. The first draft, called *Spartakus*, was completed in February 1919, one month after communists from the Spartacus Union led by Rosa Luxemburg and Karl Liebknecht occupied newspaper and telegraph offices in Berlin. The rebellion, capping revolutionary activity from the previous November, started on 5 January 1919, was crushed five days later by remobilized troops known as the *Freikorps*, and by 15 January the leaders had been murdered. At this point Brecht had never been to Berlin, but relied on newspaper accounts and took notes during raucous socialist party meetings in Munich, to which he was commuting constantly from Augsburg. Anti-bourgeois but otherwise disengaged and indifferent to even anti-bourgeois political programmes, Brecht would later write, with typical irony: 'The revolution, which had to serve as a background [to the events of *Spartakus*], was of no more interest to me than Vesuvius is to a man who wants to cook a saucepan of soup on it.'[29]

Indeed the soldier protagonist of his renamed *Trommeln in der Nacht (Drums in the Night)*, published in 1922, stirred the soup and ignored the volcano. Designed, like *Baal*, to reject the heroics of expressionism, the first Munich production of *Drums in the Night* had signs posted warning spectators to 'stop that romantic gaping'. Yet the play turns on a trite romantic scenario: a soldier and prisoner of war in Africa returns after four years to find that his fiancée, Anna Balicke, has become affianced to and pregnant by Murk, a newly successful war profiteer in the mould of her father. After shocking Anna's parents at home (Act I), Kragler, shaky and wild, confronts Anna and Murk in the fancy Piccadilly Bar (Act II). Rejected, Kragler stumbles into the street (Act III), with Anna in pursuit. Kragler is led by a sympathetic prostitute to a workers' 'gin mill' (Act IV), where he becomes part of a rag-tag drunken crew. They set off toward the riots in the newspaper district but Anna finds them first. Reunited with Anna (Act V), Kragler bitterly rejects both the ideals of the 'red' Spartacists and the brutality of the *Freikorps* (historically known as the 'whites'). Instead he decides to take his pregnant fiancée home, to bed. Brecht represents his disgust at the human waste of war by having Glubb, the gin-mill proprietor, open Act IV singing his 1918 *Ballade von dem toten Soldaten*. But as one biographer notes, the song Brecht debuted (and later suppressed) in January 1919, *Gesang des Soldaten der roten Armee*, was more to the point: it mocked soldiers marching 'behind the red inhuman flag' while a 'red moon swam over the oat-fields' (Hayman, *Brecht, a Biography*, p.41).

Indeed that 'red moon' alerts us to the play's complex use of primitivist signifiers. In an ironic echo of the dadaist Huelsenbeck, Brecht's Babusch, a journalist and friend to the Balickes, views *Spartakus* as primitivist spectacle: 'Friends, the Reds are having a witches' sabbath (*roten Hexensabbat*) but you're nicely fortified in here.'[30] And as Kragler approaches, the red moon starts to 'glow' – a reference not only to the communist project about which Brecht was ambivalent, but also to the jungles of Africa.[31] Kragler's African tour of duty where he was apparently called upon to defend the German colonies – possibly German West Africa (though he was imprisoned in Morocco) – is the obsessive topic of the *petit bourgeois* Balicke family. He is, for Mr Balicke, not only a rotting corpse, but one whose proximity to the primitive has produced a race change: 'Does she [daughter Anna] want a nigger?' (*Muss es ein Neger sein?*). As critics have noted, the play's numerous references to Kragler as undead corpse or 'ghost' (*Gespenst*) who haunts the greedy Balickes – allude both to ghostly soldiers from traditional ballads who come back from the dead to claim their faithless brides and to the 'haunting spectre of communism'.[32] Indeed Balicke almost immediately links the Kragler as ghost to the Spartacus rebels: 'Are you drunk? Pauper! Anarchist! Soldier! Pirate! Moon ghost! Where'd you leave your sheet?' (Brecht, *Drums in the Night*, p.76). But while Kragler initially claims his social identity ('*Mein Name ist Kragler*'), he is quickly transformed by the others into a bizarre, primitivist object, his face the 'colour of a rotten fig' (*verfaulte Dattel*)', his body covered with an 'African hide' (*afrikanische Haut*). Herr Balicke goes right to the heart of Kragler's sins: he's a 'nigger tramp' (*Negerkutsche*) come to disrupt his and Murk's new money-making venture after years of successful war profiteering selling ammunition boxes. 'Pack up your moon', Balicke snarls to Kragler, 'and go sing to your chimpanzees.'

Kragler quickly slides down the evolutionary ladder. Borrowing Balicke's epithet, he names himself a *Negerkutsche* with 'nigger language in his throat' (*Negersprache im Hals*), 'webs' between his fingers and 'crocodile skin' (*Krokodilhaut*). Now of indeterminate race *and* species, Kragler gazes out the window: 'It's only the red moon, I've got to think out what it means.' But Brecht leaves no time for thinking. As Hurston's cakewalk interlude blasted open the folk play, Brecht pushes his characters into a wind that stirs up not revolution, but the unsorted curiosities and temporal collisions of international primitivism. A jazz band at the Piccadilly Bar plays 'The Lady from Peru' while Murk dances the 'Boston', the latest import from black America. Anna, with Babusch and Murk in tow, runs run toward the conflagration in the newspaper district to parodic strains of Wagner's 'Ride of the Valkyries', and Kragler spits out allusions to Büchner's *Woyzeck*. Like *Color Struck*, as well, *Drums in the Night* contains two emblematic statements, one that concludes the local story and one that attests to what primitivist signifiers, once destroyed, make visible. As John's moralizing judgment in *Color Struck* ('She so despises her own skin that she can't believe anyone else could love it') crystallizes the folk-play plot, so Kragler speaks for romantic individualists amongst the disaffected post-war German youth: 'Do they want my flesh to rot in the gutter so their ideas can go to heaven?' (*Mein Fleisch soll im Rinnstein verwesen, dass eure Idee in den Himmel kommt?*) (p.106).

Kragler's second statement is a proto-*Gestus*, that is, a gesture, or gestural language, that, as Brecht will explain in the late 1920s, expresses the social attitudes of the play. As I have noted elsewhere, a *gestus* explains the play and it exceeds the play.[33] It produces what Walter Benjamin calls 'dialectics at a standstill',[34] when the constructions of the historical force-field in which the play is embedded suddenly emerges. And what emerges here are the strange racial configurations of Germany's post-war history. Retrieving the revolutionaries' drum, Kragler raps out denunciations of himself and his audience, then flings the drum at the red moon, '*which turns out to be a Japanese lantern*' – another item in the primitivist grab bag – then '*drum and moon fall into the river, which has no water in it*' (p.106). All revolutionary politics would appear to be theatrical nonsense, 'a few boards and a paper moon' that conceal the 'only thing that's real...the butcher's block in the background'. Yet this analysis is incomplete. The destruction of the red moon is juxta-posed to Kragler's now firmly chosen destination – 'I'll lie in bed tomorrow and multiply, so as not to perish from the earth' (...*ich liege im Bett morgen früh und vervielfältige mich, dass ich nicht aussterbe*). Kragler's 'big, white, broad bed' should be taken ironically. Like Murk, who also speaks of a white bridal bed, Kragler and Anna's union can hardly symbolize purity. Kragler asserts that he and Anna will multiply, though it is equally crucial that the first evidence of multiplication, Murk and Anna's child, will not belong to him at all. Actually, Kragler's baby *must* be deferred. Africanized by all, including himself, 'black' Kragler coupling with his white woman hints dangerously at miscegenation. Indeed at the moment Brecht was drafting *Drums in the Night*, public horror of the mixed-race bed had become the obsessive topic of the German press.

In the wake of Germany's defeat in World War I, France occupied the Rhine and Saarland with vast numbers of soldiers – 25,000 to 40,000 – from the French African colonies of Morocco, Algeria, Tunisia, Mada-gascar and Senegal. According to historian Sally Marks, the Senegalese arrived in Germany in January 1919 – the month of the Spartacus uprising.[35] By the end of the occupation in 1925, six to eight hundred mulatto children had been born from liaisons between German women and non-white occupying soldiers. Newspapers, especially those in Munich, Berlin and Hamburg, hysterically bruited the entire action as the 'Black Horror on the Rhine'. Following standard racist (and primitivist) procedure, the press lumped together all the nationalities of the French occupying force as '*coal black savages from the African jungle...one hundred percent of whom were afflicted with syphilis, skin disease, and parasitic worms'* (Marks, 'Black Watch on the Rhine', p.301; my italics). If Brecht keeps the 'red' uprising in the background of *Drums in the Night*, inserting only a few journalistic announcements about the uprising in the newspaper district, he makes black 'Afrika' the imposing subtitle to Act I and perhaps hints at the French occupation by having *'die Marseillaise'* played in Act V of *Drums in the Night*. Just prior to Kragler's first entrance in Act I, Balicke borrows the rousing *'Marchons!'* from the anthem's final lines, and repeats the command to urge Frau Balicke to flee Kragler's presence. Kragler, viewing himself as a primitivist object, notes his own skin aberrations: 'I've got skin like a shark. Black' (p.77). 'Now do you see my face? Is it like crocodile skin?...I've been in salt water' (p.78). At the end of Act II, as the Balickes see that Anna will choose the 'nigger tramp', Frau Balicke echoes the newspaper hysteria of 1919: 'They're all of them sick. They've all got something. Syphilis! Syphilis! They've all got syphilis!' (*Die sind ja alle krank! Die haben ja alle was! Syphilis! Syphilis! Alle haben sie die Syphilis!*) (p.84). And Kragler's first speech includes the wonderfully inverted notion that he is so hungry he could eat the worms, which, as a corpse, should be eating him. Of course the reference to syphilis and to the corpse-like soldier point to the condition of demobbed soldiers and to Brecht's imagery in *Ballade von dem toten Soldaten*, not to mention the writer's brief World War I service in an Augsburg clinic that treated soldiers with venereal disease. If the Black Horror on the Rhine penetrates Brecht's second play, he settled 'Afrika' by destroying the primitivist body and reasserting the correct colour. Brecht will not allow Kragler to contribute to the *Mulattisierung* of the German race – Anna has a white baby in her womb. As Kragler and Anna walk off, they hear a wild scream from the newspaper district, but now the scream is 'white': *ein weisses, wildes Geschrei* which continues until the stage goes dark.

* * *

If Brecht was colour struck in *Drums in the Night*, the effect was no less revealing than the formal cacophony of Hurston's *Color Struck*. In abjecting Kragler, in making him a primitivist object, Brecht contributed to the aesthetic logic of primitivism by removing from view and from critique the social violence of racism. Produced a year after *Drums in the* Night, *In the Jungle* (later *Im Dickicht der Städte*) is also preoccupied with skin, but the colourized one is Shlink, Garga's orientalized antagonist, and in *Man Is Man* (*Mann ist Mann* 1926), racial others are entirely subordinated to the transformation of a folkloric individual into a protofascist machine man. For Brecht, race had to be sublated in order to create the aesthetic politics of what would become epic theatre and its canoncial plays (*Mutter Courage* 1941; *Der gute Mensch von Sezuan* 1943; *Leben des Galilei*, 1943; *Der kaukasische Kreidekreis*, 1944). For her part, after the 1920s, Hurston stopped thinking about the folk as the proletariat, definitively so after the Marxist Richard Wright accused her of presenting minstrel images of poor southern Negroes in *Their Eyes Were Watching God* (1937).[36] No communist, yet impressed with the new vein of 'serious' literature, Alain Locke wondered in print when Hurston would 'come to grips with motive fiction and social document fiction'.[37] But Hurston persisted in rejecting the 'inner psychology of characterization' just as she resisted the one-statement folk play form decreed by her admired teachers and friends. To promote images of racial uplift meant to accede to the idea that racial feeling must be framed as a social and political problem. If Brecht suppressed race for the Marxist politics of epic theatre, Hurston abjured politics for the exploration of a racial aesthetics – most notably in her well-received folk concert *The Great Day* (1932; variously performed under the titles *From Sun to Sun*, *All De Livelong Day*, and *Singing Steel*) which honored the labor and leisure of black Americans in a typical southern railroad camp.

Their mature theatre work suggests why Hurston and Brecht deployed and destroyed the primitivist body in *Color Struck* and *Drums in the Night*. In these early plays they began to search for ways to make visible and palpable the distinctively modern experiences of urban and semi-urban subjects, and those 'farthest down'. For both writers the hyperbolic torquing of representation in avant-garde performance was unproductive. And yet Hurston knew that there was no model for an emancipated working-class Negro in the United States in the 1920s. Similarly, given the political violence in post-World War I German society, Brecht would wait several years before proposing an alternative to Kragler's melancholy egoism. For both it was impossible to *see* the characters they were beginning to imagine, except in motion, in fragments, in borrowed bits of primitivist colouration.

Notes

1. Cited in Carla Kaplan, ed., *Zora Neale Hurston: A Life in Letters* (New York: Doubleday, 2002), p.116.
2. F. T. Marinetti, 'The Variety Theatre', in Umberto Apollonio, *Futurist Manifestos*, trans. R. Brain, R. W. Flint, J. C. Higgitt, C. Tisdall (Boston MA: MFA Publications, 1973), pp.129, 126.

3. See, for example, Hurston's, *Cold Keener, Woofing, Lawing and Jawing*, all copyrighted in 1931, at the Library of Congress.
4. 'Natural' is a complex keyword in Hurston's vocabulary and important to distinguish from Brecht's usage. The title of her famous essay of 1928, 'How it Feels to be Colored Me', contains a pun on what 'nature . . . has given [us]': 'colored' is both adjectival (the me who is coloured) and a passive verbal construction (the me who is coloured [by you]). Hurston further plays on the gap between 'to be colored' (how society looks at her) and 'me', sometimes by closing the gap ('I am colored' and happy to be so); sometimes by opening it wide ('At certain times I have no race, I am *me*'). And in her final, oft-quoted paragraph, this 'me' is no more definable than the apparently random contents of a paper bag, hers a brown bag; others a yellow, white or red one. (In *Zora Neale Hurston: Folklore, Memoirs, and Other Writings*, ed. Cheryl Wall, New York: Library of America, 1995, pp.826–9. Hereafter known as *ZNH.*) In this emphatically modernist essay, identity is one performance among many, a consolidation, at a given moment, of paradoxical or contradictory elements. Brecht makes a similar judgment in an interview in 1926: 'The continuity of the ego is a myth. A man is an atom that perpetually breaks up and forms anew' (*Brecht on Theatre*, ed. John Willett, New York: Hill & Wang, p.15).
   But while for Brecht, in the 1930s, 'natural' behaviour was historically determined, the visible symptom of bourgeois ideology, Hurston presented a complex view. In the early 1940s, she insisted on ahistorical characteristics of 'the natural Negro' ('Concerts', in *ZNH*, p.808). '[T]he natural Negro' is someone not 'tampered with' by musical training. 'Conservatory' music was 'a determined effort to squeeze all of the rich black juice out of the songs and present a sort of musical octoroon to the public' (p.805). But in 'Characteristics of Negro Expression' (1934) she argued that 'permeat[ing] the Negro's "entire self" is drama', that which impels him to create through 'mimicry' and 'modification' (pp.830, 838). In other words 'natural' for Hurston was as dialectical as it was for Brecht, but the axes were different. In Brecht's dialectic, the bourgeois natural opposes the historical (false vs true); in Hurston's dialectic, the natural opposes the bourgeois historical (true vs false.). One could say this chiasmus depends simply on the difference between races. Black Americans had had their 'nature' defined and distorted for centuries; thus to give content to 'the natural Negro' was a strategic as well as an aesthetic act, and no less complex than naming, as Brecht did, 'the children of the scientific age' as his ideal audience. Both terms were critical performatives intended to carve out aesthetic space for new theatrical work.
5. Cited in Vincent Crapanzano's 'The Moment of Predestidigitation', in Elazar Barkan and Ronald Bush, eds, *Prehistories of the Future: The Primitivist Project and the Culture of Modernism* (Stanford University Press, 1995), pp.106–7, 395.
6. Allison Davis, 'Our Negro 'Intellectuals' ', in Sondra Kathryn Wilson, ed., *The Crisis Reader*, (New York: The Modern Library, 1999), p.327.
7. James Clifford, *The Predicament of Culture* (Cambridge, MA: Harvard University Press, 1988), p.9.
8. See David Graver, *The Aesthetics of Disturbance: Anti-Art in Avant-Garde Drama* (Ann Arbor: University of Michigan Press, 1995), p.50.

9. See Raymond Williams, *Keywords: A Vocabulary of Culture and Society*, rev. edn. (New York: Oxford University Press, 1985), p.126.

10. Hurston alludes to a possible production by the Negro Art Theatre of Harlem in a letter dated 10 November 1925. But as Carla Kaplen notes, the theatre did not offer a full production of any drama until 1929. See *Zora Neale Hurston: A Life in Letters*, pp.68–9.

11. Zora Neale Hurston, *Mules and Men* (New York: Harper Collins, 1990), p.9.

12. Cited in Robert Hemenway, *Zora Neale Hurston: A Literary Biography* (Urbana: University of Illinois Press, 1980), p.91.

13. Wallace Thurman, who headed the editorial board of *Fire!!* (consisting of Hurston, Langston Hughes Bruce Nugent, Gwendolyn Bennett and Aaron Douglas), described the journal's policy: 'Hoping to introduce a truly Negroid note into American literature, its contributors had gone to the proletariat rather than to the bourgeoisie for characters and material, had gone to people who still retained some individual race qualities and who were not totally white American in every respect save color of skin'. Cited in Hemenway, pp.44–5.

14. Kathy Perkins, *Black Female Playwrights: An Anthology of Plays before 1950* (Bloomington: Indiana University Press, 1990), pp.1–7.

15. Fritz Richard Stern, *The Politics of Cultural Despair: A Study in the Rise of the German Ideology* (New York: Anchor Books, 1965), p.147.

16. Barbara Kirshenblatt-Gimblett, 'Folkore's crisis', rpt. *Journal of American Folklore*, 11: 441 (Summer 1998): 283.

17. Richard M. Dorson, *Folklore in the Modern World* (The Hague: Mouton Publishers, 1978), p.12.

18. Alain Locke, 'The New Negro' and 'Negro Youth Speaks', in Alain Locke, ed., *The New Negro* (New York: Atheneum, 1992), pp.7, 48 respectively.

19. Zora Neale Hurston. *Color Struck*, in Perkins, *Black Female Playwrights*, p.89.

20. Sandra Richards, 'Writing the Absent Potential', *Performativity and Performance* (New York and London: Routledge, 1995), pp.74–5.

21. *Plantation Revue*, starring Florence Mills, was produced by Lew Leslie, a prolific generator of the generic black musical – light on libretto, heavy on song and dance numbers. Others in this vein include the famous Sissle and Blake's *Shuffle Along* (1921), *Put and Take* (1921), *Strut Miss Lizzie* (1922), *Runnin' Wild* (1923), *Chocolate Dandies* (1924), *From Dixie to Broadway* (1924). See Allen Woll, *Black Musical Theatre: From* Coontown *to* Dreamgirls (Baton Rouge: Louisiana State University Press, 1989), p.75 ff.

22. Cited in Glenn Watkins, *Pyramids at the Louvre: Music, Culture, and Collage from Stravinsky to the Postmodernists* (Cambridge, MA: Harvard University Press, 1994), p.101.

23. Michael North, *The Dialect of Modernism: Race, Language, and Twentieth-Century Literature* (Oxford: Oxford University Press, 1994), p.176. In contrast to the commercialized cakewalk, see Anthea Kraut's discussion of Hurston's staging of vernacular dance in *The Great Day* in 'Between primitivism and diasposa: The dance performances of Josephine Baker, Zora Neale Hurston, and Katherine Dunham', *Theatre Journal*, 55 (2003): 433–450.

24. Zora Neale Hurston, 'My People! My People!', in *ZNH*, p.726.

25. See Lynda Marion Hill's still unmatched discussion of Hurston's performative writing in *Social Rituals and the Verbal Art of Zora Neale Hurston* (Washington,

DC: Howard University Press, 1996). David Krasner makes Emmaline's apostrophe the basis for his thematic reading of *Color Struck* in 'Migration, fragmentation, and identity: Zora Neale Hurston's *Color Struck* and the geography of the Harlem Renaissance', *Theatre Journal*, 53 (2001): 533–550. Krasner's contention–that we should read *Color Struck* as the victimization of Emmaline by John, and by the historical circumstances of migration of which black women bore the brunt – is important, notwithstanding several problems in his argument. First, there is no evidence in the play for Krasner's repeated assertion that 'John ... leaves with Effie for parts north' (p.542), nor does Krasner comment on John's own statement, that the woman he married was 'jus' as much like you [Emma] as Ah could get her' (p.99). Second, he interprets Hurston's stage direction: *'[Emma] buries her face in the moss'* to mean that Emma has been 'thrust to the ground with her face in the moss' (p.547). Spanish moss is a hanging plant that grows on trees and in the play is clearly *'along the wall'* (Hurston's stage directions, p.97). Thus Emma has turned her face to the wall, she isn't lying on the ground, a strong semiotic difference when reading the cakewalk scene. Finally, while *Fire!!* was certainly addressed to Harlem Renaissance intellectuals, Krasner's assertion that it was 'intended primarily for African Americans' seems to me to be dubious. *Fire!!* intended to defy the 'uplift' positions taken by *Opportunity* and *Crisis*, but to be black literary radicals, which was certainly the editors' self-description, is to announce *how* one wants to be read, not who should be reading.

26. Cited in Brenda Dixon Gottschild's excellent study, *Waltzing in the Dark: African American Vaudeville and Race Politics in the Swing Era* (New York: St Martin's Press, 2000), p.168.
27. See Andreas Michel's discussion in 'Formalism to Psychoanalysis: On the Politics of Primitivism in Carl Einstein', in S. Friedrichsmeyer, S. Lennox, and S. Zantop, eds, *The Imperialist Imagination: German Colonialism and Its Legacy* (Ann Arbor: University of Michigan Press, 1998), pp.141–61.
28. Cited in Watkins, *Pyramids at the Louvre*, p.107.
29. Cited in Ronald Hayman, *Brecht, A Biography* (Oxford: Oxford University Press, 1983), p.40.
30. Bertolt Brecht, *Drums in the Night: Collected Plays*, vol. 1, ed. Ralph Manheim and John Willett (New York: Vintage, 1971), p.67. *Trommeln in der Nacht. Gesammelte Werke in acht Banden* (Frankfurt: Suhrkamp Verlag, 1967), p.78. While I consulted the 1922 edition of the play, the argument here did not depend on citing differences between the texts.
31. Another connection, out of Brecht's ken, but interesting for my argument, is *The Red Moon*, one of the first black musicals, written and performed by Bob Cole and Rosamund Johnson in 1909. It was billed as a 'sensation in red and black'. In Woll, *Black Musical Theatre*, p,24.
32. See Ronald Speirs, *Brecht's Early Plays* (London: Macmillan, 1982), pp.33ff. See also Astrid Oesmann, *The German Quarterly*, 70.2 (Spring 1997): 141 and David Bathrick, *The Dialectic and the Early Brecht: An Interpretive Study of* Trommeln in der Nacht (Stuttgart: Akadmisher Verlag Hans-Dieter Heinz, 1975), pp.67–98.
33. See Elin Diamond, *Unmaking Mimesis: Essays on Feminism and Theater* (London and New York: Routledge, 1997), p.53.

34. Cited in Susan Buck-Morss, *The Dialectics of Seeing: Walter Benjamin and the Arcades Project* (Cambridge, MA: The MIT Press, 1991), p.219.
35. Sally Marks, 'Black Watch on the Rhine: A study in propaganda, prejudice and prurience', *European Studies Review*, 13 (1983): 297–334. On the various ways Brecht 'misrecognized the racial discourse of his time', see Kattrin Sieg, *Ethnic Drag: Performing Race, Nation, Sexuality in West Germany* (Ann Arbor: University of Michigan Press, 2002), pp.63ff.
36. See Wright's review of *Their Eyes Were Watching God* in *New Masses*, 5 October 1937, reprinted in Henry Louis Gates, Jr. and K.A. Appiah, eds, *Zora Neale Hurston: Critical Perspectives Past and Present* (New York: Amistad Press, 1993), p.17.
37. See Locke's review in *Opportunity*, 1 June 1938, of *Their Eyes Were Watching God*, in Gates and Appiah, *Zora Neale Hurston: Critical Perspectives*, p.18.

8
John Cage's Living Theatre

Marjorie Perloff

> Where do we go from here? Towards theatre. That art more
> than music resembles nature. We have eyes as well as ears, and
> it is our business while we are alive to use them.
>
> (John Cage, 'Experimental Music', 1957[1])

When asked by David Shapiro whether he considered himself 'as
antitheatrical the way Jasper Johns is sometimes called antitheatrical',
John Cage responded emphatically:

> No. I love the theater. In fact, I used to think when we were so close
> together – Earle Brown, Morton Feldman, Christian Wolff, David
> Tudor, myself [in the early and mid-1950s] – I used to think that the
> thing that distinguished my work from theirs was that mine was
> theatrical. I didn't think of Morty's work as being theatrical. It
> seemed to me to be more, oh, you might say, lyrical...And
> Christian's work seemed to me more musical...whereas I seemed to
> be involved in theater. What could be more theatrical than the
> silent pieces – somebody comes on the stage and does absolutely
> nothing.[2]

Yet the same Cage repeatedly insisted that, when it came to the real
theatre, he could 'count on one hand the plays I have seen that have
truly interested me or involved me' (*Conversing*, p.105). As he explained
it to Richard Kostelanetz:

> when I bought a ticket, walked in, and saw this marvelous curtain go
> up with the possibility of something happening behind it, and then
> nothing happening...the theater was a great disappointment to

133

anybody interested in the arts. I can count on one hand the perform-
ances that struck me as being interesting in my life. They were
Much Ado About Nothing, when I was in college; it was done by the
Stratford-upon-Avon players. Nazimova in *Ghosts* by Ibsen, Laurette
Taylor in *Glass Menagerie*. The Habima Theater's *Oedipus Rex* in 1950
or thereabouts [Pause]. I run out.[3]

These theatre epiphanies are obviously responses to individual memorable
performances rather than reasoned appraisals of dramaturgy or
dramatic theory. It is the mimetic contract of most Western drama that
seems to bother Cage. Even theatre in the round, so seemingly innovative,
irritates him: '[it] never seemed to me to be any real change from the
proscenium, because it again focused people's attention and the only
thing that changed was that some people were seeing one side of the
thing and the other people the other side... More pertinent to our daily
experience is a theater in which we ourselves are in the round'
(*Conversing*, p.103).

But in that case, what does Cage mean by his appraisal of his own
work as inherently 'theatrical'? Among his incredibly varied productions – productions in many media and genres – there is only one work
that can be strictly called a 'play' in the usual sense, and even here the
voice of the narrator all but overwhelms the 'speaking' characters. The
work in question is *James Joyce, Marcel Duchamp, Erik Satie: An Alphabet*,
which was first produced as a *Hörspiel* in July 1982 in Cologne on the
WDR (*Westdeutscher Rundfunk*) programme *Studio Akustische Kunst. An
Alphabet* had its stage première in February 1987, again in Cologne: the
actors included Dick Higgins, Gerhard Rühm and Cage himself playing
Joyce. The performers sat on the stage in a semicircle before their music
stands and read their texts. Klaus Schöning reports that 'The light of the
stage would cause the event to be imagined as if in a dream, which went
well with the origin of this 'spirit' play, which Cage had written in a
state between sleep and wakefulness. The play began in the dark; it grew
gradually brighter up to the middle and then faded slowly back into
darkness – **NightCageDay**.[4] In 1990, the play was performed at the
Whitney Museum of American Art in New York, as part of the second
Acustica International festival. In this performance, which has been
recorded by Wergo (see note 4 above), Klaus Reichert plays the
narrator; Alvin Curran, Satie; Charles Dodge, Duchamp; and Cage
himself again plays Joyce. There are cameo appearance from Jackson
MacLow as Brigham Young, Jerome Rothenberg as Robert Rauschenberg,
with Dick Higgins as Buckminster Fuller, and Mimi Johnson as

Rose Sélavy. And more recently (2001–2) the 'play' has toured the United States and Europe, as part of the repertoire of the Merce Cunningham Dance Company, with Cunningham himself playing the part of Satie.

But what does 'playing a part' mean in *An Alphabet*, given the work's total absence of characterization in the usual sense? In his Introduction, which is reprinted along with the text itself in *X: Writings '79–82*, Cage refers to the play as a 'lecture' or 'fantasy'. 'Alphabet', he admits, is a misnomer since the names of his three protagonists – James Joyce, Marcel Duchamp, Erik Satie – as well as the play's minor characters generate the text's structure, not alphabetically, but as follows:

> To outline the entire text by means of chance operations was not difficult. There were twenty-six different possibilities: the three ghosts alone, each in combination with one to four different beings, the ghosts in pairs with one to three different beings, all three with one or two. I used the twenty-six letters of the alphabet and chance operations to locate facing pages of an unabridged dictionary upon which I found the nonsentient beings, which are the stage properties of the various scenes (I through XXXVII) that follow. For the sentient beings, the other actors, I also used the alphabet, but only rarely as a means of finding a person I didn't know in an encyclopaedia. Mostly the other actors are people with whose work I've also become involved, sometimes as deeply as with Joyce, Duchamp, and Satie.[5]

This, like many of Cage's 'factual' accounts of his modes of operation is more pataphysical than logical: one thinks of Duchamp's arithmetic in the *Large Glass* and Satie's *Furniture Music*. The fact is that there is no neat succession of ghosts alone, in combination with one to four others or in pairs, and the 'non-sentient' beings – curtains, radio, Vichy water, gas and so on – seem to be chosen quite arbitrarily, as are the cited individuals, who range from Brigham Young to Buckminster Fuller to Heidegger.

The structuring principle is the familiar Cagean mesostic, a term the artist has frequently defined as a vertical acrostic – an acrostic, that is, in which the capitalized letters of a given name, run down the centre of the text. In a 100 per cent mesostic on the name JAMES JOYCE, for example, neither the J nor the A can appear in the 'wing' words and phrases between the J and the A, and so on. In a 50 per cent mesostic, which is what we have here, only the second letter, in this case **A**, cannot appear between the two. For example (*X: Writings*, p.56):

> Jump
> alternately fOrth and back and forth
> verY slowly
> in time with the Curtain's
> phrasEology

Here the **O** but not the **Y** of the name 'JOYCE', is allowed to appear between **O** and **Y** of lines 2–3: witness 'forth'.

The three names generate sets of five-line (J-A-M-E-S J-O-Y-C-E), four-line (E-R-I-K S-A-T-I-E) and six/seven line (M-A-R-C-E-L D-U-C-H-A-M-P) stanzas, with a few couplets (for two of the first or last names) used for variation. But ingenious as the resulting patterns are, mesostics are, of course, designed for the eye rather than the ear: when the piece is spoken, whether by one reader or by a set of actors, one doesn't hear the mesostic string although there may be an unusually high incidence of prominent **J** and **K** sounds. Then, too, *An Alphabet* differs from most of Cage's mesostic texts in that it isn't a 'writing through', as in the case of the earlier 'writings through' *Finnegans Wake*, where chance operations generate mesostics like the following:[6]

> i rimimirim Jute
> one eyegonblAck
> ghinees hies good for you Mutt
> how woodEn i not know
> old grilSy

> Just
> hOw
> bY a riverpool
> Clompturf
> rEx

The brilliant onomatopoeia ('rimimirim', 'Clompturf'), phonetic spelling ('ghinees is' = 'Guinness is'), grammatical scrambling, compounding and fragmentation that results when Cage relies on a source text like *Finnegans Wake* is obviously unavailable to the creator of *An Alphabet*, where the typical mesostic on, say, 'E-R-I-K S-A-T-I-E' is formed from a set of normal sentences, as in:

wE
heaR
over a radIo
a conversation sticKing

o two wordS
fifty-five And
fifTy-four
It is
An argumEnt

(X: Writings, p.58)

When these stanzas are heard, the mesostic string is all but inaudible. Indeed, from the point of view of performance, the strength of *An Alphabet* comes less from the mesostics themselves than from the contrast between their flat language and the inserted citations (ten in all) from Satie (5), Duchamp (3) and Joyce (2). These are spoken, or rather read and recited, by the 'characters' themselves. Consider the following mesostic, with its slightly forced, slightly cute, conjunction of ghosts:

Now and then niJinsky's ghost
Appears
Bringing a telegraM
To joycE
From marShall mcluhan

(X: Writings, p.57)

This 'J-A-M-E-S' stanza is juxtaposed to a passage from Book 1, Chapter 6 of *Finnegans Wake,* in which Anna Livia-Iseult-Stella speaks seductive sweet nothings to her lover:

Do you like that, *silenzioso?* Are you enjoying, this same little me, my life, my love? What do you like my whisping? Is it not divinely deluscious? But in't it bafforyou? *Misi, misi!* Tell me till my thrillme comes! I will not break the seal. I am enjoying it still, I swear I am! Why do you preer its in these dark nets, if why may ask, my sweetykins? Sh sh! Longears is flying. No, sweetissest, why would that ennoy me? But don't! You want to be slap well slapped for that. Your delighted lips, love, be careful! Mind my duvetyne dress above all! It's golden silvy, the newest sextons with princess effect.[7]

On the Wergo CD, Cage, acting the part of Joyce, reads these lines, with their elaborate punning, compounding and phonemic play, to thrilling effect. It is an excitement, we must recognize, that has less to do with Joyce impersonation as such than with the layering that occurs when one brilliantly modulated and trained voice performs the words of a kindred artist, the combination producing 'theatre' in the purest sense. But it is only in these passages that Cage's Joyce comes alive; for the most part, the narrator's account produces gently droll effects like the following:

> Joyce
> is At work
> in a roMan bank
> mErce Cunningham
> comeS in to cash a traveler's check

> Just sign
> Giambattista vicO's name
> instead of Your own
> and I'll give you Control
> of a rEvolving fund

(*X: Writings*, p.67)

Here the linkage between Cunningham and Joyce via Vico, whose cyclical philosophy governs the *Wake*, provides the joke on 'rEvolving fund'. And similar transitions are made between Duchamp's pataphysical writing in *Salt Seller* and the narrator's account of Marcel, or again between Satie's writings on furniture music and Cage's stories about the composer's visit to Nancarrow in Mexico City. The three 'ghosts', their words sometimes in union or dialogue with other ghosts like that of Rauschenberg, also speak within the mesostics themselves. Then, too, their words are heard against the backdrop of scraps of sound fluttering around the auditorium.

As such, Cage's *Alphabet* can hardly be called theatrical. When the play was performed at the Edinburgh Festival in 2001, the *Guardian* reviewer, Elisabeth Mahoney, remarked: 'Cage's fantastical alphabet of artists who have changed the way we think and see is stylish, assured and beautifully simple, for all the lofty ideas it contains. The play's limitations are those of all ground-breaking modernism – without narrative, conventional characters, any sense of conclusion, it is hard to feel any emotional engagement.'[8] And the Berkeley performance of 2002 evoked similar response. In *Critical Dance*, Mary Ellen Hunt complained of the piece's 'static and at times confusing direction', with its 'bewildering barrage of stimuli for the ears and hardly anything for the eye'. And, having praised the role of the narrator, she continued shrewdly:

> Had this been an interactive installation in which one could wander in and out along with the Narrator and hear various monologues as you passed by, it might have been more successful, but with the proscenium separating us and them, and with everybody sitting practically immobile, there was an uneasy feeling of stagnation. With all the discussion of Buckminster Fuller's work, the configuration began to look rather like an unstable carbon – 12 atom with twelve staid protons and neutrons and one crazed electron.[9]

The proscenium separating us and them: Cage himself was quite aware of the problem he had created. Having conceived of *Alphabet* as a *play*, with the speech-making and dialogue a drama entails, he resorted to techniques he had long ago rejected because they did not allow for what he considered the necessary 'unimpededness and interpenetration'. 'Unimpededness,' as he put it in 'Composition as Process' (1958), 'is seeing that in all of space each thing and each human being is at the center and furthermore that each one being penetrated by every other one no matter what the time or what the space' (*Silence* p.46). And in the *Musicircus* he first organized in 1970, 'Interpenetration', so Cage told Daniel Charles, 'must appear *through* non-obstruction', through 'flexibility of relationships'.[10]

Given this trust in art as modelled on 'Nature in her manner of operation',[11] Cage soon came to see that *Alphabet* had a problem. 'All those scenes', he told Richard Kostelanetz referring to the 37 sections of the play 'have beginnings and ends. That's what annoys me.'[12] What Cage means here, I think, is that his conversations between individual artist-ghosts, embedded as they are in narrative, fall too easily into separate closural units. At the same time, the characters blur, all of them subsumed in the person of the narrator, whose voice is the only one to have presence and palpability. But then 'theatre', as Cage usually understood it, could not be 'drama' in the traditional sense; rather, it demanded what he had called, with reference to the *Roaratorio*, written just a few years before the *Alphabet*, a 'circus situation', a 'plurality of centers'.[13]

'A fugue', Cage explains to Klaus Schöning with reference to the *Roaratorio*, 'is a...complicated genre; but it can be broken up by a single sound, say from a fire engine. Paraphrase: *Roaratorio* is a more complicated genre; it cannot be broken up by a single sound, say from a fire engine' (Schöning Introduction to *Roaratorio*, p.19). Cage's creation of a mesostic sound field, which I have described in *Radical Artifice*,[14] is a complex orchestration of music (Irish jig, folk song), the human voice (laughing, crying, singing, shouting or whispering), the sounds of nature (waterfall, thunderclap, frog croaking, cow mooing) and occasional man-made sound (church bell, gong, shotgun). Individual place names and sound references cited in *Finnegans Wake* were chosen and recorded on multitrack tapes by a complex set of mathematical rules, and then superimposed on one another to create this Irish 'circus'.

The resulting soundscape is, as William Brooks has noted, 'pastoral, unsullied, spacious'. Technological and mechanical sources were few and there is no electronically processed sound. 'It is a soundscape for Thoreau, for Joyce, for Charles Ives: unreal, dearly loved, joyfully affirmed, but illuminated by the certainty of loss, the recognition that this place cannot be, never was, before us.'[15] The paradox, in other words, that a piece so formally generated, what with the precise transfer of a 626-page grid (the text of *Finnegans Wake*) on to a 60-minute tape segment – a piece written entirely in mesostics on the name **JAMES JOYCE**, could come out sounding like the Irish culture with which it deals, a largely rural culture, whose 'tumbles a'buckets [come] clattering down', to the tune of 'fargobawlers' and 'megaphoggs'. The figure opposite is a sample.

Note that here no two line lengths are the same: they range from three letters ('hEr) to 47: 'she swore on croststYx nyne wyndabouts she's be.' The 'stanzas' are thus enormously variable, as is the design made by the punctuation, which Joyce has moved from its place in the text itself to the page that surrounds it. Note, for example, the inverted question mark preceding 'when Maids' from p.202 of the *Wake*. Then, too, sound and word repetition are highly prominent, the *Wake* providing countless possibilities for wordplay and phonetic spelling. Thus the Js of **JAMES JOYCE** include *Jigs, jimjams, ijypt* [Egypt], *Jade, Jutty, Jub, Jude's, ubanJees*.

At the same time – and this is *Roaratorio's* distinction – the sounds so carefully chosen and layered never coalesce; they retain their individual identities. And it is the spoken/written words themselves that are the actors in this new Cagean theatre. 'Theatre', as Cage defined it for Michael Kirby and Richard Schechner in 1965, 'is something that engages both the eye and the ear. The two public senses are seeing and hearing; the senses of taste, touch, and odor are more proper to intimate, nonpublic situations. The reason I want to make my definition of

194   black mass of Jigs and jimjams haunted by
innOcence
Yield our spiritus to the wind
pole the spaniel paCk
and thEir quarry

198   iJypt
sAw
lord saloMon
hEr
bullS they were ruhring surfed with spree

200   in a period gown of changeable Jade
that wOuld robe the wood
off her nose *vuggYbarney*
hello duCky
plEase don't die

202   tapting a flank and tipting a Jutty
pAlling in and pietaring out
when Maids
wEre in arc
or when three Stood hosting

204   and me to do the greasy Jub
verOnica's wipers
theY've moist
Crampton lawn
baptistE me father for she has sinned

205   or Jude's hotel
from nAnnywater
to the lootin quarter you found his ikoM
tipsidE down
cornerboyS cammocking his guy

       the peihos piped und ubanJees twanged
with Oddfellow's triple tiara
206   she swore on croststYx nyne wyndabouts she's be
quiCk and
maguE

Figure 1 John Cage, *Roaratorio: An Irish Circus on Finnegans Wake*, ed. Klaus Schöning (Munich: Athenäum, 1985), p.46

theater that simple is so one could view everyday life as theater.' And again, 'If you're in a room and a record is playing and the window is open and there's some breeze and a curtain blowing, that's sufficient, it seems to me, to produce a theatrical experience. When you're lying down and listening, you're having an intimate, interiorly realized theater which I would – if I were going to exclude anything – exclude from my definition of theatre as a public occasion' (*Conversing*, p.101).

Something to see, something to hear, and a public occasion: by Aristotelian standards, this may be a pretty lame definition of theatre: *opsis* (spectacle) is elevated above *mythos, ethos* and *dianoia; melopoeia* over *logos* and *lexis* (style). And yet the notion of theatre as a public seeing and hearing ('an occasion involving any number of people, but not just one' – *Conversing*, p.101), makes good sense if our touchstone is Eastern rather than Western theatre. The clash of voices, languages and sound registers, juxtaposed to the text's visual performance, which foregrounds lines like 'hello duCky', where the capital C separates the two syllables of the words, producing a buried *du* (you) and a **ky** that both puns on 'key' and connotes place-name endings like 'Kentuc**ky**'.

Perhaps the *Roaratorio* is, as Cage suggests, most usefully understood as theatre. Certainly, it is not lyric: the narrator's voice refuses any personal disclosure, reciting, as he does, someone else's words. Again, the piece is not opera for there is not the slightest plot, not oratorio, for it is neither linear nor closural. *Roaratorio* subordinates the temporal to the spatial, the lateral movement of Joyce's mesostics creating a field of action that avoids one-directional movement. As in Zen discourse, it is the reader who takes up alternate positions toward what is happening. Indeed, in such related works as *Lecture on the Weather* (1976), the audience *becomes* the protagonist, in this case huddling together when a thunderstorm takes place on the sound track, or drifting apart into a set of monads in the concert hall when birdsong introduces a new dawn, even as the 'real' actors are reading from Thoreau's *Essay on Civil Disobedience*.[16]

But perhaps Cage's most successful theatrical mode is not, strictly speaking, a performance at all, but a genre he more or less invented – namely the 'italic' or semi-found text. I am referring to the many public lectures and articles Cage devoted to his various artist friends over the years. *James Joyce, Marcel Duchamp, Erik Satie: An Alphabet* is a variant on this form, but Cage's more usual mode is a lecture in which the poet holds a covert dialogue with his artist-subject by putting that subject's cited words in italics and pasting them into what looks like a seamless third-person account of his work. A brilliant example is 'Mosaic' (1966), in which Cage takes on his mentor Arnold Schoenberg, shrewdly evaluating the Viennese composer's brilliance and tenacity along with his prejudices and pet peeves.[17] But perhaps the most poignant italic text Cage wrote is the 1964 lecture 'Jasper Johns: Stories and Ideas', published with a headnote in *A Year from Monday*.[18]

In the headnote, Cage admits that he had a hard time inventing a text that 'would relate somehow to the canvases and personality of the painter. The absence of unpainted space in most of his work and, what seemed to me, an enigmatic aura of the personality produced a problem, one which I was determined to solve and which for five months occupied and fascinated me' (*A Year from Monday*, p.73). This time, accordingly, Cage did not use 'chance operations with respect to type faces, size of type, superimpositions of type, collage of texts previously written about Johns by other critics', because these would have violated Johns's notion that, in Gertrude Stein's words, 'each thing is as important as every other thing'. Rather, as Cage explains in his headnote to 'Rhythm Etc.', he used the technique that generated *Cartridge Music*: a pencil is placed on an overlay of transparent sheets on ordinary sheets bearing biomorphic forms, the outlines providing directions for the position of specific sentences on a given page (*A Year from Monday*, p.120). And to thicken the plot, quotations from Johns's own writings, placed in italics, are juxtaposed to snatches of remembered comments, made in conversation with Cage. These appear in regular type. Further: paragraph signs evidently result from chance operations, but the sign doesn't necessarily produce a new paragraph and hence remains mysterious and equivocal.

We thus have four perspectives: (1) 'normal' third-person narrative produced by Cage; (2) third-person narrative that represents Johns's own narrative, that is, *oratio obliqua*; (3) Johns's own words, rendered directly; and (4) fragments from Johns's writings. Sometimes these four angles are represented separately:

1. It does not enter his mind that he lives alone in the world. There are in fact all the others. I have seen him entering a room, head aloft, striding with determination, an extraordinary presence inappropriate to the circumstance: an ordinary dinner engagement in an upstairs restaurant. There were chairs and tables, not much room, and though he seemed to be somewhere else in a space utterly free of obstructions he bumped into nothing. (p.76)
2. His earliest memories concern living with his grandparents in Allendale, South Carolina. Later, in the same town, he lived with an aunt and uncle who had twins, a brother and sister. Then he went back to live with his grandparents. After the third grade in school he went to Columbia, which seemed like a big city, to live with his mother and stepfather. A year later, school finished, he went to a community on a lake called The Corner to stay with his Aunt

Gladys. He thought it was for the summer but he stayed there for six years studying with his aunt who taught all the grades in one room, a school called Climax. (p.78)

3. Why, he asks, was she won over? Why does the information that someone has done something affect the judgment of another? Why cannot someone who is looking at something do his own work of looking? Why is language necessary when art so to speak already has it in it? 'Any fool can tell that's a broom.' (p.75)

4. Whenever the telephone rings, asleep or awake, he never hesitates to answer. *An object that tells of the loss, destruction, disappearance of objects. Does not speak of itself. Tells of others. Will it include them? Deluge.* (p.75)

In the third case above, the discourse modulates from straight narrative (1) to Johns's actual words even though only the final sentence is a direct quotation. The difference is perhaps between habitual statement and a particular, memorable one. And in the fourth example, the third-person account frames the quoted words, which are extracted from a comment Johns made in an art interview. But the situation is complicated when the text moves back and forth, without warning, between all four of the above points of view:

Does he live in the same terror and confusion that we do? *The air must move in as well as out – no sadness, just disaster.* I remember the deadline they had: to put up a display, not in windows on a street but upstairs in a building for a company that was involved in sales and promotion. Needing some printing done they gave me the job to do it. Struggling with pens and India ink, arriving at nothing but failure, I gradually became hysterical. Johns rose to the occasion. Though he already had too much to do, he went to a store, found some mechanical device for facilitating lettering, used it successfully, did all the other necessary things connected with the work and in addition returned to me my personal dignity. Where had I put it? Where did he find it? That his work is beautiful is only one of its aspects. It is, as it were, not interior to it that it is seductive. We catch ourselves looking in another direction for fear of becoming jealous, closing our eyes for fear our walls will seem to be empty. Skulduggery.

(Cage, *A Year from Monday*, p.80)

The first sentence above is Cage's own question. The 'answer' comes indirectly in Johns's own remark about a painting, evidently one of the dark paintings of the *Watchman* period. *'The air must move in as well as out – no sadness, just disaster'* has a Buddhist ring that must have appealed to Cage: one accepts the 'disaster' of one's situation without sentimentalizing it ('no sadness'). But the next sentence, 'I remember the deadline...'. doesn't continue Cage's train of thought; rather, it shifts to Johns's own discourse, his memory of a particularly unpleasant commission in his days as window-display artist. But the embedding of this passage, culminating in Johns's memory that 'I gradually became hysterical' into the larger narrative, creates a curiously surrealist effect. It is, after all, Cage who speaks these words in the performance of 'Jasper Johns: Stories and Ideas,' without giving a clear indication that the words are not his own. We thus hear a calm, modulated voice telling us 'I gradually became hysterical', and then shift quickly to the third person, 'Johns rose to the occasion.'

But now an even odder shift occurs. In another example of *oratio obliqua*, the narrator records Johns's trip to the store to buy supplies to make the lettering. In the middle of the sentence, the pronoun shifts from 'He' to 'me': 'and in addition returned to me my personal dignity'. The question 'Where had I put it?' is thus indeterminate. Is this part of Johns's narrative or Cage's response? What is the 'it'? The passage ends, in any case, with Cage's response to the visceral appeal of Johns's work, and his generalization: 'We catch ourselves looking in another direction for fear of becoming jealous.' It is all a form of 'Skulduggery', as the italicized aesthetic statement: *'Focus. Include one's looking...'* confirms. In context, *'do what I do, do what I say'*, brings Cage and Johns together in an epiphany as to the nature of aesthetic experience.

And in a larger sense, this is what the Jasper Johns piece accomplishes. What seems at first glance a casual set of comments prompted by Cage's study of Johns's art is a curiously dramatic composition in which the two artists gradually become one. The stage directions of the opening, 'On the porch at Edisto. Henry's records filling the air with rock 'n' Roll' (p.73) – a moment where Cage and Johns are still two distinct persons ('I said I couldn't understand what the singer was saying. Johns [laughing]: "That's because you don't listen" ') – gradually gives way to the witty and moving conclusion:

> Even though in those Edisto woods you think you didn't get a tick or ticks, you probably did. The best thing to do is back at the house to take off your clothes, shaking them carefully over the bathtub. Then make a conscientious self-examination with a mirror if necessary. It would be silly too to stay out of the woods simply because the ticks

are in them. Think of the mushrooms (Caesar's among them!) that would have been missed. Ticks removed, fresh clothes put on, something to drink, something to eat, you revive. There's scrabble and now chess to play and the chance to look at TV. *A Dead Man. Take a skull. Cover it with paint. Rub it against canvas. Skull against canvas.*

(Cage, *A Year from Monday*, p.84)

It is Johns who knows the Edisto, South Carolina woods where his house is located and can dispense advice about getting rid of ticks. But Cage is the one who would have hated 'to stay out of the woods simply because the ticks are in them. Think of the mushrooms...that would have been missed.' Both men, in any case, take a pragmatic position to the day's activities, looking forward to 'something to drink, something to eat...scrabble and now chess to play and the chance to look at TV'. It all seems very *gemütlich*. But then Cage concludes with a passage from Johns's notebook, next to a sketch for the painting *In Memory of My Feelings: Frank O'Hara*, Johns's elegy for the marvelous poet-friend who died in 1966 at the age of 40. And so the text ends on a death note, 'skull against canvas', suggesting that the acceptance of death is what makes the wonderfully various life described throughout the piece meaningful.

It is a moment of high theatre. Unlike *Alphabet*, where the 'ghosts' of Duchamp and Satie remain inert *dramatis personae*, their conversations never quite creating a dramatic conflict situation, in the more modest italic lecture 'Jasper Johns: Stories and Ideas', the separate voices of Cage and Johns are carefully orchestrated so that, by the end of the piece, the audience witnesses a particular poignant moment in art-making: the double recognition, by 'Cage' and 'Johns' of art's 'rubbing' a skull against canvas, of art's inseparability, in other words, from death and hence life.

Something to see, something to hear and a public occasion: Cage's definition of the *theatrical* is curiously post-modern in that, in a text like 'Jasper Johns', as in *Roaratorio*, speaking and hearing don't coincide. When hearing Cage read the piece, the italic sections don't stand out as separate. Indeed, unless one has more or less memorized Johns's sketchbooks and interviews, one cannot be sure that the sentences and phrases in question *are* citations. When the work is read on the page, on the other hand, the shift in voices, which Cage can accomplish orally, is not marked. The prescription should thus be: 'Something to hear *or* something to see.' The public occasion, moreover, can just as well be private, in keeping with Jasper Johns's adage (or is it Cage's?), 'The situation must be Yes-and-No not either-or. *Avoid a polar situation*' (p.79). What, then, about the knotty 'character' issue? The disjunction between speaking and hearing not only undercuts the audience's ability to distinguish between the senses but also its notion of what a person, as seen on stage, really is. For Cage – and for him this is a comic, not at all a tragic, fact of post-modern existence – individuals – say, the characters in an Ibsen or Chekhov play – are no longer at centre stage. Rather, in works like *Roaratorio* and *Jasper Johns*, identity quite literally merges as if to carry to its logical extreme Samuel Beckett's question in *The Unnamable* 'What matter who's speaking?' As Cage liked to put it, citing *Finnegans Wake*, 'Here Comes Everybody.'

Notes

1. John Cage, *Silence* (1961; Middletown, CT: 1973), p.12.
2. David Shapiro, 'On Collaboration in Art', *Res*, 10 (1985); reprinted in Richard Kostelanetz, ed., *Conversing with Cage* (New York: Limelight, 1988), p.105. Subsequently cited as *Conversing*.
3. Richard Kostelanetz, 'Conversation with John Cage' (1970), in Kostelanetz, ed., *John Cage: An Anthology* (New York: Da Capo, 1991), p.24.
4. Klaus Schöning, liner notes, *James Joyce, Marcel Duchamp, Erik Satie: An Alphabet*, John Cage Trust, New York, Wergo 6310 (Mainz: Schott Music & Media, 2003), pp.26–7.
5. John Cage, 'James Joyce, Marcel Duchamp, Erik Satie: An Alphabet', in Cage, *X:Writings '79–82* (Middletown, CT: Wesleyan University Press, 1983), pp.53–101. Subsequently cited in the text as *X: Writings*.
6. Cage, 'Writing for the Fourth Time Through Finnegans Wake', *X: Writings*, p.4.
7. Cage, *X: Writings*, p.57. See James Joyce, *Finnegans Wake* (1939; New York: Viking Press, 1976), pp.147–8.
8. Elisabeth Mahoney, review of 'An Alphabet', Royal Lyceum Theatre, Edinburgh, 1 September 2001.
9. Mary Ellen Hunt, 'James Joyce, Marcel Duchamp, Erik Satie: An Alphabet', *Critical Dance.com*, 5 February 2002.
10. John Cage, *For the Birds: In Conversation with Daniel Charles* (Boston, MA, and London: Marion Boyars, 1981), p.52.
11. John Cage, *A Year from Monday: New Lectures and Writings* (Middletown, CT: Wesleyan University Press, 1967), p.31.
12. Cited by Richard Kostelanetz in 'John Cage as a Hörspielmacher' (1989), in Kostelanetz ed., *Writings about John Cage* (Ann Arbor: University of Michigan, 1993), pp.213–21: see p.218.
13. John Cage, *Roaratorio: An Irish Circus on Finnegans Wake*, ed. Klaus Schöning (Munich: Athenäum, 1985), p.107.
14. Marjorie Perloff, *Radical Artifice: Writing Poetry in the Age of Media* (Chicago: University of Chicago Press, 1991), pp.149–61.

15. William Brooks, '*Roaratorio* Appraisiated' (1983), in Kostelanetz, *Writings about John Cage*, pp.223–4.
16. I discuss this piece at length in *Radical Artifice*, pp.21–8.
17. See my 'The Portrait of the Artist as Collage-Text: Pound's *Gaudier-Brzeska* and the 'Italic' Texts of John Cage', in Marjorie Perloff, *The Dance of the Intellect* (1985; Evanston, IL: Northwestern University Press, 1995), pp.33–73.
18. John Cage, 'Jasper Johns: Stories and Ideas', *A Year from Monday*, 73–84.

9
Mallarmé, Maeterlinck and the Symbolist *Via Negativa* of Theatre

Patrick McGuinness

Aussi quand le soir n'affiche rien, incontestablement, qui vaille d'aller de pas allègre se jeter en les mâchoires du monstre et par ce jeu perdre tout droit à le narguer, soi le seul ridicule! n'y a-t-il pas occasion même de proférer quelques mots de coin du feu; vu que si le vieux secret d'ardeurs et splendeurs qui s'y tord, sous notre fixité, évoque, par la forme éclairée de l'âtre, l'obsession d'un théâtre encore réduit et minuscule au lointain, c'est ici gala intime.[1]

(Thus when the evening promises nothing, incontestably, that makes it worth one's while to hurry to hurl oneself into the jaws of the monster and in so doing lose all right to make fun of it – oneself the only ridiculous one! – is there not an opportunity even to proffer a few words at the fireside, given that if the old secret of flames and splendour that twists therein evokes, through the lit form of the hearth [*âtre*], the obsession with a theatre [*théâtre*] still reduced and tiny in the far distance, it is here the intimate gala.)

In this prose paragraph by Mallarmé (hardly less dense or allusive than his poetry), we find compressed many of the paradoxes of the Symbolist movement's engagement with theatre. The verbal play from *âtre* to *théâtre* is at the hub of the matter: a rejection of theatre that leads to – that is perhaps even the *precondition of* – a triumphant reclaiming of the theatrical. Mallarmé, theatre critic for the *Revue indépendante*, is ostensibly giving his reasons for not going to the theatre – he after all told its editor, Edouard Dujardin, that he would only agree to the job provided going to the theatre was not a condition for reviewing the plays.

149

'Sometimes', Mallarmé wrote, 'the programme alone is enough' for the theatre critic. Yet this apparent retreat from theatre is transformed, through resourceful verbal play, into an audacious advance towards it. At the risk of pre-empting our conclusion, we could say that, so far as the Symbolist avant-garde is concerned, the further one goes from theatre, the closer one gets; or, more precisely, the more uncompromisingly one dismisses theatre, the more triumphantly one can claim it back.

There are other energies at work in this passage that bear sharply on the theatrical: the tension between public and private spaces as the domestic fireside is recuperated into a great rite of primal energy, with the hearth suddenly offering, in miniature, a kind of elemental drama of fire. There is also the evocation of a theatre, 'faraway' both in place and in time, that resumes, in its hesitation between past and future, the twin aspirations of theatrical avant-gardes in general: the idealization of the past (Greek tragedy, Elizabethan drama, the Noh) and a faith (rhetorical, at any rate) in the theatre of the future. Finally, there is the startling mix of subtlety and overstatement in the image of the stage as the 'jaws of the monster', the beast that devours poetry and spits out...mere words. As Mallarmé wrote earlier in the same passage, theatre had the potential to be the *'ouverture de gueule de chimère'* (the gaping maw of dream). Such striking images of orality return theatre to the word, with the mouth as the ambiguous space of consumption and expulsion, but also of violence and danger.

Only a reader singularly unattuned to paradox would read Mallarmé's paragraph as a simple rejection of theatre. Mallarmé may be undermining the theatre, but in so doing he *affirms* the theatrical. It lurks everywhere, and the transformative power that theatre displays – but does not, Mallarmé asserts, *own* – lies all around us. That *âtre/théâtre* play suggests not just that theatricalilty lurks everywhere, but that it is embedded in the quotidian, that it lies at the heart of the everyday even as it distils and transforms it. The theatre is merely one – crude – means of locating and channelling that transformative power. Perhaps Mallarmé's *théâtre* is first and foremost a faculty of the mind, an imaginative opera-tion of which real theatre is only the brute outer manifestation. Certainly many critics are content to let it rest at that, omitting to consider the extent to which Mallarmé's ideas of reading and writing are themselves theatrically constituted. Briefly stated (this has been said elsewhere more fully[2]), reading and writing in Mallarmé articulate them-selves through theatrical models, models which originate in performance and provide the perfect means to express his ideas about the reader/writer relationship, about the poet and his medium, and about the special prestige he attaches to reading and interpretation. Mallarmé prizes the symbiotic relationship between the dramatic performance that aspires to the book, and the book that aspires to dramatic performance. The one without the other is not enough: performative reading feeds back into the reading of performance, each validating and consecrating the other. We could even argue that reading for Mallarmé only has worth if it is a sort of existential-interpretative performance of meaning, a dynamic spiritual enactment of the word in all its multiplicity and polyvalence. Poetry may be the supreme art, but it can only remain so by first absorbing and then embodying – rather than by rejecting – the theatrical.

I Symbolism and the 'rejection of theatre'

Of all the anti-theatrical literary movements, French symbolism seems the most avowedly extreme, yet it furnishes the best example of how a systematically thought out anti-theatrical position can produce constructive and innovative engagements with theatre. These engagements run not just to theory but across a range of practical dramatic issues, from acting and movement to lighting and set design. Although a few Symbolist productions were stilted affairs, more like poetry readings in an ambient décor than dramatic constructions, by far the majority were interestingly staged, innovatively designed and thoughtfully performed, with help not just from the poets and playwrights themselves but from artists and composers of the avant-garde. The irony is that this was all conducted against a rhetorical background of extreme anti-theatricality. Critics such as Dorothy Knowles and Jacques Robichez, in still unsuperseded studies, have discussed Symbolist theatre in theory and practice, and documented the performances and reception of their plays, while modern theoretical perspectives have been opened up by, notably, Frantisek Deak.[3]

Romanticism had already produced the *spectacle dans un fauteuil*, the 'armchair drama' to be read, just as, in England, Charles Lamb was to summarize these debates in his famous essay on Shakespeare. The Symbolists are different – they are obsessed with the minutiae of performance, and are often to be found advising on performance and staging, and taking an active part in productions of their own and each other's plays. The resemblance between Romantic and Symbolist attitudes to performance can be misleading. French symbolism is characterized, perhaps even constituted, by a symbiosis between textuality and performance that masquerades as conflict. The movement that more than any other espoused the idea of 'poésie pure' was, as we shall see, critically beholden to the theatrical. Let us first sketch out the lineaments of symbolism's anti-theatrical stance. There is Téodor de Wyzewa's claim, in the *Revue Wagnérienne*, that 'a play read will appear to delicate souls more alive than the same play performed on stage by living actors';[4] there is Mallarmé's assertion that '*maintenant le livre essaiera de suffire, pour entr'ouvrir la scène intérieure et en chuchoter les échos*' (henceforth the book will strive to suffice to open up the interior stage and whisper its echoes) (*OC*, p.328). Even Maurice Maeterlinck, the most successful Symbolist playwright and one of the seminal figures in modernist theatre, started out in 1890 with this unpromising opinion:

> performance of a great work using contingent and human elements is an antinomy. All great works are symbols, and the symbol can never bear the weight of the active presence of the human being.[5]

In another article, 'Menus propos: le Théâtre' (Small talk: On the theatre), Maeterlinck takes the anti-theatrical position a step further, contending that poetry and theatre are irreconcilable. Performance transgresses against the '*poème*' by transposing it back into that from which it had originally been lifted. It repollutes was has been purified:

> Performance produces in relation to the poem, more or less the same effect as would be produced if you extended a painting into ordinary life; if you carried its deep, silent, secretive characters into the midst of the glaciers, mountains, gardens and islands which they seem to inhabit, and then entered after them – an indefinable light would suddenly be extinguished...[6]

In one of the notebooks in which he would sketch his dramatic scenarios, Maeterlinck even went so far as to note down the following damning condemnation of theatre:

> All in all, theatre today is completely opposed to art, because it is the production of the artificial by means of nature itself, that is to say, the inverse of what it should be, like a statue made of flesh or fat.[7]

Theatre is an aberrant genre: performing a text, climbing into a painting, making a statue from flesh, all denote grotesque reversals of the artistic process. It would be hard to predict, from these declarations, that Maeterlinck would soon become one of the most successful dramatists of the late nineteenth and early twentieth centuries.

Another Symbolist, poet and playwright Pierre Quillard, in an important essay called 'De l'inutilité absolue de la mise-en-scène exacte' (1891) (On the absolute uselessness of exact staging), declared that 'the word creates scenery just as it creates everything else'. Alfred Jarry, perhaps the ultimate user of theatre against itself (and who dedicated *Ubu Roi* to Quillard), followed it up five years later with an essay entitled 'De l'inutilité du théâtre au théâtre' (On the uselessness of theatre in the theatre), deliberately raising the polemical stakes. Then Lugné-Poë, the great Symbolist actor-director published a response which endorsed Jarry and Quillard's ideas from – ironically enough – a performance perspective. Lugné-Poë in this and other texts described his desire to reproduce, so far as possible, 'the conditions of reading in the theatre', and advertised his disdain for what he called 'the whole material side known as theatre'.[8] And yet Lugné-Poë was an extraordinarily productive and successful actor-director, whose productions were galvanizing, radical and innovative – it was in the course of Lugné-Poë's production of a Maeterlinck play that members of the audience ran out of the theatre in terror, and it was his production of *Ubu Roi* that caused the near riot on its first night – the same performance attended by W. B. Yeats who was prompted to write: 'after us the Savage God'. It was, furthermore, in Lugné-Poë's troupe of actors that the young Artaud began his acting career, and Lugné-Poë who staged Maeterlinck's adaptation of John Ford's *'Tis Pity She's A Whore*, later to become a touchstone of Artaud's theatre of revolt.

These articles – Maeterlinck's, Quillard's, Jarry's – and the many like them that appeared at the time, are faithful to their origins in a fundamentally (fundamentalist, even) textual approach to theatre. It is not performance as such that they seek, but the staging of the Word ('le Verbe', often capitalized in Symbolist discourse with all the religious and ritualistic connotations). Villiers de l'Isle-Adam spoke for the generation of experimental dramatists that followed him when he wrote in *Axël* (quoting the nineteenth-century occultist Eliphas Lévi): 'any word, within the sphere of its action, creates what it expresses.' Alongside an elevation of the Word, there is the more straightforward phobia of materiality, a theme present throughout Symbolist poetry (its many images of virginity, whiteness, purity, tropes of the numinous, ineffable, elusive), allied to a terror of what Barthes called the '*lisibilité*' (readerliness) of theatre and the '*machine cybernétique*' of performance that threatens to swamp the verbal text under a tidal wave of signs and codes. Albert Mockel, a Symbolist writer, went so far as to argue for the removal of actors' names on posters and programmes, lest the semiotic overspill of their previous roles, their celebrity or even their names themselves, might interfere with the text's staging.[9] Maeterlinck for his part called the actors 'portants', bearers or carriers of the role, rather as semioticians of theatre such as Patrice Pavis might talk of the actor as '*porteur de signe*',[10] in what is surely a pre-emption of the vocabulary of semiotic theatre analysis.

Symbolist theatre was sufficiently self-aware to dramatize its own suspicion of theatre. Two of the most important poem-plays of the period, Mallarmé's 'Hérodiade' and Quillard's 'La fille aux mains coupées' are concerned with purity and virginity, with exactly this phobia of materiality which in poetry recoils from the body and in theatre recoils from the theatre. Both are poem-plays about virginal icy women refusing to succumb to the physical, written at a time when poetry was acutely engaged in debating whether or not to 'succumb' to stage performance. Mallarmé's Hérodiade keeps herself pure, in a great Mallarméan sexual/ textual *double entendre*, for '*le lit au pages de velin*' (the bed with vellum pages). The book is the true consummation of the dramatic encounter, while the eroticism, as so often in Mallarmé, is increased by the virginity, the almost ardent asexuality, of Hérodiade, the ultimate figure of negative perfection. She stands, we could say, for all the great plays that have defied or eluded performance. More viscerally, Quillard's protagonist prefers to have her hands severed than to be drawn by the sexual feeling she fears – hands, symbols not just of touch but of action. There is even the category of plays that take pride in their unperformability, the most prominent of which is Mallarmé's 'L'Après-midi d'un faune', described in tantalizingly perverse terms by its author as '*absolument scénique, non pas possible au théâtre mais exigeant le théâtre*' (absolutely scenic, not possible in the theatre yet demanding the theatre) (*OC*, p.1449). The essential theatricality of Mallarmé's play is measured, paradoxically, by its resistance to theatre. Just as Hérodiade's virginity is enhanced by the sexuality she both exudes and keeps at bay, so the play's purity is accentuated by the theatre it both conjures up and turns its back on.

The Symbolists' apparent rejection of theatre can be explained in part by the fact that they dramatized reading to such an extent that the theatrical was not so much expelled as gloriously sublimated. Barthes's great essay on Baudelaire's theatre suggests that the reason Baudelaire couldn't write plays was that he had such an acute sense of theatricality as lying outside the bounds of theatre.[11] In a sense that is true of

Symbolism, whose poetic and critical discourses were saturated with theatricality. They realized that theatricality, as a set of models and metaphors for intellectual action, adventure or conflict, had more to offer than any real theatre. Just as theatre itself in the nineteenth-century avant-garde is questioned and frequently undermined, so, by a sort of countervailing movement, the theatrical begins to take hold in the poetic, critical and analytical discourses of the time. One of the great theatrical models, and one that is sure to have influenced a generation of poets, is Hippolyte Taine's extraordinary extended model of the mind in his 1870 book *Sur l'Intelligence* (On Intelligence), in which the theatrical model provides an account not just of the intellect's light, but of the mind's unconscious processes in relation to it:

> We can therefore compare the human mind to a theatre of indefinite depth, whose limelight is very narrow, but whose stage grows wider and wider beyond the footlights. In front of these lights, there is only room for one actor at a time. He comes on stage, gesticulates for a moment, and then leaves; another appears, then another, and so on ... In the wings and far-off background is a multitude of obscure forms which a sudden summons sometimes brings onstage or even up in front of the footlights, and unknown evolutions incessantly take place in this teeming crowd of actors of all orders to produce the images which, one after another, parade before our eyes. What is this narrow limelight, and why is it that thought appears fully illuminated nowhere else?[12]

What need of the real theatre when theatre metaphors offer so much?

A related aspect is the sheer ubiquity of dramatic figures in nineteenth-century French poetry and prose. We could go so far as to say that the nineteenth century in France sees the increasing dramatization of the poet and his relations with his public, the growing reliance of poetic discourse upon models and metaphors drawn from the performing arts. This has not yet been traced or properly investigated, but a brief review here can set out the parameters of an area of study with much to tell. From Baudelaire's great prose poem 'Une mort héroïque' (a key text in nineteenth-century theatricality) to Laforgue's *fin-de-siècle pierrots*, by way of Mallarmé's 'Pitre chatié' and Théodore de Banville's acrobats ('Le sot du tremplin' for instance), images of performers and performance lie at the heart of French poetry. Through such images nineteenth-century poetry explores the role of the poet and addresses questions of readership and audience, as well as meditating on the nature of illusion and reality, self and mask, thought and action. A crude but efficient line can be drawn from the heroic poet-prophet figures of romanticism (the best example being Vigny's Moses in 'Moïse', interceding between God and man and preaching to a rapt audience at his feet) to the self-ironizing, isolated, often pathetic figures of Laforgue, Corbière and others towards the end of the nineteenth century. That move – a decline in stature perhaps but also a development in complexity – from prophet to *pierrot* tells a story about *fin-de-siècle* and modernist poetry that can only be expressed and understood through images of performance. There is also the romantic obsession taken up and re-emphasized by Mallarmé, whose Hamlet, poised between self and role, word and action, existence and obliteration, is *'lisant au livre de lui-même'* (reading the book of himself). Hamlet thus becomes what the poet has always wanted to be: text and performance, the outward enactment of the inner word. He is also perhaps the great hermaphrodite of art: the reader and writer of himself, actor and spectator of the interior life. In the figure of Hamlet poetry internalizes theatre and the twin obsessions of text and perform-ance, page and stage, become one.

In parallel to a sort of Symbolist recoil at the physicality of performance there develops a fascination with the seemingly limitless metaphorical possibilities offered to poetry by performance. The note, posited as a sort of stage direction, to Mallarmé's *Igitur* reads *'ce conte s'adresse à l'intelligence du lecteur qui mettra les choses en scène elle-même'* (this tale is addressed to the reader's intelligence, which will stage things on its own). The reading mind is envisaged as a stage, validating the written by reference to the performed. Mallarmé often presents solitary reading as unfolding like a play, staged in *'le théâtre que l'esprit porte'*, (the theatre carried within the mind) (*OC*, p.393). The inner theatre is the *'prototype du reste'*, a *'théâtre inhérent à l'esprit'* (*OC*, p.328), and that word 'protoype', in an age of invention and technological advance, is surely full of significance. The poet himself is akin to a director: *'le poète,...par l'écrit, ordonnateur de fête en chacun'* (the poet, through writing, the director of festivities in each of us) (*OC*, p.330). Reading for Mallarmé does not *replace* theatre by abolishing it but by providing its consummate achievement: *'un livre, dans notre main,...supplée à tous les théâtres, non par l'oubli qu'il en cause mais les rappelant impérieusement, au contraire'* (a book, in our hands, supplants all the theatres, not by consigning them to oblivion but, on the contrary, by imperiously recalling them) (*OC*, p.334). The book, for Mallarmé, beats theatre not because it rejects theatre but because it calls it back to mind, emphatically, absolutely. The motifs of text and performance in Mallarmé are powerfully brought out, and brought out as powerfully intertwined, in *'l'action restreinte'*: *'l'écrivain…doit s'instituer, au texte, le spirituel histrion'* (the writer…must insert himself, into the text, the spiritual actor) (*OC*, p.371). Poetry is at its highest pitch when conceived as performance (and indeed Mallarmé takes up, in this quotation, a notion we find in Edgar Allan Poe, the archetype of the absolute poet: the idea of the poet being the actor of his own consciousness as scripted in a poem). Performance, correspondingly, reaches its perfection when conceived as poetry. The greatest compliment Mallarmé pays to a piece of theatre is his claim that Maeterlinck *'inséra le théâtre au livre!'* (placed theatre inside the book), adding that ' *"Pelléas et Mélisande", sur une scène, exhale, de feuillets, le délice'* (*Pelleas and Melisande*, on stage, exhales the delight of the page) (*OC*, p.329).

Perhaps no other writer spends so much time thinking through and elevating to such prestigious status the metaphorical implications of a genre – theatre – whilst showing such poor regard for its actual manifestations. Mallarmé can be said to theatricalize the inner life, the life of the mind. We may now turn to a playwright who detheatricalizes the outer life.

II Maeterlinck and the detheatricaliztion of theatre

In Maeterlinck we find the Symbolist theatrical paradox embodied by a successful playwright who, for all his anti-theatrical beginnings, produced plays that were innovative and radical on the one hand, and popular and accessible on the other.[13] Maeterlinck is the only Symbolist playwright to have combined avant-garde success with widespread public popularity, and though best-known for *Pelléas et Mélisande*, it is his one-act dramas, *Intérieur* (Interior), *Les Aveugles* (The Blind) and *L'Intruse* (The Intruder) that appear today as seminal modernist plays. Recent publication of Maeterlinck's *Agendas* shows that he was writing scenarios for his early plays in the very same notebooks as he was sketching out his articles against dramatic performance, 'Un théâtre d'Androïdes' and 'Menus Propos: le Théâtre'.[14]

Maeterlinck starts, in 1889–90, by seeming to reject performance outright. By 1894, as he begins to enjoy real success on the stage (through the agency of Lugné-Poë, who directed and performed Maeterlinck's major early plays), he refines his views. By the time of his greatest avant-garde success, he is developing his seminal theory of the 'tragique quotidien', 'the tragic in everyday life'. This is allied to the radical theory of what Maeterlinck calls 'static theatre', an approach based around what we could call the 'de-theatricalization' of theatre. Briefly stated, this is characterized by the expulsion of event in favour of situation, and of instrumental dialogue in favour of 'second-degree dialogue'. Those elements which theatre had striven to ignore or downplay – waiting, inactivity, superfluous or underdetermined language, marginal or transitional spaces – become central to Maeterlinck's dramatic universe. The relationship between anti-theatrical theory, innovative play-writing and radical performance and staging practice is at the heart of the Symbolist theatrical avant-garde (as it is, later, in that of the *nouveau théâtre* in France). It is also best exemplified in the work of Maeterlinck.

Maeterlinck is a tricky figure to characterize in the sense that, at the same time as berating the concreteness and physicality of theatre, he makes great use of it. Many of his Symbolist colleagues thought his plays too concrete, too bruisingly involved with the physical dimension of theatre, to be truly Symbolist. For one thing, Maeterlinck demoted language and made too much use of stage effects, of things like lighting and sounds off, slamming doors and moving objects, which sat ill with a school of writers who sought to deny the physicality of theatre. Moreover, his characters do not express ideas through language, but transient, flickering states; there is plenty of Symbolist silence and suggestiveness, but it is the wrong sort: where the Symbolist inexpressible is beyond expression, complex and multivalent, Maeterlinck's is beneath expression, and has more to do with the inarticulacy of his characters than the elevation of their insights. In Maeterlinck's theatre, agency and expression are taken from language and its human user and transferred to the world of things: objects, sounds and off-stage space are prominent driving forces in his plays. He sought to replicate symbolist values – hiddenness, ambiguity, uncertainty – at the level of staging, set, props and lighting, by fully mobilizing the theatre's physical resources. In so doing, he showed himself ready not just to use but to *exploit* the very 'material side' of theatre that his fellow Symbolists disdained.

Maeterlinck's article 'Menus propos: le Théâtre' was published in September 1890 in *La Jeune Belgique*. Its original version was titled 'Un théâtre d'Androïdes'[15] – A Theatre of Androids – and both versions are symptomatic of the widespread vogue for marionette and puppet theatre of the period. Maeterlinck's initial objections to performance take the standard Symbolist line:

The stage is where masterpieces come to die, because performance of a masterpiece using accidental and human elements is an antinomy.

All great works are symbols, and no symbol can bear the active presence of the human being...The Greeks were not unaware of this, and their masks, which we no longer understand, were designed to attenuate the human presence and to free up the symbol.[16]

The actor, far from interceding, blocks out the role, and thus stands for the way performance in general blocks out or swallows up the text. Maeterlinck describes what he calls his *'instinctif malaise théâtrale'* (instinctive theatrical malaise) as due to this sense of theatre's imperfect doubleness, and in a passage of 'Un théâtre d'Androïdes' omitted from 'Menus propos' he had written: 'it is not yet art, but it is no longer an ordinary act of life.'[17] Theatre is not a genre in any pure sense, but a sort of imperfect transformation, frozen in mid-change. Theatre, we could say, is the art without an essence. What Maeterlinck understands, which arguably his fellow Symbolists do not, is that one must learn to work with rather than against it.

Maeterlinck therefore does not, contrary to expectation, reject perform-ance outright. Instead he asks the following question: 'If the poem rises to the level of the symbol performance must rise likewise, and might it not do so by becoming more abstract?'[18] This is a compromise, designed to pay lip-service to Symbolist anti-theatricality while safeguarding the prospect of a suitably innovative mode of performance. But compromises, too, can be radical, and Maeterlinck envisages a way out of the Symbolist *impasse*:

We should perhaps remove the human being from the stage altogether...Will the human being be replaced by a shadow, a reflection, a projection of symbolic forms? I do not know, but the removal of the human being seems to me a necessity. It is difficult to speculate about what collection of lifeless beings we should replace him with on stage, but it seems to me that the strange feelings we have when we visit wax museums, for instance, might long ago have enabled us to find the traces of a dead or innovative art. We would then have, on stage, beings without destinies, whose identity would no longer come to erase that of the hero. I also think that any form which has the appearance of life yet without being alive, can draw on extraordinarily powerful effects... it is possible, in these circumstances, that the soul of the poet or hero would no longer refuse to inhabit a creature without a jealous soul to forbid him entry.[19]

Having begun by rejecting performance, Maeterlinck finishes by envis-aging a new kind of theatre. But his principal contribution to theatre is rooted in another facet of his anti-theatrical beginnings: his theory of the 'tragique quotidien' and its attendant concepts: 'second-degree dialogue', 'static theatre' and the 'theatre of waiting'. His 1894 essay 'Le Tragique quotidien' begins:

> I have often thought that an old man sitting in his armchair, waiting simply beneath his lamp, listening beneath his consciousness to all the eternal laws that reign around his house, interpreting without understanding the silence of his doors and windows and the small voice of the light, submitting to the presence of his soul and his destiny, head slightly bent, unaware that all the powers of this world are active and watchful in his room like attentive servants, not knowing that the sun itself holds the little table he leans on over the abyss, and that there is not a single star in the sky, nor a single force of the soul which is indifferent to the movement of an eyelid closing or a thought rising, – I have come to believe that this immobile old man lives, in reality, a more human, more profound, and more common life than the lover who strangles his mistress, the commander who is victorious in battle, or "the husband who avenges his honour".[20]

These thoughts are not especially original. What makes them original is the way they are drawn into the theatre, and articulated in the language of the theatre. This is all the more unusual as, since they express a fundamentally still, silent and inward form of action, these ideas would seem at first sight largely unsuited to theatrical representation. As Artaud wrote, Maeterlinck's originality lay less in his ideas *qua* ideas, but in their application and exploration on the stage: 'One is not a great philosopher for having observed that the whole of life is a static drama in which are woven the occult encounters of the forces of destiny. Where Maeterlinck is truly great is where he analyses these encounters, when he reveals their form.'[21] Being original does not always entail making new discoveries, but in deploying them in new forms and in new spheres. What most needs to be expressed on stage, argues Maeterlinck, is what is outwardly invisible in life. If action is distraction, then language is a diversion, and Maeterlinck rejects 'contributive' dialogue in favour of what he calls *'dialogue "du second degré"'*,[22] a form of 'second-degree dialogue' freed from its plot-furthering role:

> It is only the words which seem at first hearing useless that really count in a play. It is in them that the soul of the play is hidden. Alongside the indispensable dialogue, there is almost always another dialogue which seems superfluous. Look closely, and you will see that

it is the only one that the soul really listens to, because it is only here that it is being spoken to.[23]

Maeterlinck refocuses theatre on three related planes: action to immobility, plot to situation and dialogue to silence (Maeterlinck writes of a semantics of silence as expressive as any of symbolism's most sophisticated constructs) and second-degree dialogue. 'Le Tragique quotidien', insofar as it is directly applicable to dramatic practice, argues for the elevation of theatre's intermittent parts into coherent, free-standing, dramatic 'wholes'. It is the construction of drama from those materials which are usually considered drama's accidents, what we might call the residues or by-products of conventional theatre. In a sense Maeterlinck puts to use, or recycles, the waste products of conventional drama: inactivity, silence, small talk. It also implies an attitude to stage space: the action seems always to unfold out of sight or off stage. Diegetic space presses in on the stage in a way that undermines the stage's very stability, as well as its claim to be the focus of action. In a sense this is the application to the spatial dimension (real and virtual) of symbolism's poetic obsessions with what is out of sight, intermittent, beyond reach.

A deeper analysis of Maeterlinck's theory and practice is not to our purpose here and has in any case been carried out elsewhere. What is surely significant, however, is that Maeterlinck's vision of theatre lies in the detheatricalization of theatre. 'I'm not sure it's true that static theatre is impossible', writes Maeterlinck, and here surely lies the most creative destruction of all: a theatre which abolishes the theatrical in order to *re-become* theatre. Maeterlinck's battle is not just with theatre, but with a theatricalized notion of existence, a version of human life that is beholden to the models of theatre for its validation. For Maeterlinck, theatre becomes, paradoxically, the tool by which life can be detheatricalized and brought face to face with an authentic image of itself. The question crudely posed by Maeterlinck in the 1890s is answered by Beckett 50 years later: how much can you take out of theatre while still retaining theatre? Beckett's answer – the more you take out, the more you have – was one Maeterlinck, in his own less penetrating way, was asking (and half-answering) in the 1890s.

We now come to our conclusion. This chapter has demonstrated two movements in symbolism's dealings with the theatrical. The first, exemplified in its most brilliant and subtle forms in Mallarmé, is an anti-theatricality based on the pre-eminence of the textual. But it is more than that: we have shown that this anti-theatricality is not a rejection of theatre but its opposite – the elevation of performance and theatrical metaphors into models of reading and writing. Theatricality is thus at the very core of the poetic avant-garde of the late nineteenth century – indeed, one could claim that poetry, from romanticism through symbolism and into modernism, becomes dependent on theatrical models *in direct proportion to* its rejection of real theatre. It is not enough, as so many critics of symbolism have done, to assert that the Symbolists were 'against' theatre. That is only half the story. The other half, which this essay has sketched out, is that that very primacy of the textual in the late nineteenth century can only articulate itself through theatricality, that the prestige and uniqueness of the poetic could only express itself through the borrowed terms of theatre. The interpenetration of textual and theatrical motifs in the literary discourse of the period is crucial to poetry's vision of itself in the second half of the nineteenth century.

That is the first movement. The second movement, exemplified in Maeterlinck, may be seen as the counterpart if not exactly the opposite of the first: for Maeterlinck theatre becomes a way of resisting the dramatic, of undoing the damage caused by the unchecked spread of theatricality and theatrical discourse in nineteenth-century thought. In this sense Maeterlinck is both the apotheosis of the Symbolist dramatic experiment (because of his popular success as well as his innovation) and its most sustained and powerful opponent (because his entire theory of theatre is built on the removal of action, drama, heroism, articulacy). Symbolism is based around the elevation of the theatrical at the expense of the theatre, while Maeterlinck's work is based on the elevation of the theatre at the expense of the theatrical.

Stanley Cavell, in an important essay on the philosophy of history, 'The Ordinary as the Uneventful', writes that 'there is a history of the human being to which we are blinded by the traditional histories of flashing, dramatic events'. The occasion of Cavell's essay is a dialogue with Paul Ricoeur on Fernand Braudel, the great French historian. Cavell's sentiment here we might recognize as Maeterlinckian (it is in fact Emersonian, though Maeterlinck wrote on and studied Emerson and Cavell himself has written penetratingly on Emerson's thought). Cavell's contention is that the writing of history has been limitingly obsessed not just with 'events' but with a certain conception of 'event-hood' that has prevented it, not just from understanding, but from actually perceiving the forces that shape collective and individual exist-ence.[24] Cavell quotes a passage from Braudel's inaugural lecture at the Collège de France:

> There is...a history slower still than the history of civilizations, a history which almost stands still, a history of man in his intimate

relationship to the earth which bears and feeds him; it is a dialogue which never stops repeating itself, which repeats itself in order to persist, which may and does change superficially, but which goes on, tenaciously, as though it were somehow beyond time's reach and ravages.[25]

This long unfolding sentence, its enchainment of related clauses, reminds us of Maeterlinck's lengthy paragraph about the interconnectedness of forces around the old man beneath his lamp. It resembles, too, a sentence from Proust, another writer who focuses on the interstices of life to draw out another world, a subliminal but deeply enmeshed realm of existence that lies outside the scope of conventional narrative. Braudel's great charge against conventional history, a charge applicable to pretty much all forms of narrative organization with which we work, is that events are merely the foam that feathers up from the deeper movement of the water; to mistake the foam for the wave is the great historiographical error we make when we focus only on the event.[26] A sort of literary-psychological (and pseudo-scientific) parallel might be Maeterlinck's own theory of dramatic action and human motivation as being 'vegetal', a matter of subliminal, unseen, often unconscious development that may well terminate in action, but of which actions are merely the crude, delayed, manifestations. This in turn anticipates Nathalie Sarraute's idea of 'tropisms', a term she borrows from botany to explain those imperceptible movements that conventional novelistic narratives omit but which she investigates in her *nouveau roman* novels.

We need not insist on any *rapprochements* between Braudel's philosophy of history and Maeterlinck's philosophy of drama to see that both are bent on questioning the basis on which their respective 'genres' are predicated, convinced that crucial elements of what might enrich these genres are not only ignored but obscured by traditional modes of presentation. Just as traditional history is not calibrated to take account of what Braudel evokes, so traditional theatre is not calibrated to take account of what Maeterlinck envisages. Maeterlinck is emphatic in the opening sentences of 'Le Tragique quotidien':

> There is a tragic in everyday life that is far more real, far deeper and far more true to our genuine selves than the tragic of great adventures. It is easy to feel this, but it is not easy to show it, since this essential tragic is not simply material or psychological. [...] The important thing is to show what is extraordinary in the simple fact of being alive.[27]

Maeterlinck's dilemma arises from the incompatibility of this conception of life with the demands of theatre: it is something which occurs and unfolds between or outside the boundaries of the event. It threatens to become a "content" that resists, even contravenes, any possible "form" it might take. Braudel, from his perspective, asserts:

> To the narrative historians, the life of men is dominated by dramatic accidents, by the actions of those exceptional beings who occasionally emerge, and who often are the masters of their own fate and even more of ours.[28]

This is what Braudel calls 'a first stage of history', wedded to the 'monotonous game' according to whose rules the historian ignores 'the social realities in themselves and for themselves'. Maeterlinck cannot be said to be interested in 'social reality' (just as Braudel would not have cared for Maeterlinck's drawing-room spirituality). But for both writers there exists an invisible drama, or an inaudible history, a process of 'happening' that must be distinguished from what merely 'happens'. This is what needs to be recuperated from the interstices of traditional theatre and traditional history. For Maeterlinck, this lies outside theatre's capacity yet is theatre's proper subject. Just as Braudel sees event-driven history as 'first-stage history', so Maeterlinck might be said to envisage a theatre of action and events as 'first-stage theatre'. This is a distinction that modern (we could even say moderni*st*) theatre makes between the 'event' and the process of happening, best captured in Beckett's *Endgame*: Hamm: 'What's happening, what's happening, what's happening?' *Clov*: 'Something is taking its course".[29] This is the distinction, in a sense, between the event as a discrete culminative point with defined temporal and consequential borders, and a process – expansive, numinous and impossible to pin down – that is more authentically reflective of existence.

What is apparent from Braudel's words are the underlying dramatic metaphors, as if here too the supremacy of 'generic' imperatives – drama, progression, actions, events, deeds and heroes – were stifling something altogether richer but less easily 'presentable'. In case the reader were to miss the implications of the metaphors by which Braudel characterizes these crude forms of historical writing, Cavell draws them out:

> Surely this alternative history, however briefly and polemically stated, extends its own, competing, philosophy of history, a competing conception of the human being and of the knowledge of human

existence... Braudel's opposition is evidently to a concept of event one of whose negative features is that it *theatricalizes* human existence.[30]

Maeterlinck asks:

Is it thus dangerous to affirm that what is truly tragic in life, the shared, deep and general tragic, begins only at the moment when what we call the adventures, the pain and the dangers are passed?... Is it not just when we are told at the end of the stories 'they lived happily ever after' that our worries should begin?[31]

Where Cavell follows Braudel in rejecting the 'theatricalization' of existence as a suitable model for historical enquiry, Maeterlinck – as playwright and dramatic theorist – takes the question into potentially impossible territory. And yet he succeeds, in a way: by attacking the theatricalization of theatre, and beyond that the theatricalization of life itself, he invents a new kind of play and new conception of drama, designed to show us what life was like before theatricality came to disfigure it. In Maeterlinck's theory and practice, theatre becomes its own antidote, its own counterweight. For both Mallarmé and Maeterlinck, though in different ways, all roads lead to the theatre. However, it is the negative road, the *via negativa*, that proves most rewarding in terms of dramatic theory and practice in the Symbolist period.

Notes

1. Stephane Mallarmé, *Oeuvres complètes* (Paris: Pléiade, 1945), p. 295. Hereafter *OC* in main text. For reasons of space I have only provided the original language in quotations from Mallarmé, where questions of wordplay and semantic complexity require an original to check against. For the rest of the quotations I provide only the English, with references to the original text in the notes. All translations are my own.
2. See my 'From page to stage and back: Mallarmé and Symbolist theatre', *Romance Studies*, Autumn 1995.
3. Dorothy Knowles, *La Réaction idéaliste au théâtre* (Paris: Droz, 1934); Jacques Robichez, *Le Symbolisme au théâtre: Lugné-Poë et les débuts de l'Oeuvre* (Paris: L'Arche, 1957); Frantisek Deak, *Symbolist Theater: The Formation of an Avant-Garde* (Baltimore, MD: Johns Hopkins University Press, 1993). A valuable recent contribution to scholarship on Symbolist theatre is Michael Holland's essay 'The Difficult Distance: Mallarmé, Symbolism and the Stage', in Patrick McGuinness, ed., *Symbolism, Decadence and the Fin-de-Siècle: French and European Perspectives* (Exeter: Exeter University Press, 2000).
4. Téodor de Wyzewa, *La Revue Wagnérienne* 8 May 1886: 104.

5. Maurice Maeterlinck, 'Menus propos: Le théâtre', *La jeune Belgique*, September 1890: 334.
6. Maeterlinck, 'Menus Propros', p.331
7. Introduction to 'Un théâtre d'Androides', *Annales de la Fondation Maurice Maeterlinck*, 1977: 11.
8. Pierre Quillard, 'De l'inutilité absolue de la mise-en-scène exacte', *Revue d'Art dramatique*, 1 May 1891; Alfred Jarry, 'De l'inutilité du théâtre au théâtre', *Mercure de France*, September 1896; Aurélien Lugné-Poë, 'A propos de l'inutilité du théâtre au théâtre', *Mercure de France*, October 1896.
9. Mockel's writings on Symbolism are collected in Albert Mockel, *Esthétique du Symbolisme*, ed. Michel Ottten (Brussels: Palais des Académies, 1962).
10. Patrice Pavis, *Voix et images de la scène* (Lille: Presses Universitaires de Lille, 1982), p.17.
11. Roland Barthes, 'Le Théâtre de Baudelaire, *Essais critiques* (Paris: Seuil, 1964).
12. Hippolyte Taine, *Sur L'Intelligence*, vol. I (1870; Paris: Hachette, 1920), pp.278–9.
13. See Patrick McGuinness, *Maurice Maeterlinck and the Making of Modern Theatre* (Oxford: Oxford University Press, 2000), for a study of Maeterlinck's theatre and dramatic theory.
14. The recent publication in two volumes of Maeterlinck's notebooks makes this even more apparent – see *Maurice Maeterlinck. Carnets de travail (1881–1890)*, 2 vols, ed. Fabrice Van de Kerckhove (Brussels: AML/Ediitions Labor, 2002).
15. This early version, complete with copious quotations from another upholder of reading over performance, Charles Lamb, can be found in the *Annales de la Fondation Maurice Maeterlinck*, vol. 23 (1977).
16. Annales de la Fondation Maurice Maeterlinck, vol. 23, p.334
17. Maeterlink, 'Un théâtre d'Androïdes', p.33.
18. Maeterlinck, 'Un théâtre d'Androïdes', p.33.
19. Maeterlinck, 'Menus propos', pp.335–6.
20. Maeterlinck, 'Le Tragique quotidien', in *Le Trésor des humbles* (Paris: Mercure de France, 1896), pp.168–9.
21. Antonin Artaud, introduction to Maeterlinck's *Douzes chansons* (Paris: Stock, 1923), p. 16. For an analysis of the relationship between Maeterlinck and Artaud, see Patrick McGuinness, 'Maeterlinck et le Dieu sauvage', in *Présence/Absence de Maeterlinck. Actes du colloque de Cérisy 2000*, ed. Marc Quaghebeur (Bruxelles: Editions Labor, 2002).
22. Maeterlinck, *Le Trésor des humbles*, p.176.
23. Maeterlinck, *Le Trésor des humbles*, p.173.
24. Stanley Cavell, *A Cavell Reader*, ed. Stephen Mulhall (Oxford: Blackwell, 1996), p. 258. The extract reproduced in Mulhall's selection is from *Themes out of School: Effects and Causes* (San Francisco: North Point Press, 1984).
25. Fernand Braudel, *On History*, quoted in Cavell, *A Cavell Reader*, p.258.
26. The image of foam is especially prevalent among the Symbolists, notably in Mallarmé, the opening of whose poem, 'Salut', itself the opening poem of *Poésies*, goes: *'Rien, cette écume, vierge vers à ne désigner que la coupe...'* (Nothing, this foam, virgin verse designating only the cup...). The poem plays upon ideas of form and formlessness, presence and absence, plenitude and emptiness, with the 'écume' functioning as a Mallarméan symbol *par*

excellence: the absence that defines form but is not itself substance. It makes a nice comparison with Braudel's idea of the event as the outward sign of the thing rather than the thing itself.

27. Maeterlinck, *Le Trésor des humbles*, p. 101.
28. Cavell, *A Cavell Reader*, p.255.
29. Samuel Beckett, *Complete Dramatic Works* (London: Faber & Faber, 1986), p.93.
30. Cavell, *A Cavell Reader*, p.255 (my italics).
31. Maeterlinck, *Le Trésor des humbles*, p.102.

Part III
Values

10
Narrative Theatricality:
Joseph Conrad's Drama of the Page
Rebecca L. Walkowitz

> It is the spectator, and not life, that art really mirrors.
>
> (Oscar Wilde, Preface to *The Picture of Dorian Gray*)

Joseph Conrad's dramatic adaptation of his well-known novel *The Secret Agent* (1907) was first performed in 1922, that watershed year of modernist production, and it is striking in its attempts to translate the narrative's innovative theatricality into the play's literal theatre. That the translation largely fails is telling, to be sure, about Conrad's limitations as a dramatist, but it is telling also about a misfit between the modernist content of Conrad's novel, its analysis of national characteristics and the processes of affiliation, and the (mostly) realist form of Conrad's play. The story fares better on the page than on the stage. Yet this is not because Conrad's art surpasses or precludes the theatre. Rather, Conrad's work absorbs the theatre too well: his narratives use theatrical metaphors that depend not on the absence of a stage, but on the ubiquity of staging. *The Secret Agent* is theatrical because it attributes the characteristics of natives and foreigners to the effects of social performance; but it is also anti-theatrical, because its theatre of culture resists the temporality of dramatic forms.

In the play, Conrad's modernist sensibility is most apparent when Winnie Verloc, the secret agent's wife, addresses the audience.[1] In these episodes, Winnie reminds her spectators that they are participants and interlocutors who know what she knows: her life incorporates habitual scripts, and she is conforming, against her wishes, to a melodramatic plot. From her wry comment in the first act, 'Yes, I am lucky' (referring to her marriage, in which she is in no sense lucky), to her assertion late in the play, 'No! That must never be!' (referring to prison or hanging), Winnie asks the audience to notice that conventional gestures and expectations can be recognized and sometimes manipulated.[2] As Winnie looks to the audience for sympathy, Conrad reminds his spectators that the play is invoking social roles and stereotypes with which they – and Winnie – are familiar. Conrad establishes the audience as a minor actor in his play: it serves to confirm that Winnie is choosing among established social dramas, which may be invoked and understood because they have been acted out before. The play is a social drama about the production of social dramas: a story of a woman's attempt to predict and avoid habitual narrative outcomes, and at the same time a story of a foreign embassy that stages a crime – the attempted bombing of the Greenwich Observatory – whose sole purpose is to increase anxiety about uncontrollable, purposeless crimes. Conrad is trying to dramatize, as it were, the production of literary and social effects, in which various characters perform social roles rather than merely inhabit them.

By making his audience in part responsible for the story represented, Conrad seeks to disrupt the conventional separation between actors and audience. Conrad's play thus incorporates elements that we have come to associate with modernist theatre: breaking the frame between audience and actors, forcing the audience to consider its expectations about the experience of attending the theatre and about the kinds of stories that the theatre tends to display, prompting the audience to notice what has become habitual about its own role in the theatre dynamic. These formal elements of theatrical production, which are present in Conrad's drama, have analogues in Conrad's novel, from which the drama takes not only its story but its ruptured frames as well. In fact, the novel goes quite a bit further than the drama to manipulate the spectator/reader's attention and to keep the spectator/reader aware of changes in his or her point of view; in the earlier text, the reader is made to feel like one more 'agent' in a story about social and cultural pretences – acting, deception, irony – at the heart of English life.[3] For this reason, to say that the play's form is in some way analogous to the novel's is to say too little: the literal theatricality of Conrad's drama only begins to convey the complex theatricality of culture that his narrative presents; in the drama, Conrad cannot replicate the famous delays and deceptions of the narration, in which he tells the reader, for example, that reputations are only 'nominally' what they seem.[4] The novel represents processes of showing, watching, and seeing that unfold over time: Conrad forces readers to observe their own patterns of observation and to observe moreover that patterns of observation include both conscious and unconscious acts of interpretation. Much of this chapter will focus on the narrative version of *The Secret Agent*, in which Conrad develops a narrative theatricality of culture that the modernist theatre, using narrative strategies such as stage directions, would later accommodate in drama.[5]

In Conrad's work, the possibility of performing and adapting the characteristics of native Londoners underwrites cosmopolitan practices of multiple attachment, syncretism and cultural improvisation.[6] One can certainly glimpse these practices in the drama of the period, as in Israel Zangwill's well-known play about European immigrants in New York, *The Melting Pot*, which was first performed in 1908. In Zangwill's play, an anti-Semitic Irish maid, who works for the Jewish protagonists, begins to integrate Yiddish phrases into her heavily accented English vocabulary: the British playwright seems to be suggesting that, in America at least, cultural types can blend into new amalgamations.[7] Taking on the characteristics of Jews, the Irish maid seems to become, in part, Jewish. Interestingly, a non-Yiddish-speaking audience will have to notice that the Irish maid has become, to them, less comprehensible, and thus the play's dialogue becomes less comfortable for some spectators even as the characters become more comfortable with each other. Zangwill forces his non-Jewish spectators to notice that they have been estranged by the characters' assimilation, that immigrants change English by adding themselves to it. Zangwill suggests that the newness of what he calls 'America' makes these transformations possible. Jewishness and Irishness can mix only in *The Melting Pot* (the play coined the phrase): in Europe, Zangwill implies, ethnic characteristics remain wholly identifiable and consistent.

Conrad's novel departs from Zangwill's play, proposing instead that cultural blending is the condition of culture everywhere. An immigrant from Poland to England, Conrad imagines a world not of melting but of mimicking, where defining characteristics depend on what audiences have learned to recognize. *The Secret Agent*, which made its author famous as a cosmopolitan writer, offered in 1907 a new approach to theatricality and culture: it asked readers to recognize national belonging by the performance of requisite gestures; it presented characters as actors whose skills of political manipulation rely on their knowledge of spectators rather than of life. In Conrad's novel, new theories of culture required narrative strategies that could display the process of role-playing and role-making within the life of cosmopolitan London.

* * *

To understand how the theatricality of Conrad's novel could be adapted by dramatic forms, it is important to notice that we are speaking, really, of two 'theatres': theatre as a genre of representation (a play) and theatre as a paradigm of culture, in which social categories are structured by processes of repetition and reception. In his study of 'the antitheatrical prejudice' in Western culture, Jonas Barish examines both versions of theatre, literal and metaphorical, though he tends to confuse – often, treat as equivalent – stage performance and individual acts of pretending and self-fashioning.[8] In the final chapter of his book, Barish describes the absence of strict boundaries between stage and spectator in modernist drama as a symptom of theatre turning 'against itself' (*The Antitheatrical Prejudice*, p.455). He expresses regret that many twentieth-century playwrights have renounced the 'familiar' sensibilities of the European theatre, though he is willing to grant momentarily that what seems to him like anti-theatricalism may be a 'renovation' rather than a rejection (p.464). Barish offers this optimistic tone, and yet he immediately follows with a sobering comparison between the vilification of traditional acting and the vilification of Jews and cosmopolitans in European history. He thus suggests, by the logic of association, that anti-theatricalism – including the modernist 'renovation' he has intimated only a paragraph earlier – is inseparable from anti-Semitism and extreme forms of nationalism (p.464–70).

In this transition from modernist theatre to anti-Semitism and anti-cosmopolitanism, Barish formulates his most persuasive emotional argument against 'the anti-theatrical prejudice'. He contends that anti-theatricalism is related to anti-Semitism because social critics over the centuries have attributed the same, often negative characteristics both to actors and to Jews, 'the alleged cosmopolitanism, ready adaptability, and linguistic virtuosity of the Jews being felt to have a natural kinship with the mimetic talents of the actors' (p.467). While it is true that many writers have made such associations, using anti-Semitism as an occasion to condemn other examples of heterodox culture, such as prostitution and acting, Barish's unrefined coupling of modernism and anti-cosmopolitanism implies that modernist art, in its critique of literalism and traditional theories of imitation, promotes pious authenticity and cultural dogmatism (the characteristics that Barish attributes to anti-Semitism).

As Barish confuses two kinds of theatricality, here he also confuses two discourses of authenticity. At the beginning of his chapter on modernist theatre (he discusses the work of Beckett, Pirandello, Brecht, Artaud, and others), which later segues into the discussion of anti-Semitism, Barish attributes modernist critiques of theatre to the 'search for authenticity' in representation (p.451). While it might seem at first that Barish is only unpersuaded by these theatrical innovations, his critique goes further than disaffection: as the chapter continues, 'the search for authenticity' becomes 'the rage for authenticity' (p.464), which becomes 'hard-line, fundamentalist anti-theatricalism' (p.464); Barish is suggesting that anti-theatricalism *is* anti-Semitism. The proximity between modernist theatre and anti-Semitism in Barish's account is emphasized by the fact that Barish describes modernists as 'impassioned purists' just before observing that there is a 'historical connection' between the treatment of Jews and the treatment of actors.[9] It seems likely that the word 'prejudice' in Barish's book title was intended to evoke this 'connection'.

On the one hand, the demand for representational 'authenticity' within modernism and the demand for national 'authenticity' within anti-Semitism are absolutely different, because the first demand seeks to undo conformity to types while the second seeks to assert it. On the other hand, it is important to consider these versions of authenticity together, since, as Conrad and other early modernists suggest, the desire for distinctive cultures depends on the possibility of absolute referents: anti-Semitism is grounded in strategies of representation that emphasize continuity and coherence. Barish's critique of racial purity in anti-Semitism is undermined by his embrace of 'the observed and the actual', by his sense that the cause of anti-racism will be helped by the assertion of definitive races.[10] Conrad suggests otherwise, by associating nineteenth-century racialist discourses, such as phrenology and criminology, with habitual reading and unreflective interpretation (see below). Just as one learns in Conrad's novel that conventional details do not promise what they seem to promise, that not all shops with pornography in the window intend to sell pornography, so one learns that a person with large ears is not necessarily a criminal, or that a person may become a criminal by being treated like one.

Conrad's *Secret Agent* resists the logic of racism by suggesting that all acts of cultural belonging, and not only those attributed to Jews, require habits of adaptation and virtuosity. Conrad proposes this: the cultural styles that foreigners and Jews were thought to imitate are themselves the products of imitation; put another way, the characteristics of Jews and cosmopolitans may be *exactly the same* as the characteristics of Englishmen, and both are the result of learned roles and established reputations. This new sensibility contradicts Barish's sense of theatre's essential humanism, its affirmation of already existing social worlds, and for similar reasons it disturbed Conrad's early critics, who, like Barish, perceived culture as objective and immutable. The modernist theatricality of *The Secret Agent*, as a novel of 1907 and a play of 1922, reflects a cosmopolitan theory of English culture, which Conrad demonstrates in his refusal to imagine any English character whose origins are not foreign. *The Secret Agent* conceives of theatre as constructive rather than mimetic: no longer secondary to national culture, theatre becomes integral to its production. It was Conrad's innovation to assert – and to make his readers *see*[11] – that cosmopolitan theatricality is native to England. In novels and plays, early twentieth-century writers such as Conrad unsettled national cultures by representing them as practices instead of objects. For Conrad, Englishness was a product rather than a condition of writing.

As a Polish national, later a French seaman, and even later an English novelist, Conrad came to represent English culture and English writing as few Englishmen could: as a foreigner. Conrad was widely praised by his contemporaries for his natural use of the English language, yet it was the visibility of his choice – over Polish and French – that tended to mark his foreign origins. One is reminded that to call someone 'a natural' is often to notice how effortless his or her actions appear; it is to notice not nature, but naturalness. Where naturalness is culturally and historically specific, because it depends on a projected impression, nature lays claim to timelessness, to a world apart from representation and recognition. As an English writer, Conrad understood the expectations of an English audience, so much so that he argued, writing to his French translator Hugh-Durand Davray in 1908, that his writing could not function in any language other than English.[12] The work, Conrad explained to Davray, 'is written for the English – from the point of view of the effect it will have on the English reader' (Conrad, *Collected Letters*, pp.28–9). Contrasting his interests with those of Rudyard Kipling, his most acclaimed predecessor in the English literature of empire, Conrad argued:

> A *national* writer like Kipling, for example, translates easily. His interest is in the *subject*: the interest in my work is in the *effect* it produces. He talks about *his compatriots*. I write *for them*.
>
> (Conrad, *Collected Letters*, p.29, original emphasis)

Making English novels of 'effects', Conrad asserts the reality that writing creates against the locations and national origins that situate writing. Rather than talking 'about' Englishmen, transmitting experiences and characteristics that exist before the act of writing, Conrad writes 'for' Englishmen, expressing nothing so much as the conditions of reception. It is part of Conrad's purpose to represent his effort: to show off, among his literary effects, the foreignness that is their origin.

While the difference between nature and naturalness was central to Conrad's literary project, his work was produced in the context of a literary culture devoted to categories of national distinctiveness and authenticity. For this reason, one observes in Conrad's public writings a very different set of claims than those he offers in private letters, such as the one to his translator. In his public comments, Conrad claimed to write, not for effect, but for transparency. He made these claims in response to early critics and reviewers who perceived him as a foreigner playing the role of an Englishman; the better he played this role, the more foreign he seemed. This was because – it was thought – only foreigners *have to act* English; everyone else simply *is*. Reviews of *The Secret Agent* had attributed the novel's dark view of London to the fact that its author was a foreigner to England and to English culture. These reviews often claimed that Conrad's novel was nothing more than the natural expression of his foreign self. His choice of English as his literary language was thought to confirm this fact, as it emphasized the artifice of Conrad's endeavour: only a foreigner *chooses* a language. Through the rhetoric of choice, Conrad's contemporaries registered his imposture; through the accusation of theatre, of artifice in writing and in culture, early twentieth-century critics sought to differentiate Conrad's imper-sonation of Englishness from the nature of Englishness and other national cultures.

Many reviewers of *The Secret Agent* saw the novel as a turning point in Conrad's career: with *The Secret Agent*, Hugh Walpole wrote in 1916, 'a new attitude was most plainly visible'.[13] Even those reviewers who sought to defend Conrad from the cosmopolitanism of whimsical, denationalized writing supported him by locating in his work the manifestation of an 'alien...genius'.[14] Everywhere, critics imposed the same language of inevitability: Conrad's detractors argued that he should not write in English because he was Polish; his advocates argued that his choice of English was irrelevant because the writing betrayed its author's Polishness all the same. Edward Garnett, who recommended Conrad's first novel for publication, later wrote in the *Nation* that the author of *The Secret Agent* had brought 'the secrets of Slav thought' to 'our [English] tongue';[15] a reviewer in the *Glasgow News* found it 'not an irrelevant reflection upon *The Secret Agent* that its author, Joseph Conrad, is of Polish birth';[16] and Arthur Symons, whose magazine accepted Conrad's first published short story in 1896, celebrated the novelist as a man of 'inexplicable mind' who 'does not always think in English' even when he uses English words.[17] These reviews sought to isolate cultural elements in Conrad's work, distinct from or more authentic than the English characteristics that his novels perform. The reviews are eager to keep the actual separate from the observed.

Rather than dispute the logic of these comments, Conrad spent much of his career, in prefaces and in biographical essays, insisting that his art was a product of natural inclination. This may sound like a direct contradiction of Conrad's sensibility as he described it to his translator, and in some ways it is; however, Conrad's insistence allowed him to refute the negative implications of theatricality (seen as a necessity of foreignness) while also embracing a professional ethos, for which naturalness became his principal goal. In a 1919 introduction to *A Personal Record*, first published in 1912, Conrad refuted 'certain statements' in the press: that he had 'exercised a choice' to write in English and that his work, in its sensibility and themes, reflects its author's 'Sclavonism'.[18] Conrad's refutation seems clear enough:

> The first object of this note is to disclaim any merit there might have been in an act of deliberate volition. The impression of my having exercised a choice between the two languages, French and English, both foreign to me, has got about somehow. That impression is erroneous.... English for me was neither a matter of choice nor adoption.
>
> (Conrad, 'Author's Note', pp.iii–v)

Conrad does not deny a specific interest in English so much as he denies an indulgent one, where his choice of English would suggest that he could have chosen, indifferently, another language altogether. He objects to the values associated with the ability to choose and to the notion that he might be 'able to do freakish things intentionally, and, as it were, from mere vanity' ('Author's Note', p.iii). For Conrad, denying choice and adoption becomes the only way to deny the natural foreignness ('Sclavonism') and insincerity ('vanity') that intention has come to designate. The accusation of indulgence leads Conrad to claim imperatives. The novelist conforms to the rhetoric of necessity because the alternative – artifice – would affirm the very frivolity he is trying to refute. Once artifice is deemed an attribute of foreigners, it can no longer characterize the deliberate work of an English writer. Unwilling to give up deliberate effects and unwilling to affirm the transparency of literary expression, Conrad compromises: he suggests that English is natural to his writing because, through English, through a language and culture that he has had to learn, he has found the topic of his work, that is, the fiction of naturalness. Conrad contends that his encounter with English inspired him to write: 'All I can claim after all those years of devoted practice, with the accumulated anguish of its doubts, imperfections, and falterings in my heart, is the right to be believed when I say that if I had not written in English I would not have written at all' (p.vi). Conrad proposes that writing is the agent of English 'effects', including his own; he is not interested in 'subjects' for which any language would be appropriate. He is not interested in art that merely describes, unless what art describes is the production of description.

In *The Secret Agent*, Conrad focuses on the narrative details that make nature out of theatre. Conrad's theatricality works like this: in *The Secret Agent*, English characteristics are empty signifiers – Roland Barthes would call them 'useless details' – that confirm only Englishness.[19] Conrad aligns the world he represents (arbitrary Englishness) with the world of representation (arbitrary signs), and in this sense he obscures the difference between the fictions of English culture and the fictions of his writing. By suggesting that all naturalness involves acting, Conrad proposes that national identity is structured by theatrical performance.

* * *

That the deliberate choice of English might be a defining characteristic of 'foreigners', as Conrad's reviewers affirm, the novelist suggests in and by *The Secret Agent*, the only one of his novels set entirely in London.[20] Here, the Assistant Commissioner of Police, working under-cover, transforms himself into a foreigner by adopting a caricature that the narrative has produced. The novel allows characters to detach, take up and assimilate cultural attributes – as an actor does – but it also argues that these practices constitute the repertoire of attributes to be chosen. Assuming attributes he, and we, have learned to call 'foreign', the Assistant Commissioner investigates the source of a Greenwich bombing by fitting into its milieu. This investigation takes him to the Soho pornography shop owned by Adolf Verloc, spy to the 'foreign embassy' and the most literal 'secret agent' of the novel's title. Conrad's text opens with an account of the 'customers' who typically call at the shop and whose appearance the novel configures as the manner the Assistant Commissioner will appropriate. The customers are of two main types, 'either very young men' or 'men of a more mature age' (Conrad, *The Secret Agent*, p.45). Of the latter group, it is said, they 'had the collars of their overcoats turned right up to their moustaches and traces of mud on the bottom of their nether garments'. Conrad offers this physical description two chapters before he identifies the older men, before he explains, in fact, that they are not 'customers' at all. The physical description quickly becomes an apposition, a defining characteristic: 'the evening visitors – the men with collars turned up and soft hats rammed down' (p.46) – nod familiarly when they enter the shop. Once the 'visitors' are named as 'anarchists', the apposition becomes the evidence for an identity that it has helped to create. *The Secret Agent* produces the conditions that make identities recognizable; it imagines social and cultural roles by creating their characteristics.

The Assistant Commissioner becomes 'foreign' because unremarked aspects of his person become newly meaningful as specific attributes. With a 'short jacket' and 'low, round hat', the Assistant Commissioner emphasizes 'the length of his grave, brown face'; he gives himself 'the sunken eyes of a dark enthusiast and a very deliberate manner' (p.150). This 'deliberate manner', better than a 'disguise', suits the Assistant Commissioner to his task: he becomes one of many 'queer foreign fish', he fits in among strangeness, by looking as conspicuous as possible (pp.150–1). The Assistant Commissioner becomes noticeable by taking notice of himself, for the more closely he considers his activities, the more 'unplaced' he feels (p.152). Checking his image in a sheet of glass, the police supervisor is 'struck by his foreign appearance' (p.151) and thus adopts the details the novel has attributed to anarchists and strangers. The artifice of foreignness makes the Assistant Commissioner feel foreign, so much so that the characteristics of foreigners, invented as 'characteristics' by the novel, become natural to him.

In the language of chance and opportunism, the novelist renders the Assistant Commissioner's 'inspiration':

> He contemplated his own image with a melancholy and inquisitive gaze, then by sudden inspiration raised the collar of his jacket. This arrangement appeared to him commendable, and he completed it by giving an upward twist to the ends of his black moustache. He was satisfied by the subtle modification of his personal aspect caused by these small changes. 'That'll do very well', he thought. 'I'll get a little wet, a little splashed –.'
>
> (Conrad, *The Secret Agent*, pp.151–2)

The 'subtle modification,' intentional but inspired, evokes the recognition (the 'foreign appearance') that had provoked it. Some 30 pages later, at the shop, the Assistant Commissioner is taken for the foreigner he has become. Winnie Verloc, tending the front counter, notices that

> he…wore his moustaches turned up. In fact, he gave the sharp points a twist just then. His long, bony face rose out of a turned-up collar. He was a little splashed, a little wet. A dark man, with the ridge

of the cheekbone well defined under the slightly hollow temple. A complete stranger.

(Conrad, *The Secret Agent*, p.187)

For Winnie it is not just that the Assistant Commissioner looks foreign, but that he sounds foreign as well:

> There was nothing foreign in his accent, except that he seemed in his slow enunciation to be taking pains with it. And Mrs Verloc, in her varied experience, had come to the conclusion that some foreigners could speak better English than the natives.
>
> (Conrad, *The Secret Agent*, p.187)

A deliberate and precise English, combined with a 'turned up collar' and purposefully sharpened moustache, allows Winnie Verloc to recognize, as it were, that the stranger has come 'from the Continent' (p.187). The Assistant Commissioner has performed foreignness by sounding as 'English' as possible. Speaking deliberately is not a sign that the Assistant Commissioner knows his English well so much as a sign that he knows his signs: he knows that conveying foreignness has more to do with reputed truths than with actual ones.

Conrad knows this also. In the third paragraph of his novel, Conrad describes the display window of the Soho pornography shop that serves as a cover for his secret agent's activities:

> The window contained photographs of more or less undressed dancing girls; nondescript packages in wrappers like patent medicines; closed yellow paper envelopes, very flimsy, and marked two and six in heavy black figures; a few numbers of ancient French comic publications hung across a string as if to dry; a dingy blue china bowl, a casket of black wood, bottles of marking ink, and rubber stamps; a few books with titles hinting at impropriety; a few apparently old copies of obscure newspapers, badly printed, with titles like the *Torch*, the *Gong* – rousing titles. And the two gas-jets inside the panes were always turned low, either for economy's sake or for the sake of the customers.
>
> (Conrad, *The Secret Agent*, p.45)

The pornography shop cloaks Verloc's activities because it makes the comings and goings of strange, dishevelled men seem normal. For Verloc, the shop is convenient in many ways: it allows him to pretend to his anarchist colleagues that he is hiding illicit activities from the police (in fact, he is a police informer); it allows him to pretend to the police that he is pretending to be an anarchist (in fact, he is the spy of a foreign embassy); it allows him to pretend to his wife and mother-in-law that he has a business at all. Like London, as Conrad will come to describe it, the pornography shop is made up of diverse, contradictory parts, such as the assorted paraphernalia that it sells: 'photographs of more or less undressed dancing girls', 'a few numbers of ancient French comic publications', and 'a soiled volume in paper covers with a promising title' (pp.45–6) as well as 'a bottle of marking ink' and 'rubber stamps' (p.45). In some ways, these are similar objects: the explicit pornography of the first three items is equated in its exoticism with the foreign origins implicit in the 'marking ink' (known also as 'Indian ink', made in China or Japan) and the 'rubber stamps', whose primary material is a natural product of empire. In other ways, however, the last two items are the English conveniences that aid and obscure the sale of eccentric goods. Indian ink and colonial rubber make up the products that make up England.

The foreignness of the pornography shop is reproduced in *The Secret Agent* by two other particularly English sites: the Foreign Embassy, which sponsors the novel's bombing incident, and 'the little Italian restaurant round the corner', where the Assistant Commissioner goes to polish his 'strange' appearance. The Embassy is defined by a foreignness it cannot occupy: it must reside within the geographic boundaries of one country, even as it remains the representative, by metonymy, of the other country it serves. Similarly, the Italian restaurant is a 'peculiarly English institution' (p.152), whose 'fraudulent cookery' could exist, would exist, nowhere in Italy. This fraudulence causes the patrons to lose 'all their national and private characteristics', the Assistant Commissioner observes. The people before him 'seemed created for the Italian restaurant', as if the place, in its artifice, attracts a fitting clientèle or as if it makes its patrons fit by compromising the social categories which usually define them. The local authenticities of London – the turned-up collar, the twisted moustache, the Embassy, the Italian restaurant – are assimilated fictions. What is most foreign in Conrad's novel is a strangeness invented at home, which is strange above all to those for whom things English are most familiar.

Conrad suggests in his novel that interpretation is limited by the meanings that characters and readers are able to recognize. By alternating between omniscient narrative and free indirect discourse, often several times in a single paragraph, Conrad conflates the practice of the novel with practices of social perception, such that the reader's knowledge is shaped by the way that characters read. Conrad's characters assign the individuals they meet to cultural types they have observed or imagined in the past; they make these assignments by naming incidental details as significant characteristics and by conforming these characteristics to the types they have already imagined. Like Winnie, who thinks that the Assistant Commissioner sounds strange after she has already decided that he is a stranger, Mr Vladimir of the Foreign Embassy fits Verloc's appearance to the behaviour he has diagnosed:

> ...Mr Vladimir formulated in his mind a series of disparaging remarks concerning Mr Verloc's face and figure. The fellow was unexpectedly vulgar, heavy, and impudently unintelligent. He looked uncommonly like a master plumber come to present his bill. The First Secretary of the Embassy, from his occasional excursions into the field of American humour, had formed a special notion of that class of mechanic as the embodiment of fraudulent laziness and incompetency.
>
> (Conrad, *The Secret Agent*, pp.62–3)

Mr Vladimir, who thinks from the start that Verloc is lazy, incompetent and fraudulent, confirms his judgment by finding in Verloc physical and mental characteristics that assure these behaviours. Although the passage begins with these characteristics, it is clear that Mr Vladimir has noticed only those that will correspond to the stereotype he names in conclusion. The stereotype is the perspective that organizes Mr Vladimir's judgment; it is what Roland Barthes calls a 'view', a form of description that organizes details into well-established frames.[21] In Conrad's work, the stereotype precedes the characteristics that seem to justify its invocation. Mr Vladimir's observation is ultimately both fixed and unmoored by its definitive origin: Verloc is said to be 'fraudulent', but the caricature that justifies this assessment is also something of a fiction, derived from the 'American humour' Mr Vladimir has taken seriously. Verloc embodies a falseness that is as false as the stereotype that confirms it.

Mr Vladimir's strategies of observation are comparable to those used by Verloc's anarchist colleague Comrade Ossipon, who relies on a theory of criminality devised by Cesare Lombroso. Lombroso's theory, which was fashionable in the 1880s (when the novel is set), argued that criminals could be identified by visible marks on their bodies, such as large ears or poor eyesight. Ossipon, it is said, 'was free from the trammels

of conventional morality, but he submitted to the rule of science'
(p.259). After Winnie has killed Verloc, Ossipon looks at her with new
eyes:

> He gazed at her, and invoked Lombroso, as an Italian peasant recom-
> mends himself to his favourite saint. He gazed scientifically. He gazed
> at her cheeks, at her nose, at her eyes, at her ears...Bad!...Fatal!...
> Not a doubt remained...a murdering type.
>
> (Conrad, *The Secret Agent*, p.259)

Ossipon had planned to seduce and marry Winnie for her inheritance,
but his assessment of her 'murdering type' leads him to steal the
money and abandon her on a boat bound for the Continent. Ossipon's
judgment is instrumental in his actions: as he transforms Winnie's
body into a type, he transforms his agency into an imperative. As
Mr Vladimir looks at Verloc, so Ossipon looks at Winnie: in each case,
the perception imposed reflects not curiosity but conformity; Vladimir
and Ossipon see what they expect or want to find.

At the end of *The Secret Agent*, one sees that characters, like Conrad's
readers, are reluctant to embrace their role in the production of the
novel's scenery. Individual acts are thus transformed into passive
constructions. Winnie commits suicide, and her death is reported in a
newspaper as '[a]n impenetrable mystery' because neither she nor the
cause of her distress can be identified (p.266). The last lines of the
newspaper report repeat throughout the last chapter of the novel. They
are lines that the anarchist Comrade Ossipon has memorized: '*An
impenetrable mystery seems destined to hang for ever over this act of madness
or despair*' (original emphasis). Ossipon, who had imagined a world
governed by inevitable truths, is haunted by the 'destiny' for which he
is responsible. He sees that he is the (secret) agent of the 'impenetrable
mystery'.

In Conrad's vision of English life, domestic ease exists only through
the efforts of cultivated naturalness. Winnie Verloc is noted for 'the
masterly achievement of instinctive tact' (p.172) and her husband for
'calculated indiscretions' (p.183). Winnie's 'tact' is like the other
deliberate characteristics produced throughout the novel, but it condenses
in a phrase the structure of description that Conrad elsewhere illustrates
in a paragraph or in several chapters: Winnie's tact is a characteristic
that is formative as soon as it is formulated. It is best achieved without
achievement because it is, like other local truths, a mastery that works
only by avoiding effort. These kinds of artefacts, whose agency is typically

secret, beneath notice because without noticeable history, illustrate in Conrad's narratives the obscured origins of English fiction.

Conrad's narratives are less like the urban realism of Dickens and Stevenson than they are like the aesthetic modernism of Flaubert and Wilde. This is an important distinction. As Wilde argues that fogs are the result of Impressionist painting, so Conrad argues that theatricality affirms national identity, a contention not so far from Wilde's interests as it may seem.[22] As Wilde famously puts it, with only some irony:

> Where, if not from the Impressionists, do we get those wonderful brown fogs that come creeping down our streets, blurring the gas-lamps and changing the houses into monstrous shadows?...At present, people see fogs, not because there are fogs, but because poets and painters have taught them the mysterious loveliness of such effects.
>
> (Wilde, 'The Decay of Lying', p.1086)

Wilde's 'blurring gas-lamps' and 'monstrous shadows' could have set the scene for Conrad's novel, which is full of similar, and similarly conventional, opacity. A few paragraphs after his discussion of the Impressionist fog, Wilde remarks, again prefiguring Conrad, that 'nations and individuals' like to imagine in their 'natural vanity' that art refers to *them*, but rather it is art, Wilde contends, to which 'the human consciousness' refers (p.1087).

The problem with Conrad's dramatic adaptation of his novel is that it fails in almost all ways to incorporate what I have called his theatre of culture:[23] the play unties the recursive chronology of the narrative and thus returns to a more conservative, linear development of cause and effect; spectators can no longer see that they are the subject of art's imitation. This logic of events, in which characters adjust characteristics to meet social categories, Conrad might have learned from the dramatist Wilde, a pre-eminent scholar of English norms, who knew the vital importance of seeming earnest. As an 'unnatural' Englishman (as an Irishman, a homosexual and an aesthete), Wilde had to learn, as Conrad did, how naturalness looks.[24] In the recursive wit of Conrad's descriptions, one can hear the echo of Lady Bracknell, who proposes famously that to have a fashionable address one need only change the fashion: that is, one must know, above all, one's audience.[25] To the extent that epigram in Wilde tends to surprise the reader or spectator with the habits of socialized language – habits we notice because they are imperfectly reproduced – it functions as a disruption of the theatre dynamic: the audience comes to watch its own expectations. In Conrad's novel, expectations are engaged at the level of description and sensory perception; the socialization that the reader sees and experiences is the recognition of national types and defining characteristics. Conrad proposes that English culture is made up of gestures, in speech, body and social ritual, that are regularly performed and negotiated; he shows, in addition, that these gestures achieve different meanings in different contexts, that there is no characteristic that is naturally English. Conrad integrates theatrical devices into his narrative forms, but he is less successful in creating dramatic forms for his theatrical narratives.

Conrad's strategies of description, in which national identity is neither consistent nor distinctive, make spectators *see* the habits of social perception that keep persons and cultures in place. Conrad shows that xenophobia and racism have an anti-theatrical prejudice against cultures that change and people who bring those changes. However, Conrad responds to prejudice not by describing authentic foreigners but by observing artifice at home. The novelist resists prejudice – against impersonation and against foreigners – by making naturalness his topic and his goal, by offering new models of cultural belonging, and by suggesting, finally, that cosmopolitanism has a drama of its own.

Notes

An earlier version of this essay appeared in *Modern Drama*, 44: 3 (Fall 2001) as 'Conrad's adaptation: Theatricality and cosmopolitanism'. I am grateful to Alan Ackerman and Martin Puchner for their invitation to write that essay and this one, and for their capacious advice along the way.

1. Joseph Conrad, *Three Plays: Laughing Anne, One Day More and The Secret Agent* (London: Methuen, 1934), pp.80 and 168.
2. James Richard Hand's observation that Conrad uses the audience to represent the urban crowd has been helpful to my thinking about the play's attempts to translate the novel's relationship with the reader. James Richard Hand, ' "The Stage is a Terribly Searching Thing": Joseph Conrad's dramatization of *The Secret Agent*', *Conradiana*, 32: 1 (Spring 2000): 57–66.
3. Henry James also treats spectators as actors, as Alan Ackerman wonderfully shows in *The Portable Theater: American Literature & the Nineteenth-Century Stage* (Baltimore, MD, and London: The Johns Hopkins University Press, 1999), pp.212–20.
4. Joseph Conrad, *The Secret Agent*, ed. Martin Seymour-Smith (London: Penguin, 1990), p.45. On 'delayed decoding', see Ian Watt, *Conrad in the*

Nineteenth Century (Berkeley and Los Angeles: University of California Press, 1979).

5. See Martin Puchner's discussion of Joyce's use of stage directions in the 'Circe' episode of *Ulysses* in *Stage Fright: Modernism, Anti-Theatricality, & Drama* (Baltimore, MD, and London: The Johns Hopkins University Press, 2001), pp.81–100. My discussion of 'narrative theatricality' in Conrad is indebted to Puchner's splendid account of the drama in Joyce's novel. For a later example, see Jean Genet's use of stage directions in *The Blacks: A Clown Show*, trans. Bernard Frechtman (New York: Grove Press, 1988; first published in French, 1958), p.7.

6. Conrad's cosmopolitanism does not assume that nations exist as completed entities from which one could possibly detach, as in the Kantian model. Rather, Conrad imagines a cosmopolitanism that is dialectical and critical: immigration and other practices of cultural mobility are the conditions in which national communities are formed.

7. Israel Zangwill, *The Melting Pot* (New York: Arno Press, 1975), p.170.

8. Jonas Barish, *The Antitheatrical Prejudice* (Berkeley and London: The University of California Press, 1981), pp.1 and 464–9.

9. See Barish's discussion of Jean-Paul Sartre's *Anti-Semite and Jew*, in which Barish compares the 'passion' of anti-Semitism to the passion of anti-theatricalism (*The Antitheatrical Prejudice*, p.468).

10. This blindness is also evident in Barish's readings of nineteenth-century novels, which he presents as examples of anti-theatrical prejudice. In his account of these novels, Barish makes little distinction between critiques of theatrical performance voiced by individual characters (as in Jane Austen's *Mansfield Park*, which has a famous scene of theatricals in the family home) and theatrical scenes of irony, rhetoric, wit and role-playing distributed through narration and metaphor. Joseph Litvak has argued on the contrary that in the nineteenth-century novel theatricality is regularly diffused 'throughout the culture that would appear to have repudiated it'. Joseph Litvak, *Caught in the Act: Theatricality in the Nineteenth-Century English Novel* (Berkeley: University of California Press, 1992), p.x.

11. Conrad famously announced, in his well-known Preface to *The Nigger of the 'Narcissus'*, that the sensory perception of sight is the goal of his work: 'My task which I am trying to achieve is, by the power of the written word, to make you hear, to make you feel – it is, before all, to make you *see!*' Joseph Conrad, Preface to *The Nigger of the Narcissus* (New York: Norton, 1979), p.147, emphasis in original.

12. Letter to Hugh-Durand Davray, January 1908, translated from the French, in *The Collected Letters of Joseph Conrad*, ed. Frederick R. Karl and Laurence Davies, vol. 4 (Cambridge and New York: Cambridge University Press, 1983), pp.28–9.

13. Hugh Walpole, *Joseph Conrad*, rev. edn (London: Nisbet, 1924), p.19.

14. Unsigned review, *Times Literary Supplement*, 20 September 1907: 285. Reprinted in Norman Sherry, *The Critical Heritage* (London and Boston, MA: Routledge & Kegan Paul, 1973), p.185.

15. Edward Garnett, unsigned review, *Nation*, 28 September 1907. Reprinted in *The Critical Heritage*, pp.191–3.

16. Unsigned review, *Glasgow News*, 3 October 1907: 5. Reprinted in *The Critical Heritage*, pp.195–7.

17. Arthur Symons, 'Conrad', in *Dramatis Personae* (Indianapolis: Bobbs-Merrill, 1923), p.21.

18. Joseph Conrad, 'Author's Note' to *A Personal Record* (1912), in *The Mirror of the Sea; and A Personal Record* (London: J. M. Dent, 1968), pp.iii–x.

19. Roland Barthes, 'The Reality Effect', in *The Rustle of Language*, trans. Richard Howard (Berkeley: University of California Press, 1989), pp.141–8.

20. Joseph Conrad, *The Secret Agent*, ed. Martin Seymour-Smith (London: Penguin, 1990).

21. Such description, Barthes explains, consists 'not in copying the real but in copying a (depicted) copy'. Roland Barthes, *S/Z*, trans. Richard Miller (Oxford: Blackwell, 1992), pp.54–5.

22. Oscar Wilde, 'The Decay of Lying', *Collins Complete Works of Oscar Wilde* (New York: Harper Collins, 1999), pp.1086–7.

23. Hand argues also that the play's linear chronology is one of its principal failings, though he sees this mainly as a problem of audience interest: spectators are unable to develop sympathy with characters who die early in the story. Robert S. Ryf argues that the failure of the play may be attributed to its 'expository tone', its tendency to relate events rather than perform them. Robert S. Ryf, '*The Secret Agent* on stage', in *Modern Drama*, XV: 1 (May 1972): 62–3.

24. Francesca Coppa argues that Wilde's plays, as well as his phrases, function as epigrams, because he has mastered the conventions of late nineteenth-century theatre as well as he has mastered the language of social ritual. Coppa defines epigram as the citation and negotiation of one or more previous formulations of knowledge: to master epigram is to be theatrical, as Coppa suggests in the subtitle of her article. Francesca Coppa, ' "I Seem to Recognize a Device that Has Done Duty in Bygone Days": Oscar Wilde and the Theatre of Epigram', in *Reading Wilde, Querying Spaces* (Fales Library, New York University, 1995), pp.11–20.

25. Oscar Wilde, *The Importance of Being Earnest* (Oxford: Oxford University Press, 1995), p.266.

11

The Curse of Legitimacy

David Savran

During the 1920s, theatre flourished as never before during its long history in the United States. Broadway was the vibrant centre of theatrical activities, a 'paradise for playwrights', in Brenda Murphy's words.[1] On the average, more than 200 new productions opened each year on the Great White Way.[2] By 1927, there were 76 theatres in New York City used for plays and musical comedies, twice as many as had been available only 12 years before.[3] Although playwrights such as Elmer Rice, Philip Barry and George S. Kaufman became certified Broadway favourites, they all were overshadowed by a relative newcomer, Eugene O'Neill, who was repeatedly singled out, even during the 1920s, as the inheritor of the mantle of Shakespeare, Ibsen and Shaw, and the chief native architect of what one well-regarded critic, Walter Prichard Eaton, called 'the true theatre, the true spoken drama'.[4] O'Neill, more than any other playwright, succeeded in establishing 'America's kinship', in the words of one of his earliest champions, 'with the stage of the modern world'.[5] With O'Neill's long string of Broadway successes during the 1920s, from *Beyond the Horizon* to *Strange Interlude*, 'American drama', Barnard Hewitt announced, finally 'came of age'.[6]

Despite the success of individual playwrights, the so-called legitimate theatre in the United States suffered serious economic decline during the first four decades of the twentieth century. Although the number of new productions in New York climbed steadily until 1927, they thereafter began a precipitous retreat that has continued to this day. Across the nation, the number of touring companies fell from over 300 at the turn of the century to about 20 during the first years of the Depression.[7] Cultural historians agree that the advent of the talkie sounded the death knell to theatre as a broadly popular form. But even before the widespread distribution of films with synchronized sound in the late

1920s, Hollywood succeeded in stealing the working-class and a large section of the middle-class audience from the legitimate stage by providing them with 'comfortable seats, thick rugs, elegant lounges... – all the trappings of wealth that had previously belonged to a select few in the orchestra of a legitimate theatre – and all for twenty-five cents'.[8] It is no surprise, then, that by 1925, 'the average weekly attendance' of movies 'was at least fifty-six times the maximum possible weekly attendance at legitimate plays'.[9] Legitimate theatre galleries were rarely filled after 1912 as the audience was increasingly divided by class in an institution that became even '*less* democratic...after the triumph of the movies', in part because of the high price of tickets.[10] During the 1920s, 'the average price differential' between the legitimate stage and the movies 'was five to one'.[11] And for the whole of the century, that ratio ranged between five-to-one and ten-to-one, depending on the particular venues. But ticket price was only one factor in theatre's decline. Although the success of O'Neill and his cohort with critics and upper-middle-class audiences may finally have elevated American drama above vulgar forms like vaudeville and musical comedy, many culturally progressive critics were deeply suspicious of the medium and expected – correctly – that the so-called legitimate theatre would be doomed to permanent marginalization.

The word 'legitimate' has since the nineteenth century been a key term used to position various theatrical practices (for good or ill) in the hierarchy of cultural forms. One of the most loaded metaphors in the theatrical vocabulary, it is constructed in opposition to an imprecisely defined antagonist that would never dare self-identify as 'illegitimate'. Nonetheless, the category of the legitimate, as Richard Butsch reports, has been continually 'recruited into the discourse on the relationship of theatre to art and to mass culture', two terms with which theatre has long had a vexed and nervous relationship.[12] According to the *OED*, the word 'legitimate', when applied to 'drama', designates 'the body of plays, Shakespeare or other, that have a recognized theatrical and literary merit'. (The earliest example cited is from 1855.) Alfred L. Bernheim in fact quotes an earlier American example, from an 1843 article in the *New Mirror* in which the 'legitimate' theatre is equated *tout court* with 'the drama' and hailed as a 'temple dedicated to the muses'. It is opposed to diverse entertainments presented at 'low prices' for 'low audiences': 'horses, dancing, negroes and magicians'.[13] Butsch references an 1879 column in the *New York Dramatic Mirror*, in which 'the legitimate stage' is set in opposition to 'the variety business', 'the money-making branch of the theatrical business'. Variety – that is, vaudeville, burlesque, animal shows, minstrelsy, and related forms – is first and foremost a commercial enterprise that caters to 'the popular taste' (or 'low audiences') unlike the legitimate stage which is a showcase for a consecrated universalized, sacralized art.[14]

In his 1890 memoir, the actor Joseph Jefferson notes that the designation, 'legitimate comedian', is reserved for 'those actors who confine themselves as strictly as possible to the acting of characters in old English and Shakesperean (*sic*) comedies'.[15] The legitimate theatre, unlike 'spectacle, opera, pantomime, etc.', represents a relatively elite cultural practice linked to European forms and coded as text-based and literary.[16] If, to follow through with the implications of the metaphor, the legitimate theatre is lawfully begotten, elitist, high-priced and Anglo-Saxon, then the variety theatre that opposes it must be commercial, 'low', cheap, and if not 'negro', then at least of questionable Anglo-Saxon heritage. It is merely and deplorably 'popular'. It is a 'faddist, exotic' theatre.[17] By the 1920s, the adjectives associated with the legitimate stage and its misbegotten adversary may have been repressed, but they could never quite be forgotten.

In order to compass the difference between the 'legitimate' and its implied other (whatever it is), to analyse the new settlement that was rapidly being institutionalized during the 1920s, and to understand the development of a literary drama in the United States, one must first consider theatre's uneasy relationship with motion pictures, which had by then become by far the most widely attended form of public amusement. If there is one thing on which all cultural historians seem to be in agreement, it is that Hollywood has unquestionably been the 'largest single force' shaping the American theatre at least since 1912, when 'the first full-length commercial film was shown in America', *Queen Elizabeth*, starring (not by accident) the most famous stage actor in the world, Sarah Bernhardt.[18] To claim that Hollywood was primarily responsible for a contraction of the theatre industries during the 1920s and that the Great Depression delivered the *coup de grâce* is by and large correct. But it is only the beginning of an interrogation of the relationship between theatre and popular culture during what was popularly known as the Jazz Age. It is only the first step in analysing how and why the triumph of American modernism required the marginalization of the legitimate stage.

Highbrow/lowbrow

With the ascendance of rationalized modes of production in the United States in the early years of the twentieth century, the Machine Age commenced in earnest. Frederick Winslow Taylor's *Principles of Scientific*

Management was published in 1911 while two years later Henry Ford built the first assembly line at his plant in Highland Park, Michigan. Mass production aligned human beings and machines by abstracting and co-ordinating 'a manufacturing project', in Ford's words, dedicated to 'the principles of power, accuracy, economy, system, continuity and speed'.[19] With the triumph of the rationalized workplace, the development of new communication technologies, and the almost frenzied growth of new popular forms (most notably movies and jazz), American cultural critics began to embrace modernism and react against the genteel tradition as well as the progressive mission of cultural uplift. So-called little magazines like the *Dial* and *Seven Arts* were committed to a self-consciously revolutionary cultural and political agenda. 'I feel a certain unholy glee', Randolph Bourne exclaimed in 1915, 'at this wholesale rejection of what our fathers reverenced as culture.' His delight, however, did not impel him automatically to embrace 'what is substituted for it'.[20] But it was symptomatic of a cultural radicalism that reassessed the value of popular forms. No longer disdaining the mass-mediated art of the industrial age, the modernists embraced a brand of populism whose Americanness is attested to by its connection with the 'spirit of Walt Whitman', in the words of one 1917 editorial in *Seven Arts*: 'What we are seeking is what he sought: that intense American nationality in which the spirit of the people is shared through its tasks and its arts, its undertakings and its songs.'[21]

During the 'teens, more and more intellectuals hearkened to the siren's songs of popular culture. Among the radicals, R. J. Coady rehearses a kind of utopian modernism that links 'the people' – always a problematic term, especially when used by writers who are manifestly not part of this collectivity – with progress, youth, kineticism, mass production and America itself. In a 1917 essay entitled 'American Art', he rejects the highbrow culture that comes 'from the Academy or the money old ladies leave' and instead finds 'enormous possibilities' in industry, modern cities, and popular and mass-mediated entertainments. 'It's in the spirit of the Panama Canal. It's in the East River and the Battery ... It's coming from the ball field, the stadium and the ring ... To-day is the day of moving pictures, it is also the day of moving sculpture ...' To fulfil the utopian promise of America is to fulfil the promise of modernity and the working classes whose machines and labour will be blissfully transformed into art. If 'taste', he argues, 'equalled [sic] the creative construction of the [Steam Hammer] we'd have a mighty art!'.[22]

The most celebrated and influential analysis of the cultural hierarchy by a cultural radical is Van Wyck Brooks's ' "Highbrow" and "Lowbrow," ', first published in 1915. Born in New Jersey, Brooks was educated there, in Europe and at Harvard, and introduced 'a cosmopolitan experience unmatched in American criticism of that day'.[23] For Brooks, like Coady, 'all that is real' does not yet exist in native culture.[24] He attributes this lack to the fact that every aspect of 'American life' is produced by a binary opposition between highbrow and lowbrow, between 'transcendent theory' and 'catchpenny realities', a 'desiccated' (but elevated) art and 'stark utility', theology and business, ideals and dollars (Brooks, ''Highbrow' and 'Lowbrow'', pp.6, 7, 14). Although he attacks *both* positions, between which 'there is no community, no genial middle ground', he is intent on envisioning some kind of synthesis, even if that synthesis is only perceptible by its absence (p.7). For there is a place-holder in the text, or rather, two of them. 'On the economic plane', he writes, 'that [middle position] implies socialism; on every other plane it implies something which a majority of Americans in our day do not possess – an object in living' (p.34). Just as 'priggishness... paralyzes life', so does the opposition between high and low squelch 'a popular life which bubbles with energy and spreads and grows and slips away ever more and more from the control of tested ideas, a popular life 'with the lid off'' (pp.29, 15). If socialism would guarantee an idealized, co-ordinated collective, then the popular – a popular whose very impossibility points to its abstraction from the working classes – promises to redeem America and its culture.

Almost a decade after the essays of Brooks and Coady, Gilbert Seldes published *The 7 Lively Arts*, which Paul Gorman describes as 'the most important work on the mass entertainments of the era'.[25] Widely and lavishly praised in the press, Seldes's mapping of American cultural production in 1924 would prove enormously influential and prescient. Not only was it at once revolutionary and emblematic of its historical moment, but it also sketched out the contours of a cultural hierarchy that has had remarkable longevity in the United States. 1924 was a banner year. It marked the end of the economic slump of the early 1920s and the enactment of the severe Immigration Restriction Act of 1924; the opening of Saks Fifth Avenue; the premières of Gershwin's *Rhapsody in Blue*; O'Neill's *Desire Under the Elms*; and the first George and Ira Gershwin collaboration, *Lady, Be Good!*; the first year that Burns Mantle selected only American plays for his *Best Plays* series; the formation of Columbia Pictures and Metro Goldwyn Mayer. Even today, many of the distinctions that Seldes draws between the 'lively' and the 'great' arts remain unexpectedly relevant. This feat is all the more remarkable when one considers that the book was written when radio was in its infancy, before the advent of the sound-synchronized motion picture, before the supersession of the acoustic by the electrical recording process, and before writers like the Gershwins, Jerome Kern and Oscar Hammerstein II, and Richard Rodgers and Lorenz Hart revolutionized the Broadway musical and produced so many of its undisputed masterpieces.

Born in 1893 into a middle-class, liberal, secularized Jewish family – like so many of the producers of the 'lively' arts he champions – Seldes first hoped to become a playwright, having been from an early age, Michael Kammen reports, 'enchanted with the works of Ibsen and Shaw'.[26] After Harvard College, however, he forsook theatre for journalism and started writing for the little magazines (most notably the *Dial*) in which he consistently staked out a position as highbrow intellectual, disdainful of what Kammen calls 'the democratization of theatre' and, in particular, of rude, noisy, lowbrow audiences.[27] But there is nothing like the zeal of the apostate and in *The 7 Lively Arts* he turned smartly against genteel, highbrow culture. His list of the 'lively' arts represents a veritable litany of what passed for popular culture in the 1920s: movies, jazz (or more properly, jazz-inflected popular music), vaudeville, musical comedy, comic strips, dance and radio – note the conspicuous omission of the legitimate theatre from the list. A polemical, irreverent and delightedly inflammatory tract, the book is divided into 29 short essays, most of which are meditations on a single art form. Considering the book's breadth, Seldes's gift for colour and hyperbole, and the fact that several of its chapters were originally written as magazine articles, it is palpably contradictory. Nonetheless, Seldes succeeds in setting forth a compelling – and influential – view of an extraordinarily productive and pivotal moment in the history of US culture.

One of Seldes's signal achievements is his explicit revision and displacement of the highbrow/lowbrow binary opposition by a three-term system: the great, lively and bogus arts. The 'great arts' are characterized by their 'high seriousness' of purpose, as exemplified by the work of Mozart, Aristophanes, Aeschylus, Rabelais and Racine. The lively arts, or 'minor arts', in contrast, have as their 'essence' 'high levity'. This characteristic he finds exemplified by the movies of Charlie Chaplin, the songs of Irving Berlin and Jerome Kern, and, reaching back to a historical antecedent, the *commedia dell'arte*.[28] The great arts represent a species of Europeanized, highbrow culture from which Seldes blows the dust of historical contingency by arguing that they 'are related to eternity'. A species of universal art, the fruits of Enlightenment, the great arts thereby attest to 'that extraordinary march of mankind which we like to call the progress of humanity' (*The 7 Lively Arts*, p.347).

The lively arts, in contrast, are slaked in temporality ('our moment', 'our lives'). They are 'fresh and transient', they carry 'a given theme to the 'high' point' (pp.347–8). Like the movies, they are 'strange and wonderful', 'an instrument of miracles' (pp.37–8). Because of Seldes's professed dislike for 'two of the most disagreeable words in the language: high- and low-brow', he attempts to place the great and the lively on equal footing ('there need be present no conflict between the great arts and the minor', pp.347, 349). Yet he continually reproduces the hierarchy he is trying to undo. For the difference, he maintains, between the two arts 'is not the degree of intensity, but the degree of intellect' (p.319). The great may not tower, but they stand, one might say, at least a head above the lively ones, which he admits, represent something of 'an opiate' (p.204). Seldes's scheme thereby unmistakably reinstates a version of the old highbrow/lowbrow binary opposition. But with a difference.

The difference between *The 7 Lively Arts* and earlier elaborations of the cultural hierarchy is Seldes's third category, 'the peculiarly disagreeable thing for which I find no other name than the bogus' (p.310). This class of indescribable things he calls the 'bogus arts' is opposed to both the great and the lively. The bogus are watered down and debased, 'easier to appreciate' since they 'appeal to low and mixed emotions' (p.349). Into this damnable class Seldes places 'vocal concerts, pseudo-classic dancing, the serious intellectual drama, the civic masque, the high-toned motion picture, and grand opera' (p.311). He condemns them all for being 'dull', 'pale', 'trivial', and 'uninspired' (pp.311–14). He sees them as poised between, competing with, and imperilling both the great and the lively. On the one hand, they represent 'pretentious', 'genteel', 'dignified and artistic' – and 'dead' – versions of the great arts which appeal only to snobs (pp.336, 338, 349). Yet he maintains that they are especially dangerous less to the great arts (which are beyond the vagaries of time and taste anyway) than for 'corrupting the lively ones'. 'They pretend to be better than the popular arts, yet they want desperately to be popular.' Representing a feminized kind of imposture, they are 'the exact equivalent of a high-toned lady, an elegant dinner or a refined collation served in the saloon' (p.319). He singles out for special disapprobation the Metropolitan Opera and the legitimate stage. Indeed, the bogus for Seldes is epitomized by 'the uncommunicative, uninspired, serious-minded intellectual drama' (p.314). 'In producing serious plays', he writes, 'we will stand for a second-rateness we would not for a moment abide in the construction of a bridge or the making of an omelette' (p.133). Although the connotations of 'serious' vary for

Seldes, the word is almost always condemnatory when he applies it to the legitimate stage, 'where knowing one's job perfectly and doing it simply and unpretentiously are the rarest thing in the world' (p.255). 'Modern serious plays', he writes, like St John Ervine's *Jane Clegg* (a 1920 Theatre Guild production) make a 'spurious appeal to our sentimentality or our snobbery. It is their pretence to be a great and serious art when they are simply vulgarizations' (p.315).

Although Seldes expresses a certain reluctance to use the term 'bogus', it is, I believe, an extremely accurate indicator of those things he finds so execrable in 1920s culture. Moreover, it reveals a strategic assumption that underlies his discourse and that of so many of the radicals who more or less correctly foresaw the future of American culture. For the term betrays on Seldes's part what I can describe only as mimetiphobia, a fear of imitation itself. Of the lively arts, only three (musical comedy, movies and comic strips) are primarily mimetic. And he prizes these exemplars of what I am tempted to call the illegitimate arts for the challenges they pose to traditional forms of representation. Thus, he especially esteems George Herriman's 'Krazy Kat', the most extravagant and grotesque of the 1920s comic strips, and claims that the 'greatest mistake' the movies ever made was trying to take 'over the realistic theatre' (p.338). Because 'the camera was' developed 'as legitimately an instrument of distortion as of reproduction', film is best suited 'to the projection of emotion by means *not realistic*', namely *The Cabinet of Dr Caligari* (emphasis in original, p.339). So, too, he loves musical comedy for its musical, choreographic, spectacular and vaudevillian qualities, not its verisimilitude.

For Seldes, the legitimate stage is the emblem of mimesis gone wrong insofar as everything that materializes upon it represents a bad copy. Indeed, given the almost Platonic ontology to which he has recourse, the very phrase 'bad copy' is redundant because there can never be a good or successful copy. On the stage the 'desperate effort . . . to create the illusion of reality' suppresses the 'essential distortion, caricature, or transposition which you find in a serious work of art or in a vaudeville sketch' (p.315). Unquestionably, his contempt is in part the result of his unfortunate equations of mimesis with realism and of the legitimate theatre with the kind of play 'which[,] without wit, or intensity, "presents a problem" or drearily holds the mirror up to nature' (p.314). (So much for his former idols, Ibsen and Shaw!) He also unequivocally prefers the 'playing' he discerns in *Caligari*'s 'destruction of realism' to theatrical impersonation, also known as 'acting' (p.335). The dogged literalism of the realistic stage ensures the dullness and superficiality of theatre and theatre artists. For 'if a man has anything profound to express he will flee from the theatre where everything is dependent upon actors usually unintelligent and [where everything] is reduced to the lowest common factor of human intelligence' (p.314).

Seldes's mimetiphobia is linked to his fixation on the 'lively'. Indeed, the other side of mimetiphobia is always a desire for full presence; for pure, unmediated being; for life; for presentation without that which Derrida calls the 'menace of repetition'.[29] Seldes's choice of the word 'lively' to describe the popular arts is no accident. For his title betrays a longing for live art, art before representation, 'honest' art, the 'fresh and transient'. This art has a 'relevance not only to our life, but to life itself'. It enables one 'to live fully' in 'our moment' (pp.346–7). Indeed, it is precisely the ephemerality, contemporaneity and liveness of the lively arts that give them their transcendent qualities. Thus, for example, Al Jolson and Fanny Brice, with 'their intensity of action', perform as people 'possessed by a daemon', 'at the highest possible pressure'. Jolson 'flings' into a song with 'so much energy, violence, so much of the totality of one human being, that you feel it would suffice for a hundred others' (pp.191–2). Seldes's championing of vaudeville at the expense of the legitimate stage is in part the result of the former's comparatively spontaneous nature. For the legitimate theatre of the 1920s epitomizes what Derrida calls the theological stage, that physical – and metaphysical – space in which 'a primary *logos*' is not literally present on 'the theatrical site' but 'governs it from a distance'. On this stage, the written text of the 'author-creator' is imagined as a kind of divine injunction that turns directors and actors into 'interpretive slaves who faithfully execute the providential designs of the 'master''.[30] For Seldes, the theological, also known as legitimate, stage represents an archaic remnant of an older cultural order ill-suited to the tenor of the modern age.

The anti-theatricalism of *The 7 Lively Arts* is thus extremely selective. Seldes does not, like so many anti-theatricalists, cast moral aspersions against the theatre or against actors. They may be stupid, but they have no monopoly on public lewdness. And he clearly prizes performance for its ostentatiously civic face, its role in the public sphere. He loves its theatricality, or aura, to borrow Walter Benjamin's term, 'the intense live presence', as Martin Puchner describes it, 'that binds the actor to the audience'.[31] His prejudice thus represents simultaneously what Puchner calls 'an avant-garde theatricalism' as well as 'a modernist anti-theatricalism'.[32] On the one hand, like so many American and European avant-gardists, he eagerly champions the theatricality of the modern age and of a vast array of innovative and once-disdained cultural practices. He longs for 'a revolution in our way of looking at the arts' that will celebrate (for example) 'the damned effrontery of the two-a-day' vaudeville show and 'the shouting song of the Negro' (pp.24, 63, 249). He even argues (strangely reminiscent of his contemporary, Antonin Artaud) that 'a plea could be made for violence *per se* in the American theatre' as a way of rediscovering its 'energy' (p.193). On the other hand, Seldes's anti-theatricalism epitomizes the high modernist assault on traditional forms of representation, 'a critique of the actual theatre' – the serious, legitimate stage of the mid-1920s. Taking up the 'modernist critique of realism, mimesis, and literalism', he argues that the liveliness of the theatre has been stifled by a tendency 'to prettify and restrain' (p.193).[33]

The 7 Lively Arts would seem to address itself primarily to two classes of readers: modernist intellectuals like Seldes himself and pretentious 'middle-class' patrons who regard the lively arts 'as impostors and... contemptible vulgarisms' (p.350). The latter, after all, are the ones who champion the bogus arts, the highfalutin theatre-goers who relish serious plays for 'their spurious appeal to our sentimentality or our snobbery' (p.315). They are the consumers whom Seldes and so many other American modernist intellectuals attacked, not the 'simple and sophisticated people' at 'the two extremes', but those unfortunates who hover 'in between', those 'who can see nothing without the lorgnettes of prejudice provided by fashion and gentility' (p.23). These are the chief patrons of the legitimate stage, the ones who guaranteed its dullness, superficiality and inconsequence.

Middle-high seriousness

Gilbert Seldes's carving out a middling position in the US cultural hierarchy in which to place the legitimate theatre, between the 'simple' and 'sophisticated', ties it inexorably to the category 'middlebrow', which, Janice Radway notes, 'was apparently first mobilized sometime in the 1920s as a way of referring to an increasingly visible group of consumers who enthusiastically bought the diverse products of a growing industry devoted to the marketing of 'culture''.[34] Although Seldes does not employ the term, his portrait of the genteel, fashionable, feminized snob who patronizes the legitimate stage is closely aligned with other descriptions from the 1920s of the passive consumer of standardized art commodities. From the 1920s through the 1950s, the middlebrow was constructed as an aspiring bourgeois(e) with a modicum of education who, Radway notes, would 'read the new book-review sections' in news-papers and subscribe to 'innovative magazines like *Time* and the *New Yorker*'.[35] Yet middlebrow culture was not a 'harbinger of new mass cultural forms', but a distinctive by-product of American modernism, 'a separate aesthetic and ideological production constructed by a particular fraction of the middle class offended equally by the 'crassness' of mass culture and by the literary avant-garde'.[36] For the middlebrow consumer was routinely described as – and condemned for – being a social-climbing parvenu trying, in the words of one later writer, to 'pre-empt – the highbrow's function' and 'blur the lines between the serious and the frivolous'.[37] And because middlebrow culture, as Pierre Bourdieu notes, always references highbrow by eagerly offering up 'acceptable versions' of either avant-gardist or consecrated works, it 'encourage[s] and justif[ies] confusion of the two [middlebrow and highbrow]'.[38] The bogus sophisticate that Seldes so berates is, then, unmistakably the middlebrow consumer, the highbrow wannabe, the one fixated on those dreary and pretentious, 'arty conglomerations of middle-high seriousness and bourgeois beauty' (pp.315–16).

Despite the conflicts between residual and emergent formations, between the genteel critics and the modernists over the value of popular arts, the cultural hierarchy in the United States during the 1920s was typically imagined as being clearly delineated and relatively stable. This delineation, moreover – especially in regard to the legitimate theatre's place in it – has survived more or less intact to the present day. At the top, representing sacralized, highbrow culture, were both large institutions (like opera companies, symphony orchestras and museums filled with Old Masters) and small, independent producers (like painters, poets and composers) who vended a restricted body of goods to a high-status public. These independent producers ranged from relatively anti-commercial, avant-gardist artists to the makers or recyclers of archaic (and allegedly natural) folk cultures. Highbrow work tended, then as now, to be wrapped in mystique, trading on its purported authenticity and resist-ance to the commodity form. (Highbrow culture has changed the least in character since the 1920s.) At the opposite end of the spectrum (representing the Taylorized, unwashed, lowbrow and often romanticized masses), were found jazz, comic strips, mass-produced graphics, cheap movie houses, dime novels and, among theatre forms, vaudeville, minstrel shows, burlesque, freak shows, circuses and the like. Although these theatrical forms were not mass-produced like cinema, they were usually deemed lowbrow insofar as they were imagined as catering to the working classes and only fit for consumption en masse.

I have argued elsewhere that what I am labelling the legitimate theatre became positioned during the 1920s as a middlebrow form, committed both to art and commercial success.[39] This is not to say that all theatrical practices in the United States fell into this category. Paul DiMaggio notes that the non-commercial art theatres or so-called little theatres (whose voice and champion was *Theatre Arts* magazine, first published in 1916) aimed to produce a relatively elite product. 'But for a handful of settlement-house, leftist, and rural theatres, the little stages never tried to serve any but a high-status public', and charged admission accordingly, effectively barring 'the working or lower middle classes'.[40] And despite the Broadway success of Eugene O'Neill, the New York-centered legitimate theatre was structured precisely by the binary opposition that Van Wyck Brooks noted (and critiqued) between art and commerce. Every theatre critic weighed in, one way or the other, on the difficulty in trying perpetually to negotiate this schism. Walter Prichard Eaton, the Harvard-educated successor to George Pierce Baker at Yale and long-time contributor to *Theatre Arts* magazine, despaired at the disparity between the 'professional theatre of commerce' and that 'intellectual and spiritual aristocrat' otherwise known as 'the true theatre'.[41] And the most famous, flamboyant, and idiosyncratic of the drama critics, George Jean Nathan – who made a career out of sneeringly reprimanding nearly every playwright who had the misfortune of opening a play under his watch – was uniquely disdainful of what he called the popular theatre. In his view, the commercial theatre, because it was managed by 'a great savanna of successful business men who are mistaken for and hailed as talented producers', represents a 'refuge from art and literature, from beauty and truth'.[42]

The middlebrow status of the legitimate stage is confirmed by the renown and power of a 'warm and reasonable' tastemaker like Burns Mantle, who was theatre critic for the New York *Daily News* from 1922 until 1943.[43] He is best known, however, for his stewardship of the annual *Best Plays* volumes that he initiated in 1919 and of which he remained editor until his death in 1948. Although one might argue – and many have – with his annual selection of the ten 'best' plays (he excluded musicals until the Gershwin's 1931 Pulitzer Prize-winning *Of Thee I Sing*), his series is undeniably representative of Broadway's legitimate offerings. Included among his selections is the vast majority of now canonical plays (or rather, 'descriptive synopses' thereof),[44] along with an assortment of long-forgotten pot-boilers and 'arty conglomerations of middle-high seriousness'. In the 'Introduction' to the first volume, Mantle maps out his editorial project and his method of play selection. He claims that he has endeavoured to 'compromise between the popular success, as representing the choice of the people who support the theater, and the success with sufficient claim to literary distinction of text or theme to justify its publication'.[45] His collections thus strike 'a sanely considered compromise' between 'the popular or so-called commercial theater, which is the theater of the people' and 'the "best" plays judged by the higher literary standards'.[46] His exclusion of musical comedies, farces and 'experimental' plays guarantees the unremittingly middlebrow character of the theatre that has come down to us as representing the 'best' of its time.[47]

Burns Mantle's penchant for 'compromise,' however, conceals the social and cultural struggles taking place in and around the legitimate theatre during the 1920s. For with the brisk assimilation of new immigrants, the rapid growth of the white-collar workforce, the expansion of disposable income and leisure time in which to spend it, the rise of jazz and radio, and the boom of a popular culture industry centred in Hollywood, the legitimate theatre became a kind of battleground in which a 'higher literary' theater was becoming increasingly hostile to and isolated from 'the theatre of the people'. This struggle pitted so-called serious playwrights against commercial producers, art against business, the 'literary' against the 'lively', and the most influential critics against 'a popular theatre', to borrow Nathan's phrase, in which 'the best in drama and dramatic literature must inevitably fail'.[48] It also pitted a generation of older critics coming out of the genteel tradition, like Nathan and Walter Prichard Eaton, against a generation of young, modernist upstarts, like Gilbert Seldes. For much of the 'higher literary' theatre of the 1920s represented a sanctuary for upper-middle-class patrons, critics and playwrights, many of whom had deep roots in American soil and represented what one observer described as 'Anglo-Saxon and inherently Protestant' stock.[49] The majority of these littérateurs, moreover, came from genteel families, unlike the stars, producers and defenders of 'a popular theatre'. So many of those associated with this insurgent theatre were first- or second-generation Jewish-Americans, like Seldes, George S. Kaufman, Fanny Brice, Eddie Cantor, the Gershwins, Jerome Kern, Rodgers and Hart, plus a slew of others. Its more intellectual champions, meanwhile, like Seldes, were bourgeois rebels, intent on launching a revolution that, as C. Wright Mills points out, 'was aesthetic and literary rather than explicitly political, ... an enthusiastic revolt against "provincial" regional hankerings, against social and ideological proprieties, against gentility in all forms'.[50] These modernist anti-theatricalists represented a version of the ironic, 1920s intellectual who, Edmund Wilson notes, enjoyed 'the debauchment of American life as a burlesque show' and tried 'to get a kick out of...letting one's self be carried along by the mad hilarity and tragedy of jazz, of living only for the excitement of the night'.[51] To this extent, Gorman is certainly correct when he argues that 'Seldes and the other modernists were in effect sustaining the distance from the mass public that intellectuals on the Left had opened over the early century.'[52] In Seldes's case, however, the primary symptom of that distance is not derision but the near erasure of the working classes, the ones, after all, who 'created and admired' the popular arts that Seldes so relishes (*7 Lively Arts*, p.350).

The conflict between high and low that defined the legitimate theatre during the 1920s thus set old money against new; a Europeanized cultural tradition against a new vernacular one that was impudently laying claim to the brand names 'modern' and 'American'; and a well-established, genteel, white Anglo-Saxon Protestant elite against young, insurgent, entrepreneurial, often Jewish artists and intellectuals. It is worth noting here that although Nathan came from a Jewish family, he 'repeatedly refused to discuss his Jewishness', 'obfuscated his family background', and 'lived in dread of "exposure"'.[53] And it is no coincidence, then, that Seldes in *The 7 Lively Arts* chooses Eaton as the champion of the legitimate theatre and 'the great antagonist of the movies' in an imaginary debate he pens between Eaton and D. W. Griffith, in which Eaton is limned as an Apollonian, elitist, pompous metaphysician for whom 'the past is not dead', who glories in an 'invisible and divine' art, and longs to resurrect a sacralized, humanistic theatre in which men 'speak with the tongues of angels – and of men' (pp.29, 37–8). The Dionysian Griffith, in contrast, defines himself as one (like Seldes) unafraid of 'the very lowest', the champion of '*the* vulgar art', of 'ecstasy' and 'a Rabelaisian madness' (emphasis in original, pp.30, 35, 37, 38).

Since the 1920s, the distaste for the legitimate stage expressed by the modernist pioneers has been replicated countless times, by the anti-middlebrow, leftist intellectuals of the post-World War II years; the neo-avant-gardists of the 1960s; the cohort of poststructuralist theorists who privilege narrative at the expense of poetry and drama; the cultural studies mafia for whom mass culture is far more politically engaging and revealing than 'modern serious plays'; and performance studies scholars for whom theatricality – but not the theatre – provides a methodological template. The legitimate stage is so irredeemably middlebrow that even the major critics of middlebrow, Janice Radway, Joan Shelley Rubin and Andrew Ross, ignore it. This critical prejudice has been bolstered by the shrinking of the legitimate theatre as a field of cultural production, a steady decline in the number of new Broadway plays, a reversal in the direction of the movement of product between the silver screen and the stage (once upon a time, popular plays were routinely bought and adapted by Hollywood), and the ever-increasing colonization of Broadway by media conglomerates (like Disney and Clear Channel). Given the revolutions taking place during the 1920s in class structure, leisure technologies, and in the production and consumption of culture, critics like Eaton or Seldes must be seen less as agents of change than symptoms of cultural transformation, overseeing and managing the flight of 'the people' from the legitimate theatre. Despite their opposing positions, they were in effect secretly colluding in the elevation of the stage and its expulsion from the realm of cultural centrality and moment it had enjoyed at the end of the nineteenth century. The success of 'arty conglomerations of middle-high seriousness' (toward which they harboured radically different attitudes) unquestionably made possible the triumph of a serious literary drama of no mean consequence, but it also ensured the permanent marginalization of the legitimate stage. So it seems the bastards won after all.

Notes

1. Brenda Murphy, 'Plays and Playwrights: 1915–1945', in Don B. Wilmeth and Christopher Bigsby, eds, *The Cambridge History of American Theatre, Volume Two: 1870–1945'* (Cambridge: Cambridge University Press, 1999), p.289.
2. Jack Poggi, *Theater in America: The Impact of Economic Forces, 1870–1967* (Ithaca: Cornell University Press, 1968), p.47.
3. Poggi, *Theater in America*, p.48.
4. Walter Prichard Eaton, 'The strangling of our theatre: Dangers involved in the coming control, by film producers, of the American stage', *Vanity Fair*, April 1926: 48, 144.
5. Ludwig Lewisohn (1920), cited in Barnard Hewitt, *Theatre U.S.A.: 1668 to 1957* (New York: McGraw-Hill, 1959), p.331.
6. Hewitt, *Theatre U.S.A.*, p.333.
7. Poggi, *Theater in America*, p.30.
8. Paul DiMaggio, 'Cultural Boundaries and Structural Change: The Extension of the High Culture Model to Theater, Opera, and the Dance, 1900–1940', in Michèle Lamont and Marcel Fournier, eds, *Cultivating Differences: Symbolic Boundaries and the Making of Inequality* (Chicago: University of Chicago Press, 1992), p.29; Poggi, *Theater in America*, p.80.
9. Poggi, *Theater in America*, pp.39–40.
10. See Poggi, *Theater in America*, pp.41–5, 89.
11. Poggi, *Theater in America*, p.42.
12. Richard Butsch, *The Making of American Audiences: From Stage to Television, 1750–1990* (Cambridge: Cambridge University Press, 2000), p.122.

13. Cited in Alfred L. Bernheim, *The Business of the Theatre: An Economic History of the American Theatre, 1750–1932* (1932; New York: Benjamin Blom, 1964), p.91.
14. 'The variety theatres: Sentador's views on the decline of this amusement', *New York Dramatic Mirror* (January 18, 1879): 4.
15. Joseph Jefferson, *The Autobiography of Joseph Jefferson*, ed. Alan S. Downer (Cambridge, MA: Harvard University Press, 1964), p.312.
16. Jefferson, *The Autobiography of Joseph Jefferson*, p.50.
17. Charles Coburn, 'Our theatre fighting for its life', *Theatre Magazine*, July 1926: 9.
18. Robert McLaughlin, *Broadway and Hollywood: A History of Economic Interaction* (New York: Arno Press, 1974), n.p., 9. This book remains the most comprehensive study of the economic relationship between theatre and film.
19. Cited in Terry Smith, *Making the Modern: Industry, Art, and Design in America* (Chicago: University of Chicago Press, 1993), p.19.
20. Cited in Michael Kammen, *American Culture, American Tastes: Social Change and the 20th Century* (New York: Knopf, 1999), pp.33–4.
21. Cited in Paul R. Gorman, *Left Intellectuals and Popular Culture in America* (Chapel Hill: University of North Carolina Press, 1996), p.55.
22. R. J. Coady, 'American Art', *The Soil*, 1 (January 1917): 54–5.
23. William Wasserstrom, 'Van Wyck Brooks', in *American Writers: A Collection of Literary Biographies*, ed. Leonard Unger (New York: Scribner's, 1974), vol. 1, p.240.
24. Van Wyck Brooks, ''Highbrow' and 'Lowbrow'', *America's Coming of Age* (New York: E.P. Dutton, 1915), p.35. Further citations will be noted in the text.
25. Gorman, *Left Intellectuals and Popular Culture*, p.76.
26. Michael Kammen, *The Lively Years: Gilbert Seldes and the Transformation of Cultural Criticism in the United States* (New York: Oxford University Press, 1996), p.31.
27. Kammen, *The Lively Years*, p.68.
28. Gilbert Seldes, *The 7 Lively Arts* (New York: Dover [1924], 2001), p.348. All further citations will be noted in the text.
29. Jacques Derrida, 'The Theater of Cruelty and the Closure of Representation', in *Writing and Difference*, trans. Alan Bass (Chicago: University of Chicago Press, 1978), p.247.
30. Derrida, 'The Theater of Cruelty and the Closure of Representation', p.235.
31. Martin Puchner, *Stage Fright: Modernism, Anti-Theatricality, and Drama* (Baltimore, MD: Johns Hopkins University Press, 2002), p.3.
32. Puchner, *Stage Fright*, p.7.
33. Puchner, *Stage Fright*, pp.7, 11.
34. Janice Radway, 'On the gender of the middlebrow consumer and the threat of the culturally fraudulent female', *South Atlantic Quarterly*, 93:4 (Fall 1994): 872.
35. Radway, 'On the gender of the middlebrow consumer', p.872.
36. Janice Radway, 'The scandal of the middlebrow: The Book-of-the-Month Club, class fracture, and cultural authority', *South Atlantic Quarterly* 89:4 (Fall 1990): endnote 7, p.733.
37. Russell Lynes, 'Highbrow, Lowbrow, Middlebrow', in *The Tastemakers* (New York: Harper & Brothers, 1954), p.318.

38. Pierre Bourdieu, *Distinction: A Social Critique of the Judgement of Taste*, trans. Richard Nice (Cambridge: Harvard University Press, 1984), p.323; see also Joan Shelley Rubin, *The Making of Middlebrow Culture* (Chapel Hill: University of North Carolina Press, 1992).
39. See David Savran, 'Middlebrow Anxiety', *A Queer Sort of Materialism: Recontextualizing American Theatre* (Ann Arbor: University of Michigan Press, 2003), pp.3–55.
40. DiMaggio, 'Cultural Boundaries and Structural Change', p.25.
41. Eaton, 'The strangling of our theatre: 47–8.
42. George Jean Nathan, *The Popular Theatre* (1918; New York: Knopf, 1923), pp.9, 44.
43. Gerald Bordman, *The Oxford Companion to American Theatre*, 2nd edn (New York: Oxford University Press, 1992), p.461.
44. Burns Mantle, 'Introduction', *The Best Plays of 1919–20* (New York: Dodd, Mead, 1920), p.iv.
45. Mantle, 'Introduction', *The Best Plays of 1919–20*, p.iv.
46. Mantle, 'Introduction', *The Best Plays of 1919–20*, p.iv; Burns Mantle, 'Introduction', *The Best Plays of 1921–22* (New York: Dodd, Mead, 1922), p.iii.
47. Burns Mantle, 'Introduction', *The Best Plays of 1920–21* (New York: Dodd, Mead, 1921), p.iii.
48. Nathan, *The Popular Theatre*, p.21.
49. André Siegfried, *America Comes of Age*, trans. H. H. Hemming and Doris Hemming (New York: Harcourt, Brace 1927), p.3.
50. C. Wright Mills, *White Collar: The American Middle Classes* (New York: Oxford University Press, 1951), p.146.
51. Cited in Mills, *White Collar*, p.145.
52. Gorman, *Left Intellectuals and Popular Culture in America*, p.81.
53. Thomas F. Connolly, *George Jean Nathan and the Making of Modern American Drama Criticism* (Madison, NJ: Fairleigh Dickinson University Press, 2000), p.27.

12

Performing Obscene Modernism: Theatrical Censorship and the Making of Modern Drama

Julie Stone Peters

In December of 1893, at New York City's Grand Central Palace, the theatrical manager Adolphe Delacroix was offering an exhibit of the 'Streets of Cairo', modelled on that at the Chicago World's Fair, and featuring teenage Oriental dancers performing a *'danse du ventre'* (see Figure 1).[1] After the performance opened, with four musicians costumed as Turks seated on a divan on 'the rickety stage', the dancers emerged: Zuleika, 'arrayed in red silk Turkish trousers, a blue Eton jacket trimmed with gold, and a white gauze [sash], tight at the waist', Stella, 'a tall shapely blonde, with a face that might...captivate a soothsayer or a potentate', Zora, 'a little plump, black-eyed thing', Ferida, 'the wife of an Eastern medicine man, a dancer of renown in the Orient', and Fatma, whose name (the *New York Times* reporter commented acidly) 'is particularly well-suited to her figure'. While Ferida was 'holding her audience spell-bound', 'flouncing [her] clothing', 'wriggl[ing] and twist[ing], turn[ing], cavort[ing], and kick[ing]', one Inspector Williams advanced toward the footlights and said: ' "Stop that!" ' Defiantly continuing, the dancers were arrested and charged with 'performing a dance contrary to good morals'. The trial played to a full house: with the dancers in costumes ('short red skirts, covered with beads and gold embroidery'), the morals crusader Anthony Comstock crying out, 'I am defending womanhood in this city[!]' (he was ordered to sit down), and a 'large and burly' policeman who, after failing to describe the *danse du ventre*, attempted to demonstrate it. Against the charge that the dance was 'disgusting' and 'indecent', the defence asserted its value as art. As an 'artistic dance and the dance of our nation' (said Zuleika), the dance 'had a picturesque beauty' that 'embodied the poetry of motion'. Admired by 'many magi, soothsayers, wise men of Syria, chiefs of tribes,

Figure 2 The *'danse du ventre'* at the Chicago World's Fair (1893): a 'suggestively lascivious contorting of the abdominal muscles, which is extremely ungraceful and almost shockingly disgusting'

and Oriental potentates', it was, in effect, 'art for art's sake'. Moreover, Mrs Potter Palmer saw it 13 times in Chicago and found nothing immoral in it. The dancers were fined $50 each, and returned to the theatre with a new routine featuring a cancan, a 'Carmencita' dance, and the occasional sly 'contortio[n]' just for the police.

What we have here is a characteristic intersection: of theatricality, obscenity, censorship, the para-theatre of the courtroom, and 'art' proffered as defence (as well as an instance of the complex valences of *fin-de-siècle* Orientalism). One can see, in the Grand Central Palace '*danse du ventre*', an exemplar of the exotic nineteenth-century sex entertainments that were periodically raided by the police, and, at the same time, a prototype of the shocking modern dance that was to emerge in the decades that followed: Isadora Duncan, performing *The Rubaiyat of Omar Khayyam* for a group of society women in 1898 wearing nothing but a skimpy chemise; Ruth St Denis performing *Radha* in 1905 wearing little but jewelled breastplates and a gauze skirt, her 'bosom heav[ing]' as she kissed her fingertips and slid them down the curves of her body.[2] While serious dancers were getting seriously naked (or so it seemed), the serious drama was beginning to exploit the risqué costuming, exotic 'realism', and voluptuous sensuality of the dance. In 1890, Sarah Bernhardt shocked everyone with the lascivious abandon of her performance in Sardou's *Cléopâtre*. (A British spectator commented: 'How unlike, how *very* unlike the home life of our own dear queen!') By 1907, Colette could appear in a play entitled *Flesh*, in which the heroine's dress was ripped from her body, revealing naked breasts and an exposed expanse of skin, shoulder to ankle.[3] Equally important, as the serious drama began to talk about syphilis and abortion and other unsavoury topics, it began to come under attack from both morals crusaders and the police. Modern drama was 'unhealthy', 'disgusting', 'very demoralizing in [its] tendency', pervaded by the 'worst kind of erotic perversion', showing 'hideous nightmare[s]', 'morbid and sickening dissection[s] of corrupt humanity'.[4] The result was the banning of Ibsen's *Ghosts*, Strindberg's *Miss Julie*, Wedekind's *Spring Awakening* and the Lulu plays, Wilde's *Salomé*, Schnitzler's *La Ronde*, Shaw's *Mrs Warren's Profession* (among others), in effect, some of the most important works of early theatrical modernism.

One might associate the rise of obscenity as a specific juridical category with two major developments. First, over the course of the nineteenth century, pornography and erotic performance (products of mass culture, the rise of leisure and, specifically, the rise of erotic pleasure as a leisure activity) became important commercial enterprises.[5] Second, in the second half of the century, one could feel the first stirrings of what we might think of as sexual modernism (the notion that sex was not merely an accessory to the propagation of the species but a necessary part of physical and spiritual health), slowly beginning to enter the intellectual mainstream. State obscenity regulation (developing rapidly in the second half of the century[6]) emerged in response, as a supplement to what was experienced as general moral degradation in the corrupt metropolis. Prodded by the moral purity movements of the period, obscenity regulation (sometimes framed in the language of 'decency' or 'public morals') promised to shore up norms that seemed no longer able to do their work by means of culture.

If obscenity regulation arose to protect morals from modern pornography and mass entertainment, it also arose to protect art. As Allison Pease has argued, modern pornography, produced for a mass readership and intended as a form of private sexual practice, grew up beside, and in opposition to aesthetics as a branch of philosophy as it developed in the nineteenth century. Where art was disinterested, an end in itself, above the world of commerce and exchange, finer as it became more disembodied, and ultimately a stimulus for the rational and contemplative faculties, pornography was unabashedly a product of commerce, catering purely to self-interest, instrumental, frankly embodied, and a stimulus for bodily pleasure. Thus, obscenity as a moral and legal concept arose, in part at least, as a kind of watchdog for the aesthetic: keeping disinterested contemplation pure of bodily sensation, commercial interest and the pleasure-seeking that the sex entertainment industry represented.

The problem, in the last decade of the nineteenth century and the first decade of the twentieth, was that modern art had decided to concern itself with sex: not, as light comedy had always done, in 'profligate farces and thinly sentimentalized tom-cat love tales' (as Shaw referred to them in an early essay on stage censorship[7]), but as a moral challenge to reigning obscenity standards. Modern art would present the 'frank, scientific... discussion and presentation of all subjects pertaining to sex' to destroy 'the murky, unclean, timid and defiled mental attitudes [which make sex a] matter of shame, secrecy, uncleanness and dirty jokes'.[8] Placing sex (as image and problem) at the heart of social critique, modern art seemed to have declared itself, by definition, 'conscientiously immoral' (in Shaw's phrase [*Report*, p.48]). If the widespread vitalist discourse of sexual hygiene had begun to overtake the discourse of sexual morals, the new sex moralism could be found in advanced art. As modern art gained adherents, beginning to draw mainstream audiences, obscenity regulation increasingly focused on its products (more-or-less ignoring cheap pornography, burlesque and music halls, and 'thinly sentimentalized tom-cat love tales'). Obscenity became, principally, a problem not of working-class entertainment or even coterie avant-gardism but of mainstream culture. An early twentieth-century moral reformer like Eliza Lummis, for instance, objected to cabaret, burlesque, lewd dancing and scanty costumes, but 'problem plays' were her primary concern.[9]

The obscene theatre

Eliza Lummis's focus on theatrical obscenity is indicative of the centrality of theatre during this period to debates about obscene art. We tend to think of the high-profile obscenity cases focusing on novels as setting the terms of modern debates about artistic freedom (the trials, for instance, of Lawrence's *The Rainbow* in 1915, Joyce's *Ulysses* in 1921, or Radclyffe Hall's *Well of Loneliness* in 1928). But in the decades before these trials, debates about obscene art focused primarily on the drama.[10] France (until 1905), Germany and England had highly visible institutions of dramatic censorship, which generated heated public disputes. In the United States, prosecutions for theatrical obscenity (usually tried in public before a jury) proved magnets for public attention as scandalously entertaining as the plays themselves.[11] Discussions of theatrical obscenity (in the censor's office, the courtroom, the press, and the drama itself) helped to articulate some of the central modern and antimodern discourses about sex in the public realm: as health and illness, purity and pollution, vitality and degeneracy, nature and perversion, enlightenment and demoralization. Modern drama, steeped in the work of Richard von Krafft-Ebing, Otto Weininger, Havelock Ellis, Freud, not only talked about syphilis and abortion, but gave embodiment to the strange new figures created by modern sexology: the sadist, the masochist, the fetishist, the necrophiliac, the sexual invert (male and female). In modern drama, with its parables of obscenity, sex became character (in Weininger's theatrical language); it became a vehicle for the rebirth of tragedy; it became *the* problem for modern culture.

If obscenity was defined during this period by debates about the drama, modern drama and its institutions were equally defined by obscenity. In banning the most radical new plays, censorship forced the creation of alternative venues, producing, in effect, such phenomena as the independent theatre movement (André Antoine's Théâtre Libre, the Freie Bühne in Berlin, or J. T. Grein's Independent Theatre), which proved a galvanizing force. Such playwrights as Wedekind and Shaw (most notably) wrote in continual dialogue with the censors: probing the limits of what could be publicly staged; offering up revisions that veiled sexual content but tempted interpretation; protesting loudly in the press. Theatrical censorship created an international community of protestors in the name of art, galvanizing the liberal cognoscenti around the idea of a free theatre. While they raged against censorship, playwrights and producers also (secretly or not so secretly) embraced the publicity that censorship brought. Dramatists seeking the limelight could be 'intentionally unfortunate' in their dealings with the censor (or managers hoping to increase revenues as the critic John Palmer Wryly commented[12]). Threatened prosecutions caused attendance to soar.

What placed drama at the centre of debates about obscenity during the period was not merely its focus on serious sex but its association with the theatre. Theatre, it was said, had a 'natural propensity... towards licentiousness'[13] that made it not simply another arena for the performance of obscenity, but obscenity's natural home. Thus, it required (and had always required) more stringent censorship. Addressing an imaginary abolitionist of theatrical censorship, the defender of theatrical censorship (in Zola's mocking caricature) was a defender of 'public order':

> Don't you know that the theatre is not the book? That [if you abolish censorship], every evening you'll...inflame [2000 people], send them mad into the streets, where they'll give themselves over to the utmost excess? Are you considering the abominable licence that will be unleashed the day the theatre is free?[14]

The report of the parliamentary committee appointed to study British stage censorship in 1909, which recorded the testimony of such luminaries as Granville Barker, G. K. Chesterton, Sir William Gilbert (of Gilbert and Sullivan), Arthur Pinero, George Bernard Shaw and Bram Stoker (among others), offers what is probably the most thorough articulation of fears that a 'general Saturnalia of reckless debauchery'[15] would result from the abolition of theatrical censorship. 'In a novel one may read, "Eliza stripped off her dressing-gown and stepped into her bath", without any harm', explained Sir William Gilbert, 'but...if that were presented on the stage it would be very shocking' (*Report*, p.192). Similarly, the playwright J. W. Comyns Carr cited Maurice Maeterlinck's *Monna Vanna* (1902), whose heroine saves Pisa by promising to appear naked (under her cloak) in the tent of Prinzivalle, a mercenary besieging the city. 'Now in the written book that seems to be a matter entirely without offence', he explained, 'but when it is transferred to the stage I think it might well make the Censor pause' (*Report*, p.255).

It was, in part, the actor who gave the theatre its power of material realization, its power to bring images from the ethereal imagination and transform them suddenly into gross bodily presences: 'Ideas or situations which, when described on a printed page may work little mischief', explained the *Report*, 'when represented through the human personality of actors may have a more powerful and more deleterious effect' (p.viii). Hyper-real, transgressing the threshold between private and public, inflaming the hapless spectator: the actor (or, rather, the disturbingly naked actress) could exercise a kind of demagogic power over the audience, subjecting it to her surreal grandeur. '[Everything] comes out in letters of fire on the stage', explained Sir Herbert Beerbohm Tree. 'The perspective of the stage enlarges everything' (pp.154–5).

If theatre inflamed and enlarged (as Tree's unconsciously sexual rhetoric suggests), it did so not in the privacy of the home but 'in something corresponding to Trafalgar Square' (as G. K. Chesterton pointed out [p.344]). The public nature of theatre transformed what might be private titillation into public shame, and public shame into scandal. 'To read something obscene may do you as a private individual reader a certain amount of harm', commented the *Times* theatre critic A. B. Walkley:

> It will do you much more harm...if you listen to those indecent words being uttered in the company of some hundreds of other human beings. The thing then becomes a scandal...I might blush at something I read privately; but I should be...confounded with the greatest possible shame if I had to listen...in the miscellaneous company of hundreds of playgoers.
>
> (*Report*, p.198)

What was troubling in the theatre was not merely the individual's embarrassing exposure to private acts in public places, but the presence of the crowd more generally, 'moved by the same emotions, its members conscious of one another's presence' (p.viii). Citing 'the new science of collective psychology' (with a reference to Gustave Le Bon's *On the Psychology of Crowds* [1895] provided by the committee), Walkley explained: 'A crowd is a new entity, differing in mind and will from the individuals who compose it; just as...if you mix up oxygen and hydrogen in certain proportion you get an entirely different thing, namely, water', so, if you mix up individuals in the theatre, you get 'a new compound' (p.197).

The theatrical crowd, its 'intellectual pitch...lowered', its 'emotional pitch...raised', was 'peculiarly susceptible to what hypnotists call "suggestion" ', and tended to 'tak[e] on something of the characteristics of a hypnotised "subject" '. Hypnotized by the mesmerizing theatre, peaceful, law-abiding citizens could turn into agents of terror:

> You get innumerable instances of that in history; for example, in the French Revolution, where men in crowds committed horrible excesses which they could not account for afterwards. They were individually peaceful and harmless citizens, [until subject to] the peculiar, magnetic, contagious influence of the crowd.
>
> *(Report*, p.197)

Stuck in the middle of a terrifying theatrical crowd capable of horrible excesses, there was no exit. If one does not care for a book, Chesterton explained, 'you shut it up, and you throw it into the dustbin'. But 'if you are wedged [in] a great theatre, it is by no means the same thing' *(Report*, p.344). In the theatre, 'you crowd a mass of people together, not as you would crowd them in the streets, but as you would crowd them in a prison, in such a manner that it is humiliating for anybody to make any protest' (p.344). Subject to naked ladies, to sadism, to torture, one 'might try to get out' but would be unable to do so. 'If I open a book which is all about tortures, I shut it up again; but how can I shut up a theatre?' (p.344).

Theatrical censorship was, in effect, an attempt to shut up a theatre before any member of the audience might feel helplessly unable to do so. But the theatre seemed particularly made to evade such attempts. 'The fact is, it is virtually impossible to tell from perusing a script what effect a line or an incident in a play will produce on an audience assembled in a theatre', wrote an anonymous correspondent to the London *Times* in 1907:

> A gesture, an intonation, a movement may be immeasurably more indecent than the most brutal baldness of verbal expression. Indeed, one can easily conceive a play in which the dialogue was throughout adapted to the requirements of a young ladies' boarding school while the stage directions contained matter which, illustrated in dramatic action, would provoke a riot.
>
> *(The Times* 29 October 1907, p.15)

If theatrical obscenity was difficult to predict from scripts, it was still more difficult to prosecute in the courtroom, where *double-entendre* was easily deniable and sexual meaning always attributable to the overheated imagination of the salacious censor. The defence attorney for Clyde Fitch's *Sapho*, prosecuted in 1900 for a scene in which the heroine was carried up a winding staircase to an off-stage bedroom while 'uttering inarticulate sounds [of] intense satisfaction' declared: 'there is in it nothing questionable except what would occur to a prurient mind[!]'.[16] Attempts to re-enact the indecent passages in the courtroom could not only be highly embarrassing (as the attempted *'danse du ventre'* of the police officer in the 'Streets of Cairo' case suggests) but posed the unique problem of replaying the original violation, allowing the profanations of the theatre to penetrate the sanctified space of the law itself.

The theatrical obscene

In the 1909 parliamentary report and in similar justifications for censorship during the period one can find, between the lines, a catalogue of anxieties about the terrifying aesthetics of modern theatre: its hyper-real staging of objects; its transgression of the boundaries between public and private; its ability to arouse, offend or shame the crowd; its use of gesture to explode the formal limits of the text. But there are echoes here, too, of perennial anti-theatricalism: the fear of theatre's realization of fantasy in all-too material form; of its uncanny enlargement of the stage figure; of the seductive presence of the actor; of the threat of the aroused crowd; of the ability of performance to evade official control. That is, the aesthetics of obscenity reflected in the report and elsewhere were the aesthetics of the theatre itself. Modern drama (in testing the limits of obscenity) and modern censorship (in offering a full articulation of the nature of theatrical obscenity) made manifest the deep latent historical and structural affiliation between theatricality and obscenity (expressed in one etymology for 'obscenity': *ob* [against] and *scaena* [stage]; obscenity is that which is against or off the stage).[17] This structural affiliation had two sides: if theatre was troubling in part because it always verged on the obscene, obscenity was troubling in part because it always verged on the theatrical. Obscenity and theatricality shared an investment in the body as their primary agent of expression, exhibitionism as their central *raison-d'être*, voyeurism as their principal mode of reception, the play between concealment and revelation as one of their central techniques of producing pleasure. Both promiscuously transferred things normally private into the public realm. In both, the production of intense emotional affect was founded on a fundamental charade.

Modern obscenity off-stage often exploited this historical link with the theatre. The figure of the actress (exhibiting herself for money) had long been a suggestively erotic one. But, as Tracy Davis has pointed out, the suggestive postcards of the nineteenth century featuring actresses against theatrical backdrops became explicitly pornographic toward the end of the century. In the 1890s, one could buy postcard sets such as 'Behind the scenes at the Ballet, startling revelations' with 15 'highly erotical scene[s] between a well known [theatre subscriber and] the first star of the ballet'.[18] Drawing on the theatrical trope, pornography could attempt to replicate the kind of veiling and unveiling central to erotic dance performance. In 1896, for instance, the publisher of a theatrical newspaper called *Broadway* was found guilty of obscenity for carrying revealing pictures of women partially covered with lampblack, which could be erased with a piece of bread. As the judge commented, 'the object of sending them out in that condition was, of course, to excite curiosity to know what was thus concealed.'[19]

The association between obscenity and theatricality was still more insistently exploited on stage. The nude or semi-nude theatrical tableaux ('living pictures', 'living statues' or 'posing acts'), tastefully obscene, embraced the scopophiliac pleasures of spying on the word-less body common to theatre and obscenity. Similarly playing off this shared pleasure, Arthur Wing Pinero's *A Wife Without a Smile* (1904) showed a marionette on stage whose gyrating limbs indicated marital activity in the bedroom above (an 'erotomer', as the London *Times* theatre critic called it). 'The movements of the dancing doll [speak] in plain language of sexual intercourse taking place', wrote a concerned citizen to the Lord Chamberlain, 'Could anything be more repugnant to every sense of decency?'[20] Identified with both the erotic and the theatrical body, the marionette also served as a sly referent for censor-ship, pointing to what censorship excluded and, at the same time, to the erotic potential of sex just out of view. The suggestive, everyone knew, was more powerful than the blatant, necessary to engaging the audience in the intimate activity of the unveiling of sexual meaning. As one censorship board noted, 'frank exposure of the person is much less objectionable than the exposure which is partly hidden and partly revealed', explaining that a scene showing naked 'savages' would be preferable to a scene showing a woman 'almost wholly dressed, but yet displaying a lavish amount of lingerie'.[21]

The cult of stage Salomés during these decades suggests similar preoccupations. The theatricality of Salomé's dance-within-a-dance was part of its erotic pleasure. The teasing now-you-see-it-now-you-don't of Salomé's come-on to the audience was deeply theatrical. At the same time, in Salomé's dance, the theatrical play between the veiled and unveiled could figure the larger problem of the relationship between public and private in which both obscenity and theatre participated. If it was the work of both erotic performance and modern theatre to unveil the secrets of private life, the veil as stage object could serve as a metonymy for their simultaneous concealment and revelation (at the same time, not coincidentally, that 'privacy' was becoming a defined legal category).[22] The veil also, in a sense, acted as a trope for censorship itself, in its artful exercise defining the latitude and limits of exposure.

Art for obscenity's sake

Preoccupied with the problem of obscenity, testing its limits, representing its dilemmas on stage, modern theatre also helped to redefine it, changing its relationship to art more generally. The definitional opposition between obscenity and art that had developed in the eighteenth and nineteenth centuries had created a classificatory norm that preserved the realm of art from the obscene: if a work was obscene, it could not be defined as art. What began to emerge in the nineteenth century, in discussions of obscenity in the visual arts, were arguments attempting to reverse this classificatory norm: if a work was art, it should not be defined as obscene. Modern drama played a pivotal role in this transformation: translating the claims made on behalf of the nineteenth-century nude – through both the artfully suggestive figures of 'living pictures' and the provocative moralism of the serious drama – into the broader realm of literary and aesthetic production. In the 1890s, the paradigmatic spokesman for the position that art should be exempt from obscenity regulation was Oscar Wilde. Called upon to defend not only himself but his works from charges of 'gross indecency' during his trials in 1895, Wilde famously argued that 'art' and 'beauty' were above the crude realm of morals to which the law seemed to be bound.[23] Although the works most at issue in the Wilde trials were 'Phrases and Philosophies for the Use of the Young' and *The Picture of Dorian Gray*, Wilde became a model for the dramatist as (at once) aesthete and iconoclast, proclaiming the power of art to transcend what the Philistine might call immorality. 'The sphere of art and the sphere of ethics are absolutely distinct and separate', he had written to the editor of the

St James Gazette in 1890, in a concise statement of the basic tenet of aestheticism, 'and it is to the confusion between the two that we owe the appearance of Mrs Grundy'.[24]

In defending plays from Mrs Grundy, the aesthetic claim became as important as the age-old realism claim (that plays were merely representing things-as-they-were) or the equally venerable morals claim (that it was necessary to represent indecency in order to cure it). When Max Reinhardt wrote to the Berlin Ministry of Police in 1906 defending Wedekind's *Spring Awakening*, he argued that the status of the play as groundbreaking 'art' (he uses the word repeatedly) should protect it from censorship.[25] Although artistic value did not formally become a defence to obscenity in most places until some time in the mid-twentieth century, earlier courts did sometimes accept these arguments. During the obscenity trials in 1905–6 that resulted in the banning of Wedekind's *Pandora's Box*, the Leipzig appeals court conceded that the 'artistic tendency' and 'literary quality' of the play preserved it from 'sexual immodest[y]', although (the court explained), if one excluded all artistic works from obscenity prosecution, 'the sphere of the obscene would disappear altogether'.[26] To justify suppression, censors and critics sometimes felt obliged to argue that 'obscene' plays were not, in fact, art at all, as the prosecutors in the first *Pandora's Box* trial had, charging that the play was 'without artistic value' and therefore 'pornographic' (Wedekind, *Die Büchse*, p.12). A review in *The Stage* of an early performance of Wilde's *Salomé* declared:

> This kind of stuff has no relationship to art. It is animalism, or worse; for animals have their decencies.[27]

In one mode, the modernist challenge to obscenity regulation served to intensify the definitional antithesis between obscenity and art: art was, by definition, immune from the charge of obscenity. But in another mode, the challenge to obscenity regulation served to blur the boundaries between obscenity and art, hinting that (as Freud was to argue explicitly several decades later) beauty might be derived principally 'from the field of sexual feeling'.[28]

If modern drama as art rose above the charge of obscenity, it also seemed to undo oppositions between 'animalism' and 'art'. In the first *Pandora's Box* trial, the court had proclaimed Wedekind 'an adherent of the modern trend'. Bringing a 'reevaluation of aesthetic values into ... the theatre', modern drama broke away from 'the demands of the formally beautiful', sometimes necessarily partaking of the ugly, the grotesque, the obscene. While a Munich censorship board attacked

Wedekind's embrace of the 'repulsive', the 'base', the 'darkest nooks of vice', the 'sexual aberrations that have become familiar to medical science', the 'psychiatrically known anomalies and varieties of sexual behaviour' of a 'raw and repellant nature', the Berlin trial court could recognize these as serving 'an artistic idea', and thus implicitly acknowledge the uncomfortable proximity of dramatic art to obscenity.[29] In explaining that to grant artworks immunity from obscenity prosecution might cause 'the sphere of the obscene [to] disappear altogether', the Leipzig court inadvertently makes a similar point: modern art, dramatic and otherwise, had come to monopolize the domain of the obscene.

Parables of obscenity

Spring Awakening

Wedekind's *Spring Awakening* (1891) may be taken as an early articulation of this anti-aesthetic, at once thematizing obscenity and enacting its complex relationship to art. The play places censorship at its narrative centre, for the plot turns on Melchior's trial for creating a philosophical dialogue entitled 'Sexual Reproduction', 'embellished...with almost life-size drawings illustrating' (as Sonnenstich, the Headmaster, says) 'the most revolting obscenities, utterly shameless material that would satisfy, one imagines, the basest prurient appetites of the most degenerate, debauched, bestial pervert'.[30] It also places censorship at its thematic centre, for it is a moral tale about the social costs of censorship, dramatized in Wendla's futile requests that her mother explain how babies are made, and her consequent pregnancy and death from a botched abortion. As important, the play repeatedly exploits the shock value of sex on stage, providing an overdetermined collection of avant-garde sex topoi any one of which would have been enough to goad a censorship board to ban the play: childhood sexuality, lavatory realism, masturbation, free love, homosexuality, parent–child incest, sadomasochism, rape and abortion.

Melchior, throughout the play, seems the mouthpiece for Wedekind as the spokesman for the naturalness of the sex instinct and the irrationality of censorship. The play offers (at first) a lyrical portrait of the unfolding of adolescent sexual instinct, 'the one thing' (according to Melchior) 'we have to believe in' (*Spring Awakening*, p.5). For Melchior's friend Moritz, learning about sex is at once 'strange [and] familiar', like half-remembered memories, 'like a song you hummed as a very small child' (p.30). Sexual awakening for girls is like 'paradise burst[ing] into flower. All her feelings unspoiled, fresh, astonishing to her – like a spring gushing out of a rock' (p.31). The forces that would repress this lyric awakening are represented in grotesque caricature in the scene in which Melchior is put on trial for his treatise on sexual reproduction, which the teachers (constituting, effectively, a censorship board) confuse with obscenity:

> *Sonnenstich*: Are you the author of this obscene piece of work?
> *Melchior*: Yes. But I call upon you, Headmaster, to point out one single obscenity...I have written nothing but the simple straightforward facts, familiar to you and to every adult...
> *Sonnenstich*: This is a manual of abominations.
>
> (*Spring Awakening*, p.55)

In opposition, Frau Gabor represents the voice of liberal reason, telling Melchior, 'I know you are old enough to distinguish between what is good for you and what is bad...I would always prefer to trust your good sense, Melchior, before any pedagogue's rigid set of rules' (p.29).

And yet, Frau Gabor's smug broadmindedness turns out to be ill-equipped for the dark reality of adolescent sex. If the sex instinct is natural, represented by dreams produced by the untutored unconscious, it is naturally perverse. Moritz's erotic dreams are a surrealist vision: 'legs in sky-blue tights climbing over the teacher's desk' (p.7). Disturbingly aroused as a four- or five-year-old child by the sight of the bare-shouldered Queen of Hearts in a pack of cards (p.8), haunted by a story told by his grandmother about a beautiful headless queen, his erotic fantasies now fixate (in a series of associative transfers) on headless girls (pp.26–7). Melchior dreams of flogging his dog senseless (p.6). Georg has sexual dreams about his mother (p.7). The first scene of young love in the play ends up as a sadomasochist ritual:

> *Wendla*: I have never been beaten, Melchior ... I've tried beating myself, just to get some idea ... I suppose this switch would be the sort of thing – tough and lithe ... Melchior, beat me with it – go on – just once.
> *Melchior*: Beat you?
> *Wendla*: Yes. Me. Now ... Please, Melchior, please.
> *Melchior*: Please? I'll teach you to say please.
> (*Hits her with switch...Attacks her with fists, etc. She screams. He attacks more violently – sudden sobbing fury. Breaks away and dashes off among trees – wild sobbing.*)
>
> (*Spring Awakening*, pp.22–4)

The next scene of young love in the play, following (Wedekind suggests) naturally from the first, is Wendla's rape in the hayloft.

Wedekind slyly identifies his own play with the object of censorship at its heart: both Melchior's and his works are 'philosophical dialogue[s]' 'embellished... with almost life-size drawings'; both are contributions to the sexual education of the young. Identified with Melchior's illustrated treatise, *Spring Awakening* is also identified with its dark double: Rilow's collection of erotic art prints (Correggio's *Jupiter and Io* Bouguereau's *Amor and Psyche*, Hans Makart's *Leda*, and more). The scene in the lavatory, in which Rilow fantasizes over and then destroys an image of the Venus of Palma Vecchi (as he has done with her predecessors), both rewrites Moritz's encounter with Melchior's drawings in pornographic terms and figures the sexual violence of Melchior's beating and rape of fourteen-year-old Wendla:

> *Rilow*: Girlish breasts, so eager, so unworldly, not one bit less alluring. How giddy with joy that painter must have been when his fourteen-year-old model lay there lolling across the divan, right in front of his eyes... This dreadful pounding in my chest should assure you, I do not murder you lightly ... One more kiss. Your body is all blossoms. These dainty breasts. These moulded, smooth, torturing knees...
> (*He drops the picture into the depths. Closes the toilet lid.*)
>
> (*Spring Awakening*, pp.36–8)

Rather than saving art from the charge of obscenity (as Wedekind repeatedly tried to do in his own protests against censorship), the scene deeply implicates art: the images over which Rilow masturbates are obscene in the most visceral and fully realized sense. If the censors' most powerful argument about the danger of obscenity was that it led to real violence against women, the scene substantiates this argument through its sadistic erotics, which figure Melchior's battering and rape of Wendla. This is not the erotic art incident to healthy sexual expression, which anti-censorship vitalism promised to reclaim for a morbidly repressed culture. Instead, we have here art indistinguishable from obscenity and linked inexorably to violence.

The Lulu Plays

Returning to the problem of the obscenity of art in the Lulu plays (composed between 1894 and 1903 and continually revised over the course of the next decade), Wedekind stages obscene art, here, in explicitly theatrical terms. Throughout the plays, Lulu is identified with the theatre: as a young popular dancer in Paris where she copied the costumes of Eugénie Fougère and learned the 'Czardas – Samaqueca – skirt dance';[31] as the short-lived star in Alva's theatre in Act III; as Pierrot in Schwarz's portrait, which accompanies her throughout *Earth Spirit* and *Pandora's Box* as the central object on stage in nearly every act.

This close identification with the theatre is inseparable from Lulu's identity both as artwork and as erotic object. The male characters repeatedly insist on the separation of art from eros: Schwarz says that when one paints, 'grow warm and immediately your art grows unartistic' (Wedekind, *The Lulu Plays*, p.39); Prince Escerny insists that he is interested in Lulu purely as an art object ('Interested in art as I am', it's 'not your dancing that attracts me' [p.82]). But Schwarz is soon chasing her around the studio (pp.44–5), Escerny begging her to become his private dancer (p.81). We are first introduced to Lulu in a scene in which Schwarz and Schön salivate over the Pierrot portrait, effectively, a piece of theatrically inspired high-art pornography, showcasing Lulu's sexual allure and serving to arouse its viewers ('It makes the blood rush to my head when I think of it', says Schwarz, gazing at the portrait [p.34]). With Lulu's entrance, we are given a live performance of the portrait that falls just short of a striptease:

Lulu (*pulling the left leg up to the knee; to SCHWARZ*): Like this?
Schwarz: Yes...
Lulu (*pulling it a shade higher*): Hm?
Schwarz: Yes, yes...
Lulu: Paint my lips slightly parted... (*parting her lips slightly; to SCHWARZ*): Like this – you see? I'll keep them half parted.
(*The Lulu Plays*, pp.38–9)

If the sexy Pierrot portrait recalls for viewers the functional equivalence of theatricality and pornography, both of which frame the performing body as an image and object of desire in order to transform it into a commodity, the Pierrot costume is a theatrical fetish, whose satin Schwarz and Schön stroke longingly:

Schön (*feeling it*): Satin.
Schwarz: And all in one piece.
Schön: How does she get into it?
(*The Lulu Plays*, pp.34–5)

Both dialogue and stage directions offer a kind of costume pornography, obsessively iterating Lulu's stage attire for the excited listener:

> *Lulu*: [I wore] one with a green lace skirt down to the knees, all with ruffles and décolleté, very décolleté and terribly tight-laced, . . . a pale-green petticoat, and others that keep getting lighter on top of it, . . . snow-white pantaloons with a hand's-breadth of lace at the bottoms . . .
> *Schwarz*: I can't bear anymore . . .
>
> (*The Lulu Plays*, p.44)

In Alva's theatre, provocatively dressing and undressing repeatedly behind a Spanish screen, Lulu asks Escerny to untie her bodice knot for her, which she accidentally knotted too tightly since (she explains) 'I'm always so excited when I dress' (p.81).

Fetishism, the period's 'model perversion' (in Foucault's formulation [Foucault, *History of Sexuality*, vol. 1, p.154]), becomes thus central to an understanding of the relationship between theatricality and obscenity in the play. Like sexual inversion, fetishism was sometimes figured as a theatrical malady, as Alfred Binet had explained in 1887 in which the fetishist could be aroused only by the artificial object of desire (costumes, for instance), animated by the imagination, preferably isolated, enlarged, and highlighted by such artificial devices as make-up.[32] Fetishism, wrote Binet, 'is a play (*pièce de théâtre*) in which a mere bit player advances toward the footlights and displaces the star' (Binet, 'Le Fetichisme', p.85). If Binet argued that fetishism was particularly incident to modern decadent culture (with its 'byzantine taste for luxury, the extravagance of its fashions, and its abuse of makeup' [p.74]), what was crucial was its 'replacement of a sensation by an image' (p.77), that is, the replacement of the real or natural object of desire ('genital sensation' and '[sexual] reproduction' [pp.71, 77]) by the imaginary one. Wilhelm Stekel, the exhaustive clinician of fetishism in the first decades of the century, explained that this displacement was due to fetishism's origins in a terror of real women (which Freud was later to identify specifically with the dangers of incest and castration caused by looking up one's mother's skirts).

As we come to learn, Schwarz – a model fetishist of the type that Binet and Stekel described – is aroused by Lulu's costumes but frightened by her real offers of sex: '[he] has never felt the need for a woman', she explains, 'he's afraid of women . . . I dance the can-can in despair. He yawns and drivels something about obscenity' (Wedekind, *The Lulu Plays*, pp.60–1).

Obscenity, the play suggests, is the charge the fetishist makes when theatricality threatens to reveal the terrors that lurk beneath the costume. Emblems of fetishism's inherent theatricality, Lulu's costumes thus at the same time stand in for her sex, their charming artificiality deflecting from the dangers beneath.

In fondling the Pierrot costume, in swooning over Lulu's chemise, silk stockings and lace, the male costume fetishists in the play presage the play's true fetishist, Jack the Ripper, who, quite literally, collects the female sex (in the play's grotesque metonym). Stekel described the 'collecting [of] symbolic objects' as 'the harem cult of the fetishist': 'The fetish lover is a Don Juan type . . . Instead of collecting women, however, he collects fetishes'.[33] What the play effects is a horrifying transformation of the theatrical fetish (the costume) back into the natural object for which it stands: Lulu's sex (the 'box' of the second play's title), which Jack cuts out of her abdomen in order to add it to his collection. If Schwarz, Schön and Escerny are aroused by objects that represent the exteriority of Lulu's eroticism (its theatricality), terrified of what might lie beneath it, Jack is aroused by the object that signifies Lulu's invisible erotic interiority, seeking in effect to strip away her theatrical exterior in order to reach her sex.

In thus reversing the order of fetishistic displacement, the play enacts a reversal of the meaning and function of fetishism: rather than displacing the terrors of Lulu's sex by fixating on the theatrical paraphernalia that surrounds her, Jack's fetishism displaces the terrors of Lulu's theatricality by fixating on her sex. In this, he acts out simultaneously the 'satanical desires and puritanical tendencies' that, according to Stekel, were at war in the fetishist (*Sexual Aberrations*, p.21). Raging to possess the figure of obscene theatricality, longing to act out his 'satanical desires' with her but, at the same time, overcome by 'puritanical tendencies', he must, like the play itself, finally destroy her.

Salomé

If the cult of stage Salomés thematized the relationship between obscenity and theatricality, Wilde's *Salomé* (1891) offers a more fully articulated meditation on this relationship, as well as (like *Spring Awakening* and the Lulu plays) a commentary on the relationship between obscenity and art. Like Lulu (and Sarah Bernhardt, for that matter, for whom Wilde wrote the role), Salomé personifies both theatricality and obscenity. She is at once the consummate actress and a striptease artist. She is both palace veil dancer and obscenity's id: 'I am amorous of thy body, Iokanaan! . . . Suffer me to touch thy body . . . I will kiss thy mouth,

Iokanaan... I will bite it with my teeth as one bites a ripe fruit.'[34] The central subject of the play is, in fact, obscene performance or, rather, performance perversion, manifested in Herod's panting voyeurism and Salomé's exhibitionism, as she begs to kiss Iokanaan's mouth while Narraboth (already feverish with lust) and others look on. Personifying both theatricality and obscenity, Salomé also personifies both art and sex. She is associated with the *fin-de-siècle* aesthete, promising to give 'a little green flower' (Wilde's special symbol for both the aesthete and the homosexual) to Narraboth if he will give her what she desires.[35] At the same time, she is a sadist, fetishist and necrophiliac. Steeped in the Salomé iconographic tradition, Wilde at one point thought of asking Bernhardt to perform naked, 'but draped with heavy and ringing necklaces made of jewels of every colour, warm with the fervour of her amber flesh... Her lust must needs be infinite, and her perversity without limits.'[36] This nakedness was to be both erotically provocative and central to the play's status as art.

Wilde wrote *Salomé* only a few years before his 1895 trials, and the claims he made about the relationship between art and morality during the trials can clearly be seen as reflecting on *Salomé*. To object to his treatment of the Salomé story, he fumed in a letter to William Archer soon after the Lord Chamberlain refused him a licence for the play, was 'to object to Art entirely' (Wilde, *Letters*, p.534). Wilde tempts his audience to read the relationship between art and obscenity in *Salomé* as instantiating the principles for which he was to argue during the trials: as 'Art', naked or otherwise, Salomé's dance transcends the obscene.

And yet, we are not so sure. For one thing, Herod's evident sexual arousal challenges our ability to detach her dance from the prurient interest it stirs: 'Thy beauty has troubled me', he tells her (emphasizing the overtones of the French *troubler*), 'Thy beauty has grievously troubled me... Oh! oh! bring wine! I thirst... Salomé, Salomé' (Wilde, [*Plays*], p.87). Wilde was highly conscious of the audience's sensual experience of the play, specifying, for instance, that the performers should all be dressed in shades of yellow against a sky of 'deepest violet,' and that there should be perfume-filled braziers in the orchestra producing 'scented clouds rising and partly veiling the stage from time to time – a new perfume for each emotion!' (Wilde, [*Plays*], p.327). Intoxicated by the scent of perfume, are we too aroused by her dance? Is this pornography for us, as it is for Herod? Insofar as the play equates the two main objects of desire in the play (Salomé's dance and Iokanaan's head, displayed theatrically on the shield for Salomé's pleasure), the sadistic erotics of the display at the end of the play ask us to re-evaluate the erotics of Salomé's dance. Wilde teases his spectators, seeming to ask them to judge erotic art for its tendency to lead from arousal to gross indecency (from desires to acts that dare not speak their name). But, at the same time, like *Spring Awakening*, the play more seriously offers a challenge to the boundaries between art and obscenity: Salomé, both agent and object of arousal, is necessarily both obscene and theatrical; arousal is not merely a by-product of obscene theatre, but central to the living work of art.

Blustering that he would move to France if the play were banned, Wilde could not have been surprised by the refusal of a license.[37] Like *Spring Awakening*, the play offers a parable of censorship that is a reading-before-the-fact of its fate. The central figure of censorship in the play is the anti-theatrical Iokanaan, spokesman of moral purity and destroyer of visual idolatry: 'Daughter of Sodom', he calls out from the cistern, 'cover thy face with a veil', 'Let the people take stones and stone her... It is thus that I will wipe out all wickedness from the earth, and that all women shall learn not to imitate her abominations' (Wilde, [*Plays*], pp.72, 80). As has often been noted, the play has a strong autobiographical overlay: Salomé commits what others see as a 'gross[ly] indecen[t]' violation of the law that is, for her, simply a necessary fulfilment of her urges. It is telling that scholars have persistently wanted to read a 1906 photograph of a beefy Hungarian diva playing Salomé (in long wig and jewelled Orientalia, kneeling over Iokanaan's severed head) as a photograph of Wilde in drag.[38] Seen through this conflation of Wilde with Salomé, the killing of Iokanaan becomes a moment of wish-fulfilment for Wilde: 'Thou rejectedst me. Thou didst speak evil words against me. Thou didst bear thyself toward me as to a harlot . . . Well, I still live, but thou art dead, and thy head belongs to me[!]' (p.90). Salomé kills the censor precisely *through* her erotic performance (exchanged, in the play's economy, for the right to Iokanaan's head).

The play thus seems to suggest that, if only it could achieve the artfulness of Salomé's dance, it too might behead the censor. But at the same time it expresses a fear about obscene theatricality's destructive powers. For, just as the most rabid voices of morals reform warned, Salomé's degenerate dance leads to the weakening of the state, its king cowering in terror by the end of the play: 'Put out the torches! Hide the moon! Hide the stars!' cries Herod, 'Let us hide ourselves in our palace, Herodias. I begin to be afraid' ([*Plays*], p.91). As in the Lulu plays, the embodiment of obscene theatricality must be killed, or, rather, she self-destructs. For in killing the censor, Salomé ends up destroying herself, crushed beneath the more violent censorship of the soldiers' shields. In Salomé's self-destruction, the play enacts the necessary self-sacrifice of the obscene object of desire: Iokanaan, Salomé, the play itself, ultimately consumed in flames of its own making.

* * *

Unlike the cheeky *'danseuses du ventre'* in the 'Streets of Cairo' exhibit, tauntingly wiggling their hips at the policeman sent to monitor their compliance with the law, insisting on their gyrations as high art, Wedekind and Wilde act out a kind of abjection before the forces of censorship. If *Spring Awakening*, the Lulu plays and *Salomé* are all, in a sense, parables of obscenity, their moral is that art is, in fact, obscene, that obscenity is dangerous, and that (in the latter two) the figure of obscene theatricality must be destroyed. The subliminal anti-theatricality and anti-sex moralism lying beneath the surface of Wedekind's or Wilde's celebration of erotic theatricality – or the Puritanical anti-theatricality of a playwright like Shaw (whose *Mrs Warren's Profession* has to be the primmest play about prostitution ever written) – existed in creative tension, however, with the broader *Zeitgeist*. Erotic theatricality was, increasingly, naturalized on the mainstream stage, with such scraggly shows as 'The Streets of Cairo' going upscale in, for instance, the Ziegfield Follies, celebrating at once unabashed spectacle and the equally unabashed display of women for the pleasures of the theatrical consumer. Isadora Duncan and Ruth St Denis, body parts bared, were hailed as visionaries of the dance. The Ballets Russes' *L'après-midi d'un faune* (1912), with its brazen sexuality and its shocking masturbation scene, was a masterpiece.

If plays continued to be banned, and there continued to be periodic theatrical crackdowns, by the end of the first decade of the century one could see versions of *Ghosts*, *Salomé*, the Lulu plays or *Mrs Warren's Profession* in major cities throughout Europe and North America. By the twenties, tragic lesbians and *outré* drag queens regularly populated the stage, not without protests, but nonetheless. The category of the obscene began to narrow, as literary works (inspired, in part, by theatrical cases) began successfully to challenge earlier rulings. Prosecutions for theatrical indecency in the urban metropolis began to be seen as the work of a few moral zealots beset by a retrograde Victorianism. If theatrical obscenity cases were both traumatic and formative for early theatrical modernism, they had reshaped performance culture by the second decade of the new century. Zola,

Shaw and others maintained that theatrical censorship had rendered the drama weak and conventional, and that a new drama – vigorous, probing, morally serious – could emerge only with censorship's demise.[39] But it was, in fact, in its encounters with censorship that the modern theatre had become itself.

Notes

1. My account is based on the somewhat confused reports in the *New York Times* on 3 (p.2), 5 (p.8) and 7 (p.3) December 1893. Where I cite foreign-language texts, translations are mine. I would like to thank Minou Arjomand and Danielle Beurteaux for invaluable research assistance.
2. On Duncan, see the *New York Times* 1 March 1898, p.7. My *Radha* description is based on St Denis's scenario, Ruth St Denis, *Radha, an East Indian Idyl: A Hindoo Play in One Act Without Words* (New York: n.p.,1905, unpaginated) and Ted Shawn, *Ruth St Denis: Pioneer & Prophet; Being a History of her Cycle of Oriental Dances*, 2 vols (San Francisco: J. Howell, 1920), pp.28–9. For a discussion of the origin of modern dance in popular entertainments during this period, see Amy Koritz, *Gendering Bodies/Performing Art: Dance and Literature in Early Twentieth-century British Culture* (Ann Arbor: University of Michigan Press, 1995), especially pp.13–55.
3. For the commentary on *Cléopâtre*, see Arthur Gold and Robert Fizdale, *The Divine Sarah: A Life of Sarah Bernhardt* (New York: Alfred A. Knopf, 1991), p.245 (unfortunately, uncited). For the reference to *La Chair*, I am indebted to Rhonda Garelick; and see Jean Chalon, *Colette: L'éternelle apprentie* (Paris: Flammarion, 1998) p.134.
4. *Report from the Joint Select Committee of the House of Lords and the House of Commons on the Stage Plays (Censorship)* (London: HMSO, 1909), p.265 (hereafter, *Report*). Review of *Frühlings Erwachen*, quoted in Michael Meyer, *Theaterzensur in München: 1900–1918* (Munich: Neue Schriftreihe, 1982), pp.156. Reviews of Ibsen's *Ghosts*, quoted in John Russell Stephens, *The Censorship of English Drama, 1824–1901* (Cambridge: Cambridge University Press, 1980), pp.142–3.
5. On nineteenth-century pornography as popular mass culture, see Alison Pease, *Modernism, Mass Culture and the Aesthetics of Obscenity* (Cambridge: Cambridge University Press, 2000) (especially pp.50–6, challenging the classic view of Victorian pornography as an elite bibliophilic enterprise). While there has been a wealth of work on the history of eighteenth- and nineteenth-century print pornography (see, most notably, Lynn Hunt, ed., *The Invention of Pornography: Obscenity and the Origins of Modernity* (New York: Zone, 1993), pp.9–45, 301–9 and Walter M. Kendrick *The Secret Museum: Pornography in Modern Culture* (New York: Viking, 1987)), I have found no sustained study of pre-twentieth-century erotic entertainment, but specific studies of burlesque, music hall, popular dance, and striptease offer useful material (see, for instance, Rhonda Garelick, *Rising Star: Dandyism, Gender, and Performance in the Fin de Siècle* (Princeton: Princeton University Press, 1998); and Rachel Steier, *Striptease:*

The Untold History of the Girlie Show (New York: Oxford University Press, 2004), pp.11–66.

6. Britain passed its first national obscenity law, the Obscene Publications Act, only in 1857, and the United States Congress passed a similar law only in 1873. On comparable developments in Germany and France, see Gary D. Stark, 'Pornography, society and the law in imperial Germany', *Central European History*, 14:3 (1981): 200–29, and Annie Stora-Lamarre, *L'Enfer de la IIIe République: Censeurs et Pornographes (1881–1914)* (Paris: Imago, 1990), and on parallel developments in the regulation of sexuality, see Michel Foucault, *The History of Sexuality*, trans. Robert Hurley, 2 vols (New York: Vintage, 1980) henceforth cited in the text; and Jeffrey Weeks, *Sex, Politics and Society: The Regulation of Sexuality since 1800*, 2nd edn (London: Longman, 1989).

7. George Bernard Shaw, 'The censorship of the stage in England', *The North American Review*, 169 (August 1899): 260 (henceforth cited in text).

8. Andrea Friedman, *Prurient Interests: Gender, Democracy, and Obscenity in New York City, 1909–1945* (New York: Columbia University Press, 2000), p.50 (quoting the defense attorney for the film *Inside the White Slave Traffic* [1913]).

9. Quoted in John H. Houchin, *Censorship of the American Theatre in the Twentieth Century* (Cambridge: Cambridge University Press, 2003), p.62.

10. The following books outlining the history of theatrical censorship in Britain and the United States give a sense of the centrality of drama to obscenity debates of the period: Nicholas De Jongh, *Politics, Prudery and Perversions: The Censoring of the English Stage, 1901–1968* (London: Methuen, 2000); Houchin *Censorship of the American Theatre*, pp.40–71, Steve Nicholson *The Censorship of British Drama, 1900–1968* (Exeter: University of Exeter Press, 2003), pp.1–95; Stephens, *Censorship of English Drama*, pp.133–53.

11. In Europe, prior theatrical censorship meant that few plays actually got to the stage of being prosecuted for obscenity. France abolished formal censorship in 1905, Germany in 1918 and Britain only in 1968. Plays could, however, still be prosecuted under various 'public nuisance' laws, and sometimes stopped in the middle of a run. Since there was no formal system of prior censorship in the United States (though municipalities experimented periodically with 'play juries'), arrests and trials were frequent.

12. John Palmer, *The Censor and the Theatres* (New York: Mitchell Kennerley, 1913), p.151.

13. Shaw, 'Censorship', p.257 (satirizing the view of the 'representative Englishman').

14. Émile Zola, 'La censure', in *Oeuvres complètes*, ed. Henri Mitterand, 15 vols (Paris: Cercle du livre précieux, 1966–), p.639.

15. Shaw, 'Censorship', p.257. See also Sigmund Freud, *Civilization and its Discontents*, trans. James Strachey (New York: W. W. Norton, 1962).

16. *New York Times* 2 March 1900, p.10; 6 March 1900, p.1.

17. This derivation, suggested by Varro, is probably false, but nonetheless influential. More common is the word's association with the Latin *scaevus* (left-sided, inauspicious) and with *caenum* (mud, filth). See the *OED* entry for 'obscene'.

18. Quoted in Tracy C. Davis, 'The Actress in Victorian Pornography', in K. O. Garrigan, ed., *Victorian Scandals: Representations of Gender and Class* (Athens: University of Ohio Press, 1992), p.124.
19. *Rosen v. US*, 16 S.Ct. 434 (1896), p.434.
20. Quoted in De Jongh, *Politics, Prudery and Perversions*, pp.35–6.
21. Quoted in Friedman, *Prurient Interests*, p.45 (National Board of [Film] Censorship, Statement of Standards, 1914).
22. See, for instance, Louis D. Brandeis and Samuel Warren's seminal article, 'The right to privacy', *Harvard Law Review*, 4:5 (1890): 193–220.
23. See, for instance, Merlin Holland, ed., *Irish Peacock & Scarlet Marquess: The Real Trial of Oscar Wilde: The First Uncensored Manuscript of the Trial of Oscar Wilde vs. John Douglas, Marquess of Queensbury, 1895* (New York: Fourth Estate, 2003), pp.73–5, 80.
24. Oscar Wilde, *The Complete Letters of Oscar Wilde*, ed. Merlin Holland and Rupert Hart-Davis (New: Henry Holt, 2000) p.428 (henceforth cited in text).
25. Max Reinhardt, *Schriften: Briefe, Reden, Aufsätze, Interviews, Gespräche, Auszüge aus Regiebüchern*, ed. Hugo Fetting (Berlin: Henschelverlag Kunst und Gesselschaft, 1974), pp.97–8.
26. Frank Wedekind, *Die Büchse der Pandora: Tragödie in drei Aufzügen* (Berlin: Bruno Cassirer, 1906), p.38 (Wedekind's forward paraphrasing the trials, in which Wedekind and his publisher were charged with obscenity for the printed version of the play), henceforth cited in the text.
27. Quoted in Michael Kettle, *Salomé's Last Veil: The Libel Case of the Century* (London: Granada Publishing, 1977), p.25.
28. Sigmund Freud, *Civilization and its Discontents*, trans. James Strachey (New York: W.W. Norton, 1962), p.33.
29. Wedekind, *Die Büchse*, p.18 (paraphrasing the Berlin trial court's decision); Meyer, *Theaterzensur in München*, pp.274–5 (quoting the Munich board's 1913 report).
30. Frank Wedekind, *Spring Awakening*, trans. Ted Hughes (London: Faber, 1995), p.53 (henceforth cited in text).
31. Frank Wedekind, *The Lulu Plays*, trans. Carl Richard Muller (Greenwich, CT: Fawcett, 1967), pp.43–4 (henceforth cited in the text). I have regularized the spelling of Schön's name.
32. Alfred Binet, 'Le fetichisme dans l'amour: Etude de psychologie morbide', *Revue Philosophique*, 24 (1887), pp.36–9, 70–7 (henceforth cited in the text). For an explicit identification of the theatricality of the invert, see Havelock Ellis, *Sexual Inversion* (London: Wilson & Macmillan, 1897), pp.123–4.
33. Wilhelm Stekel, *Sexual Aberrations: The Phenomenon of Fetishism in Relation to Sex*, trans. S. Parker (New York: Liveright, 1930), p.21.
34. Oscar Wilde, *Lady Windermere's Fan, Salome, A Woman of no Importance, An Ideal Husband, The Importance of Being Earnest*, ed. Peter Raby (Oxford: Clarendon Press, 1995), pp.72–3, 90; henceforth [*Plays*]. In order to conform with Wilde's dominant spelling, I have diverged from this edition in including the accent on 'Salomé.'
35. On the green carnation, which Wilde requested that all the male spectators wear to the premiere of *Lady Windermere's Fan*, see Regenia Gagnier, *Idylls of the Marketplace: Oscar Wilde and the Victorian Public* (Stanford, CA: Stanford University Press, 1986), p.163, and see Wilde's essay, 'Pen, Pencil, and

Poison,' a 'study in green' (1889), in which he identifies love of green as characteristic of the artistic temperament and of moral decadence (Oscar Wilde, *The Artist as Critic*, ed. Richard Ellman (New York: Random House, 1968), pp.320–40).

36. Quoted in Richard Ellmann, *Oscar Wilde* (New York: Knopf, 1988), p.342.

37. Wilde, [*Plays*], p.xii. Edward Pigott, Examiner of Plays, referred to it as 'a miracle of impudence', 'written in French – half Biblical, half pornographic... Imagine the average British public's reception of it' (quoted in Gagnier, *Idylls of the Marketplace*, pp.170–1).

38. Reproduced as a photograph of Wilde in Ellmann, *Oscar Wilde*, pp.428–9 (interleaves) and Elaine Showalter, *Sexual Anarchy: Gender and Culture at the Fin de Siècle* (New York: Viking, 1990), p.157. See Holland, 'Biography', pp.10–12 for the correct identification: Alice Guszalewicz performing in Strauss's *Salomé* in Cologne.

39. Zola, 'La censure'; George Bernard Shaw, Preface to *Mrs Warren's Profession*, in *Plays Unpleasant*, ed. Dan H. Laurence (London: Penguin, 1946), pp.181–212, Preface to *The Shewing-Up of Blanco Posnet and Fanny's First Play*, ed. Dan H. Laurence (New York: Penguin Books, 1987), pp.5–73, and 'Censorship'.

13
Seeming, Seeming: The Illusion of Enough

Herbert Blau

> What was to be done? or, if nothing could be done, was there anything further that I could *assume* in the matter?
>
> (Herman Melville, *Bartleby the Scrivener*)

Wherever it comes from, morality or the aesthetic, the anti-theatrical prejudice is a conceptual vanity, subject to or victimized by theatre, while going through every nerve-end to the dubious heart of drama, which has from whatever beginnings always distrusted the theatre. I'm not merely referring here, with the author living or dead, to a certain protectionism of the text against the depredations of the stage, a tradition extending, at times with egregious vigilance, from Ben Jonson to Samuel Beckett to, recently and unexpectedly, Sam Shepard – once with-it in the counter-culture, and its polymorphous perversions – who refused to allow a production of *True West* if the combative brothers were misgendered, enacted by women. Propriety aside, and social construction, the liability of the prejudice, whose contingency is theatre, is that it's constrained ontologically even before it's thought, for as Heidegger said of language: 'Language itself is – language and nothing else besides. Language itself is language.'[1] And though it's been institutionalized, so it appears with theatre, theatre itself is tautological maybe, but in the immanence of appearance, theatre itself is theatre, *before* anything else, or – in a spectrum of apprehension from Plato to Genet (sainted by Sartre for sanctifying appearance) – with a duplicitous presence suffusing everything else. That may very well prompt, in the deepest sense, a desire for anti-theatre, which may paradoxically, in a strategic, desperate or imperious theatricality, increase the quotient of theatre, while never resolving the question of whether, in being theatrical as anti-theatre, it ought to be more or less.

Either way, in a superfluity of it or on a minimalist stage, theatricality *isn't*, in its containment or presumption of theatre, even a shadow of it, only the merest facsimile, and even then we can't be sure; for if theatre is not entropic, a sort of leak in the Real, it seems brought into being by thought – though maybe the thing itself, disappearing in the perceiving, is precisely the leak in the Real. It seems no accident that the greatest drama is obsessed with that. As it happens, the most elusively theatrical figure in the canonical drama would seem, in escaping interpretation, to have reflected on this, and if we ask the simple question, what makes theatre? the answer might be Hamletic: *thinking makes it so*. What's then to be kept in mind is the theatre's incipience as appearance, because we have it in mind, from whatever it is it is *not* (reality? experience? life?) as it must have been *if it was*, before there was any theatre, or precipitous semblance of it, no less anything like the notion that all the world's a stage or society of the spectacle or, making a non sequitur of anti-theatre, a precession of simulacra. If we're not quite at the end of the real – bereft in an imaged world, with its superfetation of signs, no referentials, no metaphysics, only the vanity of a redundancy without any substance at all, not even the imaginary substance once thought of as illusion – the undeniable truth is that we're not quite sure where we are. And so far as the theatre reflects that, we're back through whatever demystifications to its ineliminable *seeming*, or in its doubling over of life, the 'Seeming, seeming', distressingly seminal, as if precisely *Measure for Measure* (2.4.151), now you see it now you don't.

Insidious it may be, or a reprise of illusion, but it's not to be done away with by an alienating detachment or pre-emptive imitation. Nor will it be carried away or contained by a kind of Brechtian narcissism, the 'ontological-hysteric' or wired-up objectification, in the theatre of Richard Foreman, who's still there pulling the strings, but – even before the dominion of exacerbated digitality – with the video-game momentum of somewhat robotic bodies, a little sexier now, but in no way 'bodies that matter'.[2] If the Brechtian paradigm has receded, or is now so familiar it needs some A-effect itself, it was the theatricalization of theory that – with the materiality of the body linked to the perform-ativity of gender – appeared to take over the *gestus*, with a parodic amplification, as in the films of John Waters and the outrageous drag of Divine. In deconstructing Austin's notion of performativity built around the marriage vow, and imitating an origin that really never was, the '*corporeal style*' of queer performativity – truly queer, celebrating a stigma – derides the notion of a stable or coherent, self-identical body, with a pre-emptive strike at specularity in a reversal of the gaze. Making a virtue of gender trouble, the bodily inscriptions of the performative are a nuance away from performance and, in its repetitive acts ('truly troubling',[3] or so it is claimed, in the hegemony of subversion), disdainful of theatre – bourgeois theatre, of course, which has always distrusted itself.

As with modernist art and thought, which in the era of cultural studies has had a bad rap (masculine dominance, elitism, a depoliticizing formalism, and the emptying out of history), so, too, apparently commodified theatre seems at various levels to have anticipated its critique, as if the theatre itself were proposing something like anti-theatre. As for the queer reversed gaze, and its subversive look at the myth of interiority, and the inside/outside binary of what became, in the Method, the actor's psychic space, it may be that its seeming seeing is something other than that. For as queer becomes method, it discovers again – as they did in painting, since Cézanne pushed his big mountain up to the picture plane – that there is no surface that doesn't recede; and if the activity of perception changes what it sees, it's in the seeing itself that interiority persists, as it always has in the theatre, subvert it as you will. And so it may be, with all its sophistication, in a 'discursive performativity' that, in 'arguing with the real' (Butler, *Bodies*, p.189), it confronts an impasse in the parody turning back upon itself – or, as Shakespeare says in a sonnet, with a stylish riff on delusion, 'Seems seeing, but effectually is out' (Sonnet 113).

What's in, what's out is itself a dismaying problem – beyond specularity or even the simulacra – in a dromoscopic, techno-scientific, biochemical, geneticist, informational world, with everything seeming to move, in the wake of the Enlightenment, with the speed of light or, as Paul Virilio thinks it, with 'the *light of speed*'.[4] Channels, screens, PCs, cell-phones, satellite dishes, CDs, webs and weblogs, samplers, Ethernets: in the proliferous sensation of the multitudinous moment, the sheer repetitive promiscuity of the instantly mediated, what happens to temporality or, for that matter, materiality? Lady Macbeth wanted the future in the instant, but with so many futures in the infinity of instants, what passeth show would, if it wanted to show, already be far in the past – though a past is problematic, with the wavelengths and frequencies picking up speed. So it is – if we pick up on the velocity and go with the implications – that theatre/anti-theatre wouldn't even be an issue, though that wouldn't necessarily relieve Michael Fried, who worried about the degeneration of art '*as it approaches the condition of theatre*'.[5] Defending an art-as-object wholly manifest in the instant, 'a continual and perpetual *present'* (Fried, 'Art and Objecthood', p.146) insusceptible to the attritions of time, Fried insists on defeating theatre, because it is given over to 'a sense of temporality, of time both passing and to come, *simultaneously approaching and receding*, as if apprehended in an infinite perspective' (p.145). What is past, and passing, and to come might have been thus apprehended, when Minimal Art, and then Conceptual Art, first appeared on the scene, but if we're now amidst the megabytes, minimizing the instant and swifter than any thought, what perspective can be expected when what's coming has already passed and the simultaneity, if imaginable, is always already surpassed? So with theatre/anti-theatre: the binary would seem to depend on a *here and now*, but we're living acceleratingly, anaphylactically, in a *then and there*, with nothing like the memory of a Bergsonian *durée*, since, in the immediacy of the remote, light-years faster than the channel changer, *'speed is the old age of the world'*, where if you hadn't seen it all in an epiphanic flash, there was hardly even an instant for now you see it now you don't.

Is this not something more than fantasy? Or if still not unfantastic, merely the virtual truth of a prospective virtual world? Maybe yes maybe no. But if Virilio is (as he would have to be, if what he's seeing is so) retrospectively prescient, then with reality *'foreclosed'*, retracted by acceleration, 'out of time in the strictest sense' (Virilio, *Ground Zero*, p.16), any apparency of the real in the form of theatre would hardly be worth our attention, no more than a sheet of newspaper in a Florida hurricane. Or for that matter, the end of modernism, which like the end of history is always beginning again – not modernism, remember, but the beginning of its end.

* * *

But slowing down for a moment, *taking time* (or the restored illusion of it), in the recidivist way of rehearsal: a brief connection was made before between modernism and the bourgeois theatre, about which – as if in a matrix of anachronism and history (with the universe of the Matrix looming) – I want to say more. So far as that theatre is an expressive function of modernism, it was from the beginning a good deal more conflicted, aphasic, destabilizing than, with the advent of critical theory, we've made it out to be – its gravity such, if thought, that its accretions of realism, density impacted, as if becoming a black hole, were an inside-out eruption into a more far-reaching amplitude than those apparently predictable plots and box sets would seem to suggest.

The atmosphere can be oppressive, but with the constraints of space and time there is, metonymically, a kind of impacted remembrance, too, opening up as in the unconscious, or as in the modernist visual arts, to the spatialization of time. If in Cubism, however, all of history appears to be there, geometrically severed, but (in the wake of Cézanne) up on the picture plane, that would seem to be the reverse of what we have in the theatre, with its proscenium arch, teasers and tormentors, surreptitious wings and legacy of perspective. Yet I've seen productions in open spaces, indoors, outdoors or sprawling all over somewhere, the legacy there regardless, with text, without text, even through improvisation, old out-guessable reflexes, much of it banal, irredeemably locked in the brain, as if there was a proscenium there – though maybe a false proscenium with no perspective at all.

But 'Fie upon't, foh! About my brains', putting it into the plural, as Hamlet does, as if with brain damage arrested, the gaze itself is reversed, as he turns to the 'guilty creatures sitting at a play' (*Hamlet*, 2.2.573–5). In a space created, it would seem, by a high-tech Mousetrap – where the watchers are watching the watchers watch – we're talking not only of *graduated* perception, but also, in reflecting that (no less reflecting upon it), unaccountable *degrees* of theatre. As for the watchers in the audience, what brought them there to begin with, or – while digesting dinner, as in Brecht's jaundiced view – compels inert attention, tuning in and screening out? Well, we all know that from the plot-line, which has an ancient history: appearance, disguise, concealment, the lies, deceits, the overheard, the disclosed, the mortifying confession, guilt again, the cover up and (what else to be expected?) the anxious relief of exposure – that suspect heritage in the bourgeois drama of the phallic Oedipal theatre, all of which the new historicism or cultural materialism, or gendered or racial versions of the going revisionist Marxism, and with it anti-theatre, has been determined to expose. And then we go through a cycle where we want to expose the exposure. As the debates continue in theory – and now beyond theory, whose future is dubious too – no doubt about it, there is a cloud of unknowing in our now conventional theatre, as if 'the scene upon the stage', which Freud might have been describing in *Totem and Taboo*, 'was derived from the historical scene through a process of systematic distortion – one might even say, as the product of a refined hypocrisy'.[6] Or maybe, after all, not so refined. Anything can be cheapened by performance, but what's not there, and should be, preys upon the brain, all the more as you look with what, 'imagination dead imagine', Beckett called 'the eye of prey'.[7] Is it a case of anti-theatre when you want to stand up and shout, *'Use your brains!'*

We've all heard the platitudes (and may even recite them), in courses of dramatic literature, about not knowing a play until we see it staged. But much of the time, up there, we don't see it at all, not to mention the liability – even with a fine performance, and sometimes especially so, as that gets in the way (transposed now to film/video, and frequently shown in class) – of not seeing it in multiple ways, incessantly re-imagined or, as by some inquest in the cortex, otherwise rehearsed. It might be thought of as closeting the drama, or resisting theatre, but I've been telling students for years (even while staging plays, and this is important to the stagings) that they may engage with a play far more profoundly if they *don't* go to a production, and then, grasping my head to define it, I'd insist that the brain is the best stage of all, the most expansive, versatile, dynamic and volatile in containment. Think of it, I'd say, that englobed space behind the eyeballs (a site of immense 'confabulation', with never a repetition, 'unstructured immensities', and according to 'neural Darwinism', with a 'value system',[8]) – now that's what a theatre should be! inexhaustibly ideational, with a repletion of image, as if the singular brain were fractured, dialectically plural, of untold and variable magnitude, and maybe as anti-theatre, where (with all the neurons working) you can see it again and again, through every (mis)apprehension, in some other heuristic form, *but not with absent vision*. (There is, as with Charles Lamb and Goethe on Shakespeare, and particularly *King Lear*, an anti-theatrical precedent for keeping a play in the text and staging it in the mind, as with Gertrude Stein on reading, but that's not what I'm talking about.) Vision may be, as they say, a 'transcendental signifier', but then, so be it: *for* theatre, *against* theatre, *it always remains to be seen*, and so it is in re-imagining what we think of as bourgeois theatre, which was once, however impaired, also a matter of vision – and with a materialist disposition, a vision haunted by history, and its visionary gleam.

Arising from the Enlightenment with a thwarted dialectic, it's as if it were inhabited at the outset by some ghosting imminence of Ibsen's *Ghosts*, its remorseless analytic brought to unspeakable terror, with glaciers and peaks in the background bathed in the morning light. Where Peer Gynt once was, the dead may awaken, in a kind of super-theatre, site of the world beyond, but unsayable, Wagnerian, at the limit of wish-fulfilment upping the ante on theatricality, but as if the subtext of Osvald's final line, 'The sun – The sun',[9] were through the syphilitic blindness a sonorous delirium. How, really, should it be staged, and in the rush of repressed memory, what kinesthetic evocations? And would they be enough? For one can imagine that at the very dawn of the Enlightenment, embodied at dawn in the Festival of Dionysus, the first primeval murmurs were heard – the proleptic soundings of a still-unending cultural hysteria – from those sub-human figures in the caves below the mountain on which, in the Aeschylean drama, the fire-giving god of forethought, Prometheus, was bound, persisting there in a 'mad harmony'[10] with the punishing forces of nature, slashing winds, pitted clouds, lightning bolts, earthquakes, serving a higher power.

It may be that Shelley released him, or some revisionist production, but I wouldn't count on that. What is more likely, however, whatever we do in the theatre, is that at some subliminal level all of it is remembered, all the more if resisted, and if not quite of the same dimensions, the delirium surely persists. With an ongoing animus against bourgeois theatre, but nothing like Wagner's resources for hypertrophic theatricality, something like it was aroused again, in the visceral 'grain of the voice', from way down in the throat, lips, tongue, glottis, teeth, the mucilaginous membranes, and scabbily out the nose,[11] by the sound/ movement exercises of the 1960s, and the participatory mystique of their psychophysical clamor. As with *Dionysus in 69*, this was one of the ways in which performance, disavowing the conventional actor, mere menial of the authorized text, would 'escape the tyranny of meaning' (Barthes, 'The Grain of the Voice', p.185), dismantling bourgeois value and – with bodies that matter naked, and more or less *jouissance* – thus transcending its theatre, the mere 'sensuous expression of estranged human life'.[12] (Which is actually how Marx described, not irrelevantly, it would seem, the movement of production and consumption.) As for the political apotheosis of that vociferous period, there was, with bodies spelling out its title and then naked all over the stage, the Living Theatre's *Paradise Now*, which also passed for the temporal instant as a sort of anarchically mesmeric, unmimetic materialism, with its libidinal economy flowing out to the streets.

In the *Economic and Philosophic Manuscripts of 1844*, Marx spoke of the senses as direct theoreticians, each of them formed by the labour of the entire history of the world (Karl Marx, *Marx-Engels*, pp.87, 89); but he had in mind another materialism, which had to bring itself first to consciousness, in a 'fully-developed naturalism [that] equals humanism, and as fully-developed humanism [that] equals naturalism', only thence '*coming-to-be*' (p.84), through the long riddling burden of that estranging history, with paradise having to wait. And so it had been in the theatre, which is in the play of appearance the form of coming-to-be, as it is – in more than etymology, and not merely with the specular gaze – also the shadow of theory, suffused with all the senses and with a sensory life. (As I used to tell my KRAKEN group, taking that as a datum, what we're doing here is *thinking*, though some might think, in a kneejerk, that's *really* anti-theatre.) As for performance itself, the sensuous expression of estranged life may occur with a certain dispassion, or as in the anti-theatre of Brecht, by estranging the estrangement; but so with Ibsen too, in a dramaturgy that was radically other, a good long way from the boulevards and the assembly-line scriptures of Scribe. And if we now think we can predict Ibsen's moves, the degrees of estrangement and passion were once, as contingencies of the perceptual, what aroused critique in the drama, while this degree or that degree, like any gesture on stage, or even an instant of held breath (not to mention Beckett's play), may at a particular moment in history determine the force of critique, which sustains itself in estrangement because, so far in history, there is no other life. As he evolved a utopian vision, Marx was very conscious of that. As for Ibsen, it adhered like a guilty thought to the most ethereal theatricality of his most symbolic plays, as it did through the grain of the voice in the organless bodies of Artaud, and – in the consummate delirium of anti-theatre – those immemorial incantations, prodigal in the air, also betrayed by the Real.

So, down to earth again, where the cruelties are sufficient. In a remarkable early letter, meant to deflect the Young Hegelians from 'dogmatic abstraction', Marx had called for '*a ruthless critique of every-thing existing*',[13] but in this regard – if they didn't quite share a politics – it was Ibsen who virtually outdid him in conducting such a critique, which is why (historicize! to be sure, but speaking of truly troubling) one of his plays was attacked as if it were Artaud's plague, as a running sore, a wound, an open drain, a cesspool. As for the dramaturgy of his realism, or the later departures from it, the paradox was that it constituted in performance, the truth of illusion there, a devastating critique of theatre, along with the apparatus of representation we've been belabouring since, where the reality of appearance is confounded by the appearance of reality – though we're still not entirely sure which of those phrases ought to go first or (though I can see everything disappearing into the velocity of the virtual) whether there's any reality at all without the duplicity of appearance. About the future of (an) illusion, it was Freud who acceded to that, after moving, in the anti-theatre of psychoanalysis, from the *mise en scène* of the unconscious through *Civilization and its Discontents*, virtually admitting there, with a kind of tragic vision, that demystification had failed. Meanwhile, theatre persists through anti-theatre like the generic ghosting in *Hamlet* through the factitiousness of the Ghost, or, with Hegel turned on his head, through the ruthless critique like 'phantoms formed in the human brain' (Marx, *German Ideology*, in *Marx-Engels*, p.154).

* * *

It was during the period, approximately, from Freud's *Project for a Scientific Psychology* to the inconsolable prospect of unpurgeable discontents that, in a sort of Moebius warp, theatre and anti-theatre merged in the vicissitudes of critique: from the early naturalism of Strindberg – whose preface to *Miss Julie* has a surprising Brechtian strain – to Pirandello's bewildered characters and Gertrude Stein's bewildering plays that, with elisions or traces of character, were really anti-plays, where 'each one is that one and that there are a number of them each one being that one'[14] – which one is only one (and, until recently, a neglected one at that) among the avatars of anti-theatre in the modernist avant-garde? And there were various ironies there, as in Futurism's assault not only on the vacuities of boulevard theatre, but also on the naturalism equalling humanism in the fully developed realism. In refusing not only the mere mimicry, but even the accomplished mimicry that – as theory sees it today – reproduced what it critiqued, Marinetti and his cohorts actually went, with all the ferocity of his manifestos, through an exponentially manic reality theatre (with its own *Survivor* shows) after the manifest sublimity of a more immediate truth. It's as if he were anticipating – though, for all the ferocity, in a tamer version of less dimension – what Slavoj Žižek wrote about (with another performative put-on of his gleeful dialectic) after 9/11: the fundamentalist terror latent but secreted in the twentieth-century's 'passion for the Real',[15] with martyrdom not only impassioned, but real, immediate and, guaranteed houris in heaven, sublime.

There were, to be sure, Boccioni and Carrà paintings, but the theatricalized spirit of Futurism was not confined to the flat walls of museums or stage sets, but went instead (as with Tzara and Dada too), to where the real action was, in cafés and cabarets, political parlours, sporting events, the offices of hostile newspapers or out there on the streets, where in notorious spectacles, with no play-acting, they even beat people up. And while the Surrealists were enamoured of dreams and the unconscious, they also broke out of the frame of painting and plinth-based art into collage, photomontage, installations, assemblage, noise and body art, environments and, with multiple sites in the real world, not only performance art but the performance of everyday life. (As for beating people up, the only person I ever heard Beckett talk about with contempt was André Breton, because if you disagreed with him too much, he had you beaten up.) All of these, of course, are the going things today in a performative artworld that – as with the blood spatterings of Istvan Kantor or his Machine Sex Action Group, or the costumes, prosthetics and role-playing in Matthew Barney's *Viral Infection: The Body and Its Discontents* – couldn't care less about theatre. As for the traditional avant-garde, and its incursion on everyday life, they may have deranged it in the process, but what then seemed weird or strange is – on stage, off stage, even in fashion or blockbuster shows in museums – second nature now.

Or so it is until you think about it, when it may become threatening again, like the very substance of theatre, which, not unlike a viral infection, keeps itself out of sight. As for the instrumental theatricality of whatever forms of theatre – the entire repertoire of representation, its originary sources or pretensions to sacred rites – that was later exposed by exploitation demonically in Genet, who, as if nurtured by infections, sustains in the theatre's seeming what is indelibly there in life. (If that seems to be mocking deconstruction, Derrida tried to make the Genetic best of it in his mirroring *Glas*. This occurred after he already had to acknowledge, in an essay on Artaud, that to abolish representation is a tragic impossibility, that even to think its closure 'is to think the tragic: not as the representation of fate, but as the fate of representation. Its gratuitous and baseless necessity.'[16]) So it is at the end of *The Balcony*, when Madame Irma says to the audience, while closing up the Brothel, before extinguishing the last light: 'You must go home, where everything – you can be quite sure – will be even falser than here...You must go home.'[17] It may very well be, in our heart of hearts, that we really don't want to go home, which is why I've often felt that at the sticking point of the most powerful plays – say, *Oedipus* or *King Lear* or *Endgame* (among those I've directed over the years) – we tend to be most evasive, as if analysis were closing in, or in the process of absorption also blanking out, or acknowledging a profundity that really we'd rather forget – and in order to get on with it, however estranged the life, that's just about what we do. So, too, with anti-theatre, as a scourge of falsehood and lies; relying as we do on appearances, it would be hard to live with that. At the extremities of exposure, we may actually incline to comedy, so we can laugh it off, though the comedy that really gets us is when we don't know when to laugh. Is that theatre or anti-theatre, or the seeming between?

It was Freud who said we must learn to live in doubt, but the anti-theatrical prejudice, for one reason or another, has had its doubts about that – most of all, perhaps, at the intolerable limits of theatre, where we sense ourselves seeing what we maybe shouldn't see. Or through all the seeming, the indiscernible, the insidious, what we really can't. Yet what would theatre be if it didn't move toward the unbearable, unless we're prepared to abandon the greatest of all plays, especially tragedy, already much critiqued, or stage revisionist versions that arrest, expose or otherwise set it right? But that, too, is a vanity of anti-theatre, for would they really go away – that is, the rage, shame, remorse, immeasurable pain that, prior to any drama, brought them into being, insisting they be represented – if we should rewrite or abolish or parody Lear's howls or his never never never never nevers, or even, in some mind-blowing enraptured form of belated epic redemption, substitute for them Molly Bloom's 'yes I said yes I will Yes?' In all this we might remember that it's not only anti-theatre or a strategic theatricality that deters what's so overpowering in performance that you almost can't think about it, but simpler things, like bad acting or directing or – again light-years from what charges the theatre, its grievous mortality and invisible wounds – lightweight production concepts, anti-theatre by default.

Having said that, I may now retract it, or at least qualify the apparent fault. For while I think I know bad acting when I see it, or an overcharged or slovenly or empty production, the issue that determined my own rethinking of what I was doing in the theatre – after more than 20 years of doing it, radically changing what I did – is this: what do we mean by acting? *where? why? how? for whom? and to what ideological end?*[18] Answering any one of those questions may mean that you're for or against theatre, at least *that* theatre; and indeed, there is a sense in which the anti-theatrical prejudice, or the deployment of theatricality, becomes an issue of this form of theatre against that form of theatre. From the outset, however, I have not been thinking so much of theatre forms as about the troubling question, undispelled by the correlative notion, in the becoming of theatre, that theatre *is* itself, of the materialization of theatre – unless it's *all* theatre, reality, appearance, whatever – from whatever it is it is not. Where theatre happens in its emergence, as itself or not, it's *something else again*, or at least would appear to be, which – like the 'Nothing that is not there and the nothing that is',[19] or the activated nothing in the 'Nothing to be done'[20] – baffles perception itself, and again demystification, or the distantiation of that Brechtian A-effect.

This is theatre at ground zero, or like the concept of zero itself, about which it has been said: 'If you look at zero you see nothing; but look through it and you will see the world.'[21] And beyond mathematics, you may see more than that, or rather see it and not see it, as in *Hamlet's* closet scene, where Gertrude says, all that is she sees, which, even if he's hallucinating, and nothing is there to be seen, is existentially something more – what he sees, what she doesn't – than mere coinage of the brain. And so it is with what's palpably there that none of us can see, neither the characters, nor the actors, nor those of us in the audience, in looking directly at it, or eyes with gazing fed, and no form of anti-theatre can do anything about that, though it might break the gaze or intensify it, cutting to the brain. And that's no coinage either, or the accursed commodification. Thus, when I've written before that the entire institution of theatre, with all its apparatus, is a historical cover-up for the ontological fact that the one performing there, that one, is dying in front of your eyes, I was not, as with queer performativity, talking of corporeal style, but rather – in the bodies that matter, the matter that makes the body – the theatre's generic substance, inarguably there but imperceptible, compelling the specularity that it will never satisfy. Yet, if I can believe what I read in the newspaper, what passeth show may be, and sooner than we think, another passing phase.

* * *

In his apocalyptic imaginings, which he would insist is the virtual truth (quite literally so), Virilio had already foreseen a super-digitized world whose high frequencies would invalidate the body as an encumbrance, requiring, perhaps, the semblance of a biological body with a body art that mirrors its inexistence (Virilio, *Ground Zero*, p.72), with dying then irrelevant. Now we actually hear from (maybe way-out) geneticists – as from molecular artists like Joe Davis, who has made art of DNA by inserting coded messages into bacterial genes – that defeating death may be in the offing, or that, shy of total victory, a life expectancy of 4000–5000 years is now a prospect, and in the sights of the avant-garde. When, moreover, we hear from Whitfield Diffie, chief of security of Sun Microsystems, that 'we live, largely speaking, in the last generation of human beings', and that there are people alive today who will have unlimited life spans,[22] well, that's really likely to change our thinking about theatre as anything but a residual seeming, since the apparatus of representation on which the institution is predicated, even as anti-theatre, becomes itself obsolete, as representation itself, reproducing what otherwise disappears, would itself more or less disappear into the *interminable* – which was in that other life the fate of psychoanalysis, in the vanity of interpretation of the dramaturgy of the unconscious.

Meanwhile, as if to augment these prospects there was a production called *The Hanging Man* – brought over recently from England to BAM (Brooklyn Academy of Music) – in which dying becomes impossible through a series of events that are eccentrically, obsessively, and decidedly theatrical, no question of it. The production was developed by The Improbable Theater, which would seem to be a more sanguine mutation of my own *The Impossible Theater*. Subtitled *A Manifesto*, that book was written with an unyielding reality principle that the theatre itself is a form of impossibility, though impossibly so, or despicably, in the American theatre, at the time I was writing the book, after the emergence of the Cold War. At one point, merging a phrase from the Cold War with terms from the New Criticism, I made this observation: 'The ritual balance of power, the maintenance of ambiguity in perilous tension, has also been one of the major preoccupations of art in the twentieth century.'[23] And now in the twenty-first century, what we're calling an age of terror, it would seem for the time being, which is the time of theatre, that the perilous tension is worse, even more ambiguous, with innumerable bodies dying, whether they matter or whether they don't. Whatever the reasons for it, *mea culpa* as we wish, orientalism, occidentalism, the paranoia is growing, what with tunnelled networks, stateless, like dreadnaughts spreading dread, with conspiracy theories and secrecies, homeland security dubious and everything out of sight. If you really think it over, how does any theatre, by whatever theatrical means, really match up with that, or the pervasiveness of seeming that, in the material world, not virtual at all, appears *in actuality* – now a perversion of seeming? – to make it nothing but theatre.

In this regard, mirrored (paranoia in abeyance), there is a level of behaviour in theatre that, like a subatomic particle, a muon or charmed quark, would – if there were an electronic microscope powerful enough to bring it into focus – disappear in the energy required for you to see it. (Which we can only hope won't happen with the indeterminate jihad, Al Qaeda or the suicide bombers.) Materializing as disappearance, theatre escapes us in being theatre, though we might think of it then as anti-theatre or, corporeal as it is, a correlative of anti-matter. As for actual theatre practice, to the degree that it persists through the self-reflexive impasse of an ethos of suspicion, it may acquire a certain energy from what will never be resolved, which is how to determine though all the seeming whether at any historical moment there is an insufficiency or overdose of what we think of as theatre. That we can do without it is absurd, since – if we're to engage the issues at the level at which Plato introduced the prejudice, and Socrates pursued it – we have no choice in the matter; and we've had a form of theatre that, in the perverse excess of its apparent undoings, or nothings to be done, was predicated on the absurdity, though some of the cruder theatricality, and its repetitive acts, appeared to overstate a case that can't be overstated. Still, if we think we have it right, there's nothing more certain in the seeming than the future of illusion, the insubstantial pageant fading, leaving not a wrack behind – except the empty space that, for Peter Brook, is (again) the beginning of theatre if an actor enters the space. My own view has always been that it needs no more than a look.

More theatre, less theatre. Actors have always proceeded on that wobbling pivot, which also defines historical periods, either acting too much or acting too little, though who in the world can say – actor? director? audience? – what is really enough? Every aspect of theatre can be thought of the same way, from scenery, lighting, costumes, sound, to the timing of a play, its two-hour traffic or the aestheticized soporific of Robert Wilson's earlier stagings, attenuated, aphasic, repetitive as a raga, with imperceptible permutations, seen unthinkingly as afterthought. Or, as the theatre expands to operatic dimensions, there may very well be, even there in its grandeur, too much to be seen, which was actually an issue in the news the other day – the case of Deborah Voigt, resounding voice, oversized body – the right weight for a soprano to be singing Ariadne, no less (*auf Naxos*) in a cocktail dress. What this suggests, even in the reduced proportions of other forms of theatre, is that aside from too much acting there can also be too much actor, literally so, psychically so, which we've heard in a tradition from Gordon Craig to Roland Barthes.

When I said a moment ago that the empty theatre space only requires a look, it was not from a desire to create an impersonal art, like Mallarmé and others since, who, in attempting by diverse means to void representation, have wanted the actor out of it in a vanity of poesis opposed to mimesis. For even when the acting is reduced to the gestural or the ideographic, even when in fact the actor is not there, but replaced by a puppet or other non-human figure, the mimetic is not extinguished, representation prevails, and if the human figure seems erased, it is there as on the mystic writing pad, if only as a trace. theatre remains to be seen because it is *as remainder*, and it wouldn't be thus at all if it didn't smell of mortality, something to be seen *feelingly* (as the blind Gloucester does in *King Lear*) in or out of *the* theatre. As for Barthes's essay on the Bunraku, it is also in the tradition of critique that finds nothing more discreditable in the theatre, no mode of theatricality, than that associated with mimesis and – with a repertoire of hapless gestures and self-indulgent mannerisms, even when focused in character – the corporeal presence of the actor. For all his exhortation of the grain of the voice (sidelined with the musicians in the Bunraku), Barthes prefers on stage the black-robed anonymous figures manipulating the puppets to the psychologized human body, which is no more than an execration in its posturing mindlessness. In the crossing of theory by practice, I must admit at times, as I've watched or worked with certain actors, sharing this view, though the preference for puppets is sometimes there when certain authoritarian directors push the actors around.

Where the actors are presumably liberated by sense and emotional memory, they would be doubly anathema to Barthes, not only because of their physical presence, and with it the smell of mortality, but maybe even worse, the inside risk of narcissism. As for the Actors' Studio actor, with a technique disguising mimesis, or any appearance of theatre, the liability in performance is – beyond that in the play – still another illusion, when the refusal of theatricality becomes, as iconically with Marlon Brando, a conspicuous symptom of it. If, meanwhile, there's a certain jeopardy in casting, aesthetically or conceptually it may also be judicious, as a means of augmenting or minimizing theatre, and thus, whether or not by intention, an incursion of anti-theatre. As for what happens in a rehearsal, the degrees of appearance there: 'Do it again!', the director says. What 'it', and how much? 'It all. [*Pause.*] It all',[24] or some intangibly furtive part of it? which, as in the Beckettian scene, can nearly drive you up the wall. What wall? Hollow, like the one Hamm insisted on going to, before being returned to the centre – 'Bang in the center!'[25] – in the bottoming out of illusion. And how many times does one hear in rehearsal, 'No! that's not it at all, you're merely repeating yourself.' Or, 'you're merely acting'. Which is, one would think, what you're supposed to do in the theatre.

What I'm essentially saying here – in a period of jaundiced value, where the familiar is distrusted, as 'natural', taken for granted and essence disqualified – is that the theatre is *essentially*, in every nuance, the site of anti-theatre, and would hardly exist without it, no more than those subatomic particles without their anti-particles. But then, at a last psychic extremity of the anti-theatrical prejudice, another nuance of seeming, there's something we tend to forget: another doubleness in the actor, not that of character but of wanting to act and not. And I'm not speaking of the desire, out of technique into performance, for a consummate realism, but once again of the Real, the datum of any acting, ineliminable in the theatre, the reality of stage fright. Shakespeare had it exactly when he spoke (in the best manual of acting

I know) of 'the imperfect actor on the stage,/Who with his fear is put besides his part' (Sonnet 23) – the implication being that there is no other actor. If that appears to confirm again that the theatre is inseparable from some instinct of anti-theatre, it leaves us with the question out of which – through whatever imperfection, in the actor, in reality, in theatre itself – the most powerful theatre is made: *why theatre at all?*

Notes

1. Martin Heidegger, 'Language', in *Poetry, Language, Thought*, trans. and intro. Albert Hofstadter (New York: Harper, 1971), p.190.
2. Judith Butler, *Bodies That Matter: On the Discursive Limits of 'Sex'*, (New York and London: Routledge, 1993).
3. Judith Butler, *Gender Trouble: Feminism and the Subversion of Identity* (New York and London: Routledge, 1990), p.139.
4. Paul Virilio, *Ground Zero*, trans. Chris Turner (London and New York: Verso, 2002), p.15.
5. Michael Fried, 'Art and Objecthood', in Gregory Battcock, ed., *Minimal Art: A Critical Anthology* (New York: Dutton, 1968), p.141.
6. Quoted by René Girard, *Violence and the Sacred* (Baltimore: Johns Hopkins University Press, 1979), p.202.
7. Samuel Becket, 'Imagination Dead Imagine', in *Samuel Beckett: The Complete Short Prose, 1929–89*, ed. and intro. S. E. Gontarski (New York: Grove, 1995), p.185.
8. 'The Brain? It's a Jungle in There', *New York Times*, 27 March 2004, Arts & Ideas, national edn: A17, A19.
9. Henrik Ibsen, *Ghosts*, in *Six Plays by Henrik Ibsen*, trans. and intro. Eva Le Gallienne (New York: Modern Library, 1957), p.153.
10. Aeschylus, *Prometheus Bound*, in *Greek Teagedies, Vol. 1*, trans. David Grene, ed. Grene and Richmond Lattimore (Chicago: University of Chicago Press, 1968), p.104.
11. Roland Barthes, 'The Grain of the Voice', in *Image-Music-Text*, trans. Stephen Heath (New York: Hill & Wang, 1977), p.183.
12. Karl Marx, *The Marx-Engels Reader*, ed. Robert C. Tucker (New York: Norton, 1978), p.85.
13. Letter to Arnold Ruge, *Marx-Engels*, p.13.
14. Gertrude Stein, 'Plays', in *Look at Me Now and Here I Am: Writings and Lectures, 1909–45*, ed. Patricia Meyerowitz, intro. Elizabeth Sprigge (London: Penguin, 1967), p.75.
15. Slovoj Žižek, *Welcome to the Desert of the Real!* (London and New York: Verso, 2002), p.9.
16. Jacques Derrida, 'The Theater of Cruelty and the Closure of Representation', in *Writing and Difference*, trans. and intro. Alan Bass (Chicago: Univ. of Chicago Press, 1978), p.250.
17. Jean Genet, *The Balcony*, trans. Bernard Frechtman (New York: Grove, 1960), p.115.
18. See the chapter on 'Ghosting', in the book written – in that uncertain period when I thought it might start again – around the work of my KRAKEN

247 of Enough 247

group, *Take Up the Bodies: Theater at the Vanishing Point* (Urbana: Illinois University Press, 1982), pp.78–144.

19. See Wallace Stevens, 'The Snow Man', *The Palm at the End of the Mind*, ed. Holly Stevens (New York: Vintage, 1972), p.54.
20. Samuel Beckett, *Waiting for Godot* (New York: Grove, 1954), p.7.
21. Robert Kaplan, *The Nothing That Is: A Natural History of Zero* (New York: Oxford University Press, 2000), p.1.
22. *New York Times* 1 November 2004; national edn: A15.
23. Herbert Blau, *The Impossible Theater: A Manifesto* (New York: Macmillan, 1964), p.21.
24. Samuel Beckett, *Footfalls*, in *Collected Shorter Plays* (New York: Grove, 1984), p.240.
25. Samuel Beckett, *Endgame* (New York: Grove, 1958), p.27.

Index